MW01613629

I Bloom
Not for Thee

Kihyon (Kim) Kim

김기현

Mental Health Counselor

&

Rotary International District Governor 2014-2015

District 6760

Tennessee, USA

Copyright ©2020 Kihyon (Kim) Kim

All right reserved. No part of this book may be used or reproduced by any means, graphic, electronic, or mechanical, including photocopying, recording, taping or by any information storage retrieval system without the written permission of the publisher except in the case of quotations embodied in critical articles and reviews.

ISBN: 9798551118213

Printed in the United States of America

ALSO BY KIHYON (KIM) KIM

My Life in Letters: The Extraordinary Journey of an Ordinary Man from Korea

I Am a Rotarian

We are Rotarians

Words That I Live By

Words That You Live By

Ahrahm Kim

Hannie Kim

Doun Kim

Books published by Kim Kim are available at quantity discounts for educational, fundraising, and special sales use. Please email: rotariankim@yahoo.com

or write: Kim Kim, 146 Chipwood Dr. Hendersonville, TN 37075. USA

TABLE OF CONTENTS

About the Title of the Book: I Bloom Not for Thee

"I came across a wild flower, marveled at its beauty and at the perfection of all its parts, and exclaimed: 'But all this in you and in thousands like you blossoms and fades; it is not noticed by anyone and in fact is often not even seen by any one.' But the flower replied: 'You fool! Do you imagine I blossom in order to be seen? I blossom for my own sake because it pleases me, and not for the sake of others; my joy and delight consist in my being and in my blossoming." Arthur Schopenhauer.

I say, "A rose is beautiful because it blossoms in thorns."

You say, "A rose is ugly because it has thorns."

You and I are looking at the same rose, but I choose to see its beauty, and you choose to see its ugliness. It is not because a rose is either beautiful or ugly.

A rose does not care what we think of it.

A rose says, "I don't bloom just for you. I am neither beautiful nor ugly. I am that I am, and I am not what you think I am. I bloom and fade away according to my nature."

"If you find me beautiful, that is a reflection of your true nature."

"On the other hand, if you find me ugly, that is what you carry inside of you."

"Oh, if you can see the beauty of a rose, you must love me for my thorns, too."

Dedication

I dedicate this book to all my sons and daughters of past, present, and those in heaven who came into my life and left a giant footstep in my heart. I hope this book would help you to live a life worth living!

Introduction

I know a New York Times best seller who has published more than a dozen books over the course of a decade. She told me that as a mystery writer, she always writes the introduction for her books before she starts the first chapter. The reason for this being, she said, "I know exactly how my story begins and ends."

My first two books took me seven years to write. When I finally finished my first draft, it was over eight-hundred pages long. I was told, "Even if you might write as good as Shakespeare wrote plays or Hermann Hesse wrote Demian or Henry David Thoreau wrote Walden, no one is going to read that long of a book!" Sadly enough, it was true on both accounts: I am neither Shakespeare nor would my book be on a New York Times Best Seller list. According to research, the average American reads four books a year, and it is very unlikely one of them would be a long book written by an unknown writer who learned English as a second language at the age of seventeen! To make matters worse, I decided to publish my book in two parts: please forgive me for each book still being over 300 pages long. What can I say? I had so much I felt lead to write!

I have been given a lifetime to become who I truly am in the space between birth and death. Ever since I was a child growing up in a Buddhist monastery in Korea, my beliefs have been naturally formed and mostly influenced by Buddhist teaching, its natural surroundings, and traditional Korean culture. One of these beliefs were that scholars and teachers must be treated with the utmost respect and valued highest. My family used to call me Sunbi (an old Korean name for scholar) as I was growing up. I was a rather odd kid who cared less about things that most people desire and conform to, and more about pursuing wisdom and spirituality.

I have always held the mindset that if I stop learning and growing at any point in my life, whether at sixteen or sixty years of age, from that moment on I have started dying and chose to be ignorant. I truly believe the end of knowledge is the beginning of ignorance and living life as a fool. Existing day by day with a weary physical body is certainly not my ideal way of living. I have seen so many rich, famous, and powerful people living miserable lives because they have not found the meaning of their existence. They hold the mistaken belief that their earthly achievements define their lives. I bluntly refuse to live without reaching for my purpose. I have a professional writer friend who lives to publish his novels, for he believes that his life is defined through successful and popular books. My writing, on the other hand, helps me to find my true self, and I have been given a lifetime to do just that.

I want my life to be experimental, adventurous, creative, and most of all, aligned to the Lord, going through trials and tribulations to reach my final destination, which is to become the truest and highest version of myself as a human being. I am not there yet, but I feel I am getting closer and closer. I want readers, too, to feel inspired and gain a different perspective on life so they can find their purpose and live a life worth living. In order to achieve my mission, I have to live a life worth living myself, first, so I can tell all about my worthy journey on earth as I have experienced it. This way, readers will find their answers in my book. I always think about how my book will impact a reader, "If a book we are reading does not rouse us with a blow to the head, then why read it?" I want to make sure I do that with this book!

As I am writing the introduction for my 9th book after my draft was submitted to an editor, I am keenly aware of what a different person I have become. I used to think that I was not good enough, not accomplished enough, and not extraordinary enough to write a book. My sojourn on earth is so brief, and it goes by in the blink of an eye. A day is still long when I work a twelve-hour shift or on a day that I announce to my wife "it is not my day." Nevertheless, as I get older, a day turns into a week, a month a year, shorter and shorter in the blink of an eye! I did express already how quickly time goes, didn't I?

So, please don't remind me how precious the time is. I feel it in my bones! Between the man I was four years ago when I started writing this book to the man I have become now, there is quite a noticeable gap. I can say with full confidence that I have been reformed to a more mature, compassionate, understanding, and over all, better person. More importantly, I am getting closer and closer to assuming the role of the man I was born to be, and everything that was unknown and unexperienced has started making sense to me now.

I humbly but proudly say that this is a huge accomplishment on my part, and I am much more near to becoming a self-fulfilled man within a short period of time, all while some spend their lifetimes struggling to reach that goal in life. That is what writing has done for me the past four years when I was devoted and committed to creating this book. I have been reading and writing for many years. One of the biggest reasons this book is so special compared to my previous books is that I focus on a singular mission: to write for adolescents whom I counseled at the hospital. Henry David Thoreau said, "The woods would be silent if no bird sang but the best." All I really want for these youth is to find their voice and sing while the music is still in them. I want to encourage them to live their God given lives no matter what, for life is truly worth living. This is it, guys! This is the only lifeform we have as physical human beings.

I conclude my introduction to this book by saying that I hope you will find my book to be your companion and encouragement. "Every lover of books has authors whom he reads over and over again, whom he cares for as persons and not as sources of information, who are more to him, possibly, than any person he sees. He continually returns to the cherished companion and feeds eagerly upon his thought. It is because there is something in the book which he needs, which awakens and directs trains of thought that lead him where he likes to be led." — Charles Horton Cooley, Human Nature and the Social Order

If this book has become your life companion and helped you find a life worth living, I would feel more fulfilled being your secret admirer rather than being on New York Times best seller list and having my book read by total strangers. This book might not change the world, but I believe it might change the world for one person. That is enough for me, and that is enough a reason to write this book for you.

PART I: SELF

What is Your Name?

"Words are things. You must be careful, careful about calling people out of their names, using racial pejoratives and sexual pejoratives and all that ignorance. Don't do that. Someday we'll be able to measure the power of words. I think they are things. They get on the walls. They get in your wallpaper. They get in your rugs, in your upholstery, and your clothes, and finally in to you." Maya Angelou

Can you find the common denominator in these words: Muzungo, Jackie Chan, Chino, ShelterBox, and Rotarian? One Mississippi, two Mississippi, three Mississippi……. Your time is up.

Those are a few of my names, none of which include my given name that my father and his father assigned for me long before I was even born. Nonetheless, those are the names I am grateful to respond to when I volunteer to serve people around the world.

When I went to Uganda to save children from polio, they called me Muzungo, which meant "white," even though I am a Korean born American. Ethnicities other than their own are called such a name. As a Muzungo, I witnessed volunteers saving children from polio and replacing the despair and nightmares of parents and their children with hopes and dreams.

I have been to Guatemala numerous times to do dental, medical, and vision missions in different villages. None of the villages have had televisions or computers, not even a movie theater, but children called me in unison, "Jackie Chan." I still have no idea how children in this isolated village knew who Jackie Chan was, yet it is within those communities that I and other volunteers have witnessed joy where there was sadness.

I have been to Honduras with groups of people to install electricity and to provide clean and drinkable water. Hondurans called me "Chino." I must look Chinese! In remote areas where their own government could not reach to help its own people, strangers from another country brought light where there was darkness, one village at a time.

13

I am one of two hundred selected ShelterBox First Disaster Response team members in the world. I have been deployed four times to save disaster victims, from an earthquake in Haiti to typhoons in the Philippines. Whether I am in a disaster area saving lives or at a conference in the States speaking about my personal experience, I am known as a "ShelterBox." In the midst of despair and fear, I have witnessed volunteers giving love and faith where there was destruction and uncertainty.

I have been a Rotarian ever since 2000 and have made the personal commitment to be a light where there is darkness, to love where there is hatred, to hope where there is despair, and to spread joy where there is sadness, no matter how small the act is. Rotarians did not start doing extraordinary things all at once. The random acts of kindness that ordinary Rotarians have been doing without being noticed or given recognition were the tiny snowflakes that later became a massive avalanche.

The ancient Greek scientist Archimedes once said, "Give me a place to stand and I will move the world." Less than one percent of people in any community in the world have chosen to be Rotarians. It is my privilege to serve because these small groups of committed and dedicated Rotarians have been changing the world. American cultural anthropologist Margaret Mead said, "A small group of thoughtful people could change the world. Indeed, it's the only thing that ever has." Having witnessed Rotarians doing good in the world for the past twenty years, it is my proudest name yet.

I have been called these names while traveling six continents for mission trips. In the States, I'm called different names as well. Ever since my children were in elementary school and up until high school, I was a soccer coach and referee. So, I am called "Coach Kim" or "Referee Kim." Sometimes, grown-up strangers still come up to me in public and say unabashedly,

"Hi, Coach Kim! Do you remember me?"

I do not always recognize the full-grown adult standing before me, once a child. Now, I cannot recollect all of the kids I coached. However, I am so grateful for those that remember me still as "Coach

Kim."

For over fifteen years, I have been a mentor for elementary students who are raised in single mother households with no male figures in their lives. Many are now in college or in the work force and remember me as "Mentor Kim." I have also been participating in developing future leaders by teaching and counseling hundreds of high school students at Austin Peay State University during the summer. A mother of one of students who graduated from the program called me to attend a special ceremony for her daughter after she became a successful businesswoman. It has been eight years since I met her daughter for the first time, and she has not forgotten me as "Teacher Kim." She and her family still want me to be a part of her life as always. What a blessing it is for me!

Abraham Lincoln once said, "Every man over forty is responsible for his face." Growing up in Korea I often heard a profound proverb that taught the importance of our own names. It says, "A tiger dies and leaves his skin; a man dies and leaves his name." Obviously, Lincoln was not talking about a man's looks. You can't judge a person by his looks. You could be born poor and have had humble beginnings. As you live your life, you face many adversities and challenges. By the time you reach forty years of age, you are responsible for who you become, and your life experience has shaped the man you want to be. Therefore, your character—who you really are when others are not present and your reputation—who others think you are, are imprinted in your face.

I was raised in the Korean culture where it is imbedded that your name is your identity. For the sake of both the family and society, you are to honor and preserve your family name, and never to bring shame to it. Living in America, I had limited connection to my heritage and cultural family values. In fact, I felt it was fading away rather quickly with each time my name was mispronounced. Also, I felt embarrassed and ashamed for having a difficult and uncommon name. Hence, my self-esteem was slowly chiseled away and the link to my own identity was damaged heavily.

More often than not, I was asked what my American name was and told that I should have one. I would be more "acceptable" and "fit in" more they said. I thought about names such as David, John, Tom,

15

and other popular American names for the sole purpose of "fitting in." In fact, when I was granted a naturalized citizenship after I fulfilled the requirements, I was to have an American name. Nevertheless, I could not and I will not change my given name, not because I refuse to assimilate into American culture, or not being proud to be an American. Nothing could be further from the truth. It is because of my belief that I was given an identity through my given name whether I accepted it or not, and I was to make a name for myself. In addition, I feel as though changing my given name to another one, I would be synonymous as having no name at all, for I would not only lose my own identity but lose my link to the past, present, and future.

You might not fully understand the significance of your name and connect your name to your identity, for you have every right to choose whatever name you want and the freedom to change it anytime you want. You may not be able to imagine such a time that you might be forced to give up your given name or to change it without your own consent. However, it was only a few decades ago that my parents and my grandparents were forced to take on Japanese names.

When Korea was invaded and colonized by Japan for thirty-six years from 1910 to 1945, the very first thing that Japan did was forbid Koreans from speaking their mother tongues and systematically prohibited using Korean names. Newborn babies had to be named Japanese names in their own land, and those who had Korean names before Japan colonized had to accept Japanese names. Speaking Korean was strictly forbidden, and if they were caught using their Korean names, they were not only humiliated and beaten but were sent to prisons or even sentenced to death. Many Koreans chose to take their own lives to honor and preserve their family names instead of living with shame. Families of those who gave up their Korean names or willingly accepted Japanese names were marked and treated as traitors even long after Japan surrendered in 1945.

The goal of Japan during the colonization and the purpose of these drastic measures was to demoralize Korean spirits and their values, to suppress tradition and to destroy much of Korean culture in order to implant Japanese beliefs, customs, and thoughts in Koreans' minds.

There was a time that I felt that living up to my family name was overwhelming; I tried to run away from it. I have finally accepted that my given name is the one connecting the past, present and future in my family, in this society, and who knows, in the world. Johann Wolfgang von Goethe said, "A man's name is not like a mantle which merely hangs about him, and which one perchance may safely twitch and pull, but a perfectly fitting garment, which, like the skin, has grown over and over him, at which one cannot rake and scrape without injuring the man himself."

By accepting your given name, you are accepting your role in your family and in society. You will be proud of your name and will do things to gain honor and to leave a legacy, not to bring shame or dishonor. Your name becomes your identity. Your identity becomes your character. Your character becomes your reputation. Your reputation becomes your destiny.

When I came to America, it did not start that way. I was lost. I remember my first day in high school in America. A teacher motioned me to come to the front and introduced me to the class. As he was writing my name on the board, he said,

"His name is 'Kim Kim from South Korea.'"

Suddenly everybody burst out laughing.

"Kim Kim?"

"Hey, Double Kim!" "KK." Someone said in the back, mockingly.

I mumbled my name in broken English, "My nam iz Kim Kihyon, no Kim Kim."

I became afraid that people might laugh at whatever I said, and I had no courage to correct them. I became silent on my first day in school and the days, months, and years after. Some people really thought I was dumb or mentally impaired because I could not speak any English, and in fact, I began to believe them because I was indeed a foreigner from a strange land. I accepted that as my sole identity. It did not take long for the entire school and later, the community I lived in and the job I worked at to catch on, calling and labeling me, "Dumb,

17

Idiot, Stupid Chinese." I became silent to protect myself from humiliation, but worse than that, I had become invisible.

Ralph Ellison said, "I am an invisible man. No, I am not a spook like those who haunted Edgar Allan Poe; nor am I one of your Hollywood-movie ectoplasms. I am a man of substance, of flesh and bone, fiber and liquids — and I might even be said to possess a mind. I am invisible, understand, simply because people refuse to see me." When I mispronounced a word, which happened often, I was called, "Stupid, it is sheet of paper, not shit of paper!" I again became invisible.

When I made a reasonable comment, but they could not understand me, they said to the group, "He don't count." I became silent, thinking about the irony of their improper grammar, but once again I became invisible. "Why bother?" I did not correct them because my voice and my existence did not matter.

I did not know exactly what I wanted to be and what my dreams were, but I wanted to succeed in life regardless of what I was to become. However, my self-esteem was crushed when they said, "You won't amount to anything." I suddenly became invisible.

President Robert F. Kennedy once said, "Few of us will have the greatness to bend history, but each of us can work to change a small portion of events, and in the total of all those acts will be written as the history of this generation." You are that tiny snowflake that later becomes an avalanche. People won't remember a tiny snowflake that disappears as soon as it touches the earth. One snowflake, two snowflakes... think of the force, power, and beauty when snowflakes join together. You and I must use our God given talents to leave massive imprints in people's hearts, together. Even if they do not remember your given name and only remember you as Muzungo, Jackie Chan, Chino, ShelterBox, and Rotarian, that is enough "to change a small portion of events."

Have you thought about what kind of life you want to live, what legacy you want to leave behind, and what you want to be remembered by? Proverb 22:1 reads, "A good name is rather to be chosen than great riches, and loving favor rather than silver and gold." Your existence on earth is no accident. You are chosen to be here to make a difference, and you are to show how your life has brought joy and honor both to the name which has been bequeathed to you and to the next generation after you.

Are you able to proclaim at the end of your journey, "I have fought the good fight, I have finished the race, I have kept the faith?" 2 Timothy 4:7. In order to fight a good fight and to finish your own race, you must first believe you are the most precious and unique human being. You are given a life only you can fulfill and complete; hence be thankful for being used and chosen by God.

I know you are scared, nervous, and afraid. Bad habits may be creeping up on you tempting you to fail. People may be telling you to give up because your mission is not worthy or that you are not worthy. Vittorio Alfieri once said, "Often the test of courage is not to die but to live." You know you are headed in the right direction when people are trying so hard to bring you down. All you have to do is take one step at a time. You don't know yet but believe me that your first small step in the right direction will end up being the biggest step of your life. You might feel like you are walking on thin ice or hanging off a cliff, but that is okay. As long as you keep taking a step in the right direction, no matter how fast or how far other people are ahead of you, you will meet your destiny in the end. Your name will be remembered as a gentle wind and light rain, when your physical presence is gone. You still leave behind the mark of your legacy in people's hearts.

Your given name is not only your identity but also everything that makes you who you are. William James once said, "The sum total of all that a man can call his, not only his body and his psychic powers, but his clothes, and his wife and children, his ancestors and friends, his reputation and works, his hands and horses, and yacht and bank account."

Dear Kim Kim,

It's not often that I'm impressed by people, especially adults. I often find people to be unauthentic with themselves and others. You are truly one of the most authentic people I have met. Your humbleness inspires me to serve people more. I can see the light of Christ shining through you. I want to someday acquire the gift of learning from others like you do, of serving others like you do. Your voice runs through my head when I believe for a moment that I am worthless. I was that sticky note with 0% on it, but you have made me believe that I truly am worth 100%. Thank you for teaching me and talking with me. I value everything you say very much. I want to be just like you when I grow up (but my English might be a little better than yours! Hahaha) — Adolescent

My Unanswered Prayers

I asked for serenity that I might live in peace, free from chaos.

God put me in a sinful world to ight my candle rather than to curse the darkness and do nothing.

I asked for strength that I might not be weakened by all these trials and hardships.

God gave me obstacles that I could handle and failures in order to learn to humbly obey.

I asked for wisdom that it might set me free.

God said I was born free and allowed troubles in my life in order for me to seek the truth. Now I have learned that wisdom in my head meant nothing if I did not live by it. All wisdom should lead to virtuous actions.

I asked for happiness that I might not have pain, sadness, nor despair.

God had me serve special needs and troubled people to make me feel special, grateful, and blessed so I could find happiness despite pain, sadness, and despair.

I asked for love that I might feel God's presence.

God said that even though people had done many wrongs and hurtful things, to forgive them and love them anyway, in the same manner He loves those who persecuted Him, not in word or in tongue, but indeed and in truth.

I asked for health that I might live a long life and do many great things.

God made me weak and poor so I could do many small and unremembered acts of kindness to strangers with great love.

I asked for power that I might change the world.

God said the world would not be changed unless I am changed, and I can create the world I want to see by changing my way of thinking.

I asked for riches that I might live comfortably without worries and build buildings named after my name.

God gave me hands and brains to work. He said he did not build a physical building but the foundation in order to build relationships with people that leave a giant footprint on their hearts.

I asked for all things that I might enjoy life.

I was given life to fulfill His will through me, and that made all the difference.

In the end, I received nothing I asked for.

But I received everything I needed. Amen!

Dear Kim Kim,

As I was standing there looking outside of the window in room #410, it hit me.
I am so glad to be here!
This is why I am alive.
This moment right here.
The way the colors of the sky intertwine, the way the light shines through the clouds.
The beauty of the outside.
This sunset will always hold a special place in my heart.
This sunset is the one that created my will to live.
I want to be alive to see many more.
I am so incredibly grateful to walk this earth to see God's beautiful creation, to walk on the best art project known to man.
I get to see this beauty every day.
I no longer want to die.
Death scares me now.
There's so much I want to do, so much I need to do before I perish.
Thank you, God, for this day.
I pray that you let me live another.
--Adolescent

Who Is the Most Important Person in the Whole Wide World?

When my family gets together, we naturally talk about the good, bad, ugly, and mostly fun memories of the past: raising our young children, supporting my extended fam ly under one household, and trying to survive in the business world as a minority Korean and newlywed couple of a family arranged marriage. Neither my wife nor I could say we knew each other well enough to even fall in love at first sight as a married couple, how to raise family, or how to live happily ever after.

Our circumstances had brought us the hardest and most difficult trials and tribulations of our lives, yet those difficult times are usually the talk of my family gatherings. Looking back, those trials and tribulations in our lives were truly happy and good times.

You do not have to nurse a baby to know how frequently infants wet their diapers. Child development experts and doctors say babies urinate approximately twenty-times and have three to four bowel movements a day for the first several months of their lives. That is a lot of diaper changing to think of it, let alone all other unpleasant things babies do! However, that one smile and hearing the word "Dada" from my babies were worth at the stinky diapers!

Now, if I were to say that I changed my three kids' diapers only once the entire time they had to wear ciapers, you would not believe me, right? Or you might think that I AM THE WORST FATHER IN THE WORLD! I love my children more than life itself. They are gifts from God and the best thing that ever happened to me. Hands down! Still, I am going to write to defend myself and more importantly to explain how this seemingly untrained and unfit father taught his children to accept who they are, to trust their importance in this world, and to believe that they are persons that have a purpose.

Of course, my three children were too young to remember how many times I changed their diapers and I assure you they care less by whom their butts were wiped. But they said it like they were right there having lived through it and swore they witnessed me changing their diapers only once. I promise you they were brainwashed by their mother and grandmother because my wife and my mother talked about that incident so many times that my innocent children who love their father so much believed that to be true. My wife said to them, "Your father is the only father who has ever done it only once and get away with it." Oh, how unfair it is for a poor father like me! So, they never fail to mention over and over again one particular incidence that occurred only one time in our lives. Nevertheless, I guarantee my children would be sharing it with their children. How embarrassing it will be knowing that my grandchildren talk about me changing my own children's diapers only once even after I departed from this earth!

Since my parents lived with me all of their lives and my sisters had to move back in with me from time to time due to marriage difficulties or financial struggles, my children were never left alone. They have always been in the hands of a competent and willing mother, grandmother, and aunts who would do anything and everything for them from changing diapers, to spoon feeding and cooking, to washing their clothes. Don't assume they are mother's boys or spoiled rotten. That is completely mistaken. I assure you that they are independent and have become complete and matured adults.

You are likely wondering what my place was then, in this well-functioning-female-run-family dynamic. You could argue I was raised in old Korean custom living in America. Men are the breadwinners and carry the responsibility of teaching their children the values of family and of society outside of the family environment. A man is a member of the family, and a family is the basic unit of society. If a family is broken and dysfunctional, society is broken and dysfunctional. I am not saying that they are not to learn those values from a female perspective, but those principles, values, and virtues are heavily influenced by fathers, wouldn't you say? Throughout this book and all of the books I have written, I have emphasized values and principles, the meaning and purpose of life, and more than anything, belief and faith in God.

Hence, as a father, I was more interested in shaping their young minds and building their characters to be men before they dreamed their dreams of whatever they wanted to become when they grew up. They had to learn how to crawl first before they walked, which means they had to become a man before a doctor, lawyer, or whatever they wanted to be. Friedrick Nietzsche once said, "He who would learn to fly one day must first learn to stanc and walk and run and climb and dance; one cannot fly into flying." I truly believe a father must walk the walk and talk the talk: be an example, do what you say and follow through with it no matter how difficult the situations are. The most honorable lesson should be for children to be like his or her father.

I was not there for my children every moment of their lives. As with everything else in my life, I was working long hours and spent many nights away from home. I owe my wife many thanks because she was the one who played my role while I was absent. I am married to an amazing woman. She works as much and as hard as I have ever since we married and still manages to take care of not only our three children but everything else that needs to be done around the house. I have never forgotten how blessed I am for marrying such a wonderful wife and mother to our children.

My youngest son was crazy about his mom and completely dependent on her. She was the most mportant person in his whole world, and he admitted it, no matter whom asked. Truthfully my heart was hurt a little because I wanted to hear my kids saying, "My Dad is the most important person in the whole world."

When he was about four or five years old, I remember asking him who the most important person in his life was. He said immediately, "Mommy." Peanut M&Ms were his favorite candy, and I was determined to win his heart over Mommy. I opened the bag of M&Ms and started putting pieces in my mouth. While I was eating his favorite candy, I asked him who the most important person in the whole wide world was. He hesitated a little, but he still answered "Mommy" while staring at the bag of candy. I gave him the whole bag and asked him again. I said, "Mommy is not home. So, tell me who the most important person in the whole wide world is." He looked at the kitchen and the hallway to our bedroom to make sure the coast was clear; then, he whispered in my ear, "Daddy."

Shaking my head, I said, "No, no, no, it is not Mommy or Daddy." Then, I looked directly in his eyes, and I asked him with a firm but gentle voice, "So, who is the most important person in the whole wide world?" He paused a few seconds thinking, then pointed his finger at himself and said, "Me."

That was one of my greatest and proudest moments as a father: teaching my son of his own importance and value as young as he was. As long as he knew who he was and believed in himself, he would not be easily influenced by negative people and their words. He would find his place in this world regardless of obstacles, failures, and the tribulations life threw at him. I felt that the basic foundation as a human being was having self-worth and living as such.

I wish I could say that from that moment on, everything was changed for good, and he always believed how special of a person he was and how much he was worth. However, all of my three children experienced trouble with self-acceptance and self-doubt because no matter how they felt inside, society would not accept or see them as parts of the whole.

The sociologist Robert Merton came up with the Strain Theory to explain the phenomenon of why there exists a gap between society's expectations and individual's goals to achieve them. He said that there is a gap or imbalance between culturally-valued goals and culturally-valued means and abilities to achieve those goals. Those goals are based on socially acceptable beliefs, conformity, and shared assumptions of what members of society should strive for in order to conform and to achieve the so-called American dream.

In other words, society defines the expectations and goals of the collective population, and people are supposed to meet those expectations and goals to be accepted and happy regardless of their backgrounds. It should not matter what my children look like. They are Americans because they were born right here in Nashville, Tennessee and English was their mother tongue. However, from the earliest of ages, they learned that they were treated differently and given unfair playing fields, for society excluded some people as outsiders and did not provide the means to achieve their goals no matter how hard they worked to obtain them.

Hundreds of thousands of people from all over the world still flock to America knowing there might be invisible gaps and invisible walls to overcome, but I stand here to tell you that America is still the greatest land of freedom, of opportunity, and where dreams do come true for anyone anywhere in America. Having said that, it took a while for my Korean American children to find their place in this country.

After graduating from high school, my son Doun went to Korea as a youth exchange student for one year. He did not want to go at the time, but I felt he needed to go to find his own identity, and if not, he would continue to feel like an outcast in America.

Even if our family spoke Korean, ate Korean foods, and lived by Korean traditions at home in order to teach our children Korean values, as soon as they stepped outside, it was a completely different ball game. The only way for my youngest son to learn about himself was to face it. My relatives in Korea were excited to see my son, but I told them not to visit or to contact him while he was there. The reason for this was that if he stayed with his relatives, they would do everything for him; then, he would not have to learn to step out of his comfort zone, which was why he was in Korea in the first place. I kindly explained this to them and asked my cousin to take him to his grandparent's house for the new year so that he could then meet the rest of his relatives.

I have been a member of Rotary Club since 2000, and there are over 35,000 Rotary Clubs in the world. I contacted a Rotary Club in Korea and we decided to exchange students. Even though I had never met his host families in Korea, I knew he would be in good hands as I have also hosted more than a dozen kids from other countries during the past fifteen years or so. Oh, I have so many stories to tell from hosting youth exchange students! They come to America and expect to live with Americans so they can learn about American culture. It is priceless to see them with my family, eating nothing but Korean foods and living a traditional Korean lifestyle in America! So far, every one of them has loved Korean foods including sushi and kimchi and never asked to be transitioned into other American families! In fact, several of them have visited us many times since and always call me their Korean Dad. I thought I would make an impact on their lives when I decided to open my house and host them, yet it was the other way around. Our family is the one impacted greatly by them.

Except for our family vacations to the beach in Florida or the Smoky Mountains, my son Doun had never ventured outside our neighborhood by himself. My wife was so worried that she did not want him to go. "What if something goes wrong!" She said, "I will never be able to forgive myself." I, however, had total faith in him, this youth exchange student program, and complete faith and trust in God that allowed me to throw my son into uncertainty. Of course, I was scared to death and doubted if I was doing the right thing for him. Having my family live through this life changing experience with him, I truly believe that not only my son, but my faith also had been tested during this time.

He was seventeen-years old when he left Nashville on August 13, 2013 by himself and arrived in Seoul, Korea two days later. His host family that lived in Pusan, a five-hour train ride from Seoul, came to the airport to pick him up. Obviously, he looked Korean so they started speaking Korean to him. However, he could not read or write in Korean, let alone communicate with them.

My wife and I were waiting for a phone call from him as soon as he arrived. His host family called to say he arrived safely and that was it. Youth exchange students were discouraged to contact their biological families too often. The more they did, the less they would learn in a foreign environment. A month later, he texted us in Korean how he was doing in detail, and we could sense he was settled down already.

He said that he went to school six days a week from 7 am until 9 pm! Seniors were to stay an extra two hours to study in school, voluntarily. He said it really was not voluntary because all seniors stayed to study for the college examination. Because he was a youth exchange student, they let him out at around 3 pm. He had been learning Korean traditional music, Tae Kwon Do (Korean martial arts), and was to visit Japan and Philippines. He had to learn the Korean language really quickly so as not to be embarrassed by not knowing any as a Korean. He also wanted to help the nine other youth exchange students from other countries who came at the same time, as they all looked towards him as an interpreter and a source of guidance.

His uncle, living in Seoul, traveled to my son's host family in Pusan to take him to his grandparents' house on the new year in February 2014. The new year is the most important holiday in Korea, and because it is based on the lunisolar Chinese calendar, it falls on a different date each year. The last time he was in Korea was when he was only three years old, and he had no recollection of his relatives. He said he met twenty relatives he had never seen.

After ceremonial bows to ancestors and the big meals, his grandfather took him alone to a remote area. His grandfather stopped to show him the view of endless rice fields and beautiful mountains laying before them. Pointing his finger, his grandfather said, "My grandson, do you see all these rice fields and those tall mountains? These are your lands and your mountains!" My son thought he did not hear correctly. So, he looked at his grandfather confused and unaware of what he was talking about.

"When I was about your age, my grandfather brought me here and said the same," said his grandfather.

"I inherited these beautiful lands and mountains from our ancestors, and I passed it along to your father when he turned twenty-one."

"You are soon to be twenty-one, an adult. Then all of this will be yours!"

My son said back to his grandfather, "Grandfather, how could that be? I have never been here before, and I did not even know these lands existed until now. It has to be a big mistake."

Grandfather said, "Listen to me, my grandson! We, the Kim family, have owned this land for hundreds of years. Your ancestors paid in full a long time ago and it is yours now and when you have your own son, you will pass it along to your son."

My son thought that he had to do something to earn it and kept arguing that he did not deserve this gift.

His grandfather said, "Whether you earn it or not, and whether you deserve it or not, none of that matters. It was paid in full before you were even born and now it is yours. All you have to do is to accept your blessing."

When he turned twenty-one, I received a thick yellow envelope from Korea. I knew exactly what it was. I took my son to my lawyer's office and had him sign. He saw his name on the bottom of the papers, and above it, my name, his grandfather's name and his great grandfathers'. He finally understood that the beautiful land and mountains belonged to him now. The only difference between him and you is that he was born into the Kim family, and that is all.

The land was worth fighting for and he accepted the responsibility honorably without question of what he had to do.

He could have turned around and sold it all to be rich quick. He had every right to do so and no one would be able to stop him. But he did not do it. In fact, he had matured overnight as he realized his position in the Kim family. He is now responsible not only for taking care of the lands that were handed down from his ancestors but more importantly, he had to make it better than how he found it for the generations to come. That was a huge responsibility. My son had not felt as though he deserved to receive his inheritance because he thought he had to earn it, yet after he accepted his place in this world, he was able to find who he was. He believed he was chosen by God to carry out his responsibility and he felt blessed.

I stubbornly convinced my wife and my son to participate in a yearlong youth exchange program because my son had to find his own identity through his own eyes and experiences. I still remember what my wife said to me the night before my son left. She said, "If anything happens to him, I will never forgive you." That was pretty harsh and painful, and it hurt my feelings deeply because I was truly doing what I believed was best for our own son. The reason why I persisted despite wife's pleas was for my son to ask profound questions and to seek the answers. Who am I? Why am I here? What is the purpose of my life? What do I believe in? What should I become when I grow up and what must I do to get there? That is what I experienced while growing up in a Buddhist temple in Korea.

I do not recall whether our family were already Buddhists before we moved into the Buddhist temple or whether we were converted. It really is not an important matter to me whichever happened to be the first, for I was merely a child who could not yet form my own religious beliefs or philosophical thoughts to live a complete and meaningful life. I was easily influenced by my environments and accepted them as my fate.

I was living in a Buddhist temple, but my parents sent me to a Christian school which was an extraordinary, unconventional, and even unthinkable decision on my parents' part. You might not find the significance of it, but normally, parents would not create such a spiritually conflicting environment for their son to grow up. My mother and father had only elementary school educations and were very poor; hence, people perceived them to be uneducated and uninterested in investing in education and the betterment of their children's futures.

At home, I was totally submerged in Buddhism. I lived, breathed, and dreamed of being a Buddha, an enlightened one. At school, preacher-teachers started each morning with prayers, hymn, and bible studies. You could argue that I was lost between two different religions but for me, I found oneness between both religions and was able to accept both flawlessly.

I was just an ordinary and simple-minded boy. There was no way a boy like me could ever be a Buddha, an enlightened one. It had to be someone who was extraordinary. So, on this particular day, I did nothing but contemplate whether I should confront my master with the dire question I had been torn over for days. I found my master sitting in Mahavira Hall (the main hall of the temple) meditating with the beads of a rosary in his right hand. When he came out, I went in and said I wanted to ask how to become a Buddha. He gave me a curious and interesting look then followed me inside.

I said, "I want to be a Buddha, an enlightened one, but I don't know how. Can a boy like me be a Buddha?" He could have brushed me off and ignored my nonsense since I was merely a child. Instead, he lowered himself to my eye level and looked at me like he was about to tell me the most important message in the universe. He said, "If you look for Buddha outside of you, you will never find him. In every person's heart, there lives a Buddha. All you have to do is to look within and connect to your true self. That is how you become what you are looking for."

I had been learning scriptures from a Bible at school and reading and memorizing Bible verses every week for homework. I read the words but didn't understand their meaning. When my master said that Buddha lives inside of me and to look within to connect to my true self, I finally understood what my preacher was saying in school. When the preacher said that man is created in the image of God, he was saying the same thing. Buddha, God, or the Higher Power you are seeking resides in all of us.

It requires a lifetime of learning to become what you are looking for, and we must let go of all things and thoughts that prevent us from connecting to our true selves. The beginning of the journey to self is believing you are a special and unique person. You must believe that you are the most important person in the whole wide world; then, you are going to speak, walk, and act like that. Only then will people start believing in you and treat you like such. Even if people don't treat you the way you should be treated, that is okay, because their opinion does not matter to you anymore. You are not here to live their lives for them; you are here to live your own. You don't need their approval of you to go out and live your God given life. God resides in you. Who could destroy you and bring you down? No one and nothing can!

Dear Kim Kim,

I'm supposed to leave tomorrow I believe. So, I wanted to say thank you.
You don't know me too well, so let me tell you a bit about myself.
I was the awkward shy girl that had no confidence whatsoever.
 I was that girl that didn't speak up about what she believes in.
I was that girl that would sit and cry because she didn't know how to handle anything.
Notice how I used past tense?
I am worth it.
I am strong, and I decide my own life.
I am unique, and I am imperfect.
Imperfection is beauty.
Kim Kim, I would like to thank you for not helping me out of the cocoon.
I would like to thank you for letting me fight to become stronger and to become a beautiful butterfly. Thank you for letting this ugly little caterpillar turn into a beautiful butterfly. Love --Adolescent

Starfish, a Bird, & David

I've studied now Philosophy

And Jurisprudence, Medicine,

And even, alas! Theology

All through and through with ardour keen!

Here now I stand, poor fool...

In Goethe's Faust

"You are my starfish!" As soon as I say this catch phrase indicating the start of my group session, adolescent-patients including those who have been labeled ADHD (Attention-Deficit/Hyperactivity Disorder) in a noisy and disarrayed room are suddenly quiet and walking toward empty seats in a circle. All the curious eyes are on me now, waiting for my next words. This phrase has surprisingly been one of the most effective attention getters for me to tell the story of a young man who unexpectedly received three life altering gifts from a little girl, a wise man, and Michelangelo all in different stages of his life.

The majority of adolescents age thirteen to eighteen are admitted involuntarily without their consent because they have suicidal ideations or have attempted suicide. So, they have to be removed immediately from their dangerous and serious circumstances and are brought to the hospital to be placed under twenty-four-hour surveillance. We are to keep them safe for a minimum of seventy-two hours to a week or two until they are no longer a threat to themselves or someone else. In consequence, the most important duty is to keep patients safe from harming themselves or somebody else in my Adolescent Unit at the acute hospital.

Thus, the number one priority is keeping patients safe from harming themselves until they are discharged. That is our main duty, but I want to do more than just manage them and keep their body unharmed. I must do more than what is expected of me as a counselor, for I understand what patients and their families are going through at one of the lowest and hardest points in their lives. My heart goes out to them, and I truly want to transform them to live a life worth living. They have been living in a body fighting for survival behind the fake smiles and hoping for the pain inside to miraculously disappear. They carve their bodies to have physical pain rather than feel the deep wound inside. At the same time, their minds and thoughts in their heads are telling them to die because their lives are not worth living.

If they were my sons and daughters, what would I do to help them overcome these obstacles that life throws at them? When I ask myself that question, I have a clear vision and purpose of what I ought to do. I want to reach their hearts and plant a seed of self-worth and self-love so that I can prevent them from having such toxic and negative thoughts which would lead to such toxic and negative actions. Ralph Waldo Emerson said, "The ancestor of every action is a thought." In that case, an action is manifested by a thought in their minds. Hence, I emphasize and put all my effort into teaching them in a group and through one on one conversation.

Teaching is my most favorite and the important part of my job at the hospital other than keeping them safe. I admit there were a few close calls, but I promise nothing bad is going to happen to my patients under my watch even if they still carry suicidal ideations and want to end their lives. Nevertheless, if you really think I could make suicidal thoughts and all the problems disappear while they are with me in a very short period of time, and if you really think I could make them believe their lives suddenly got better, and they start believing their lives are worth living, I would be a miracle worker. I would bottle the cure and give it to all adolescents and their families for free because that is what they are going through in that stage of life.

It would be beneficial to all concerned if I and the adolescents whom I am trying to save from suicidal thoughts, see eye to eye and have the same level of understanding why they are here and know what they have to do to change their behaviors. But many of them just want to go home while nothing has truly changed. Well, you know what happens: if nothing is changed while they are in the hospital, nothing will be changed when they are at home either. In addition, they don't want to be here in the first place and have given up on life already. They think there is nothing wrong with them. They say, "She hurts me so bad that I want her to suffer by me hurting myself." What kind of toxic thinking is that? Also, they say it is always somebody else's fault why they are in a locked-up facility like this, and it is simply a "mistake" what they did to themselves or that they sent naked pictures and suicidal messages on social media.

With this kind of mentality and behavior, they are not willing to accept they need help, and they are very reluctant to learn anything to change their way of thinking to have a life worth living. It is the most critical time in their lives, and I, as a counselor and father, want to do anything to save them because I see the worth and potential in each and every adolescent coming to my hospital. I have a personal mission statement for adolescents at work. It says, "My mission is to inspire and empower adolescents to reach within themselves and to find their purpose in life and transform them to live a life worth living." If I can somehow inspire them to see their worth and potential in themselves, they would see things differently and would try to work on changing themselves first instead of blaming others and trying to change them. If they do that, I feel like they are well equipped to handle their current dysfunctional family situations and environments which cause all these problems. I just can't accept that they want to give up because the past was too painful and unbearable to go on living when they have not lived their full life yet.

Then, what advice can I give to an adolescent who believes his or her life is not worth living, going on is pointless, and is giving up? I would like to ask them, "What do you know about life? You have not lived your full life yet and haven't used any of your God given potential. So, how can you say your life is not worth living, you have no hope, and you are destined to fail, when you are created in the perfect image of God and God resides in you? All the struggles and obstacles you are facing right now are preparing you for your successful future that is yet to come. Life is meant to be lived no matter what. You can never, ever turn your back on life no matter how difficult it is. It is your job to find your passion in life and keep it lit to brighten up this world."

Someone once said, "Life is full of disappointments, failures, and setbacks. None of those things can permanently stop you. You have the power in you to overcome anything that life throws at you. There is nothing as powerful as a made-up mind. Surround yourself with people who remind you that you matter and support you in the ways that matter most to you. No person, situation, or circumstance can define who you are. Do not give up, cave in, or stop believing that it is possible. It is not over until you win, and only you get to decide when that starts."

Thus, it has been challenging to talk about the most important matter in their lives when they don't see it. I can pretty much predict where some of them are heading if they don't change their behaviors and their mindsets right now. At the same time, I know I can help them discover why they did what they did and how they go about changing their thoughts, feelings, and behaviors so they will live a life worth living. I learned from my own mistakes that adolescents are just not interested in being lectured by a shrink. They see all staff at the mental hospital as shrinks. Through my own trial and errors, I have learned that telling them stories are the easiest and best way to not only build positive relationships with them but also to connect with them and open their minds to different thoughts. This helps them to re-examine their lives at their lowest point. These are three separate stories that I tell in one group, and I walk them through how a young man found his identity and purpose in life from a little girl, a wise man, and Michelangelo.

All the knowledge in our head is information, ideas, philosophy, and theories of someone else's unless we make it our own by experience and application into our own lives. In order to truly understand, accept, and see life for what it is, we have to personally experience what we learn and apply it to our lives. Only then does it become our belief and principles and will we find it worth living and dying for.

Knowledge in our head is not only useless but also blinds us from seeing the simple truths in life if we only try to attain knowledge without putting it into action. All knowledge should lead us to virtuous actions, period. Otherwise, knowledge is no more than items we voraciously collect, hoping they may bring happiness and believing the bumper sticker, "One who has the most toys wins." Knowledge comes with responsibility, and it should be treated like water. Water itself is neutral: neither bad nor good. It solely depends on who drinks it. If a snake drinks it, it becomes deadly poison, but if a cow drinks the same water, it turns into sweet and nutritious milk. The same knowledge that some use to become villains like Hitler and Stalin, others use to become heroes like Gandhi and Martin Luther King, Jr. It is the same knowledge, but produced completely different outcomes depending on how and who used it, and why and what purpose they were using it for.

The more knowledge we have, the more responsibilities we must take on. That is why knowledge is power. It does not mean you will be the most powerful person because you have accumulated all the knowledge in your head. Self-knowledge, knowing about yourself, is self-empowerment which is the greatest knowledge of all. I emphasize again, all knowledge should and must lead to virtuous actions. If not, it is as good as dead languages in your head and the same as having learned nothing at all.

How many times have I heard these stories growing up? Because I heard them too many times to count, I lost the true meaning and value of them until I personally experienced the effectiveness in my adult life. Sharing my testimony with others about how these stories have influenced me and shaped me into the man I have become is my most effective way of teaching.

Kim Kim,

You reached me!
I have a hard time with most authorities/adults. But you are just a big kid at heart. You have somehow gotten through all my walls, which is shooting on so many levels. You radiate positivity and there is an unspoken peace when you are around. This time I'm not coming back. I know you will miss me, but I still remember the words you told me on that sheet of paper, "Any father would be lucky to have you." That makes me feel worth something when society tell me I'm nothing. I still have so much left to learn. Please always tell your children that they are enough even if they fall or are told otherwise. You are worth love, and you deserve the world. I really love you, that is why I'm a pain when you get inside of my walls (Haha). That is my way of showing love. You really struck a chord with me. You are just so confident in yourself. I aspire to be just like you. I wish that you could stay in my life, but I know all good things must come to an end. I'm excited to end

37

this awful chapter of my life. Mental health has always been an interest in my life. I want to be just like you.

The way your groups make me feel is so crazy. I have never felt so much fire inside of me. It's only when you tell me I'm worth it do I believe you. You work so hard to be here for all of us. You constantly are challenging us and pushing us out of our comfort zone, and that is when we get getter. You make us better. You have made me better. I just wanted to thank you for everything. —Adolescent

Starfish

There once was a man. He worked so hard to climb the ladder of success and achievements. Everything was going right for him, and everybody thought that one day he would take over the entire company and would be their boss. As he got promotions one after another and was getting closer to the top, he worked much harder than anybody else. However, he could not help but feel that something was missing in his life. He was very successful, and everybody envied him because sooner or later, he would take over the entire company, becoming the most powerful and influential man they knew. Nevertheless, he felt he was in a rat race. Even if he won every race, he was, after all, just a rat chasing an empty dream. He thought he had everything any man could ask for but felt empty inside. He could not understand why he felt that way.

So, he took some time off for the first time in his career and went to the beach to clear his mind; most of all, to search for what was missing in his life. He got up early in the morning, just as the sun was about to rise. He was walking along the beach all alone, and waves were coming in and out silently and effortlessly. In the far distance, he saw a little girl bending down to pick something up on the sand and gently throw it into the ocean. He was curious as to what that little girl was doing this early chilly morning. As he was walking toward her, he began to see several dozen starfish washed out from the ocean. He did not bother to save them because they were just starfish, and after all, there were far too many of them. In a short minute, the sun would rise and these starfish would dry up and die anyway so why bother, he thought carelessly.

When he came near her, he saw hundreds of thousands of starfish. The little girl was picking up starfish one by one and throwing back into the ocean. He could not help but laugh at her. He said, "What are you doing, little girl?" She said, "The sun is about to be up and the tide is going out. If I do not throw them back, they will die." He burst out laughing and said, "Don't you see there are miles and miles of beach and hundreds of starfish. Who do you think you are, God or something? You can't possibly save them all! It is no use. Give it up!" After listening to him patiently, the little girl bent down, picked up another starfish and gently threw it into the ocean. Then, she smiled at the man and said, "I made a difference for that one."

For the first time in his life, he had aha moment, and embarrassingly it was from a little girl. He was so driven to succeed that he had to be the first to do everything he did; being second meant being a failure in his opinion. Hence, if he thought that the task or project was too big or impossible to solve, he did not even try because he knew it was unsolvable. He realized then how many chances he missed that would allow him to make a difference in the lives of countless others no matter how small a task it was. He went home and threw himself into study, searching for the truth that would set him free.

Kim Kim,

I am writing this not, so you remember me, but so you know I'm another starfish saved. You did it. You helped. Now, from your inspiration and knowledge, I can live. You make me believe I am so grateful. You have taught me to carry myself like I am worth it because I am. You have taught me, "seek to understand, than to be understood." I have learned so much. You have changed my life. I believe in myself. I can do this. I want you to know you are amazing! Without your impact, I may still be stuck; I may still be broken so terribly with no hope. You have given me hope. I may have only known you for two weeks, but...it may be the most significant two weeks I've ever lived.
I probably won't ever see you again. That's okay. You will always be in my memory alive and inspiring. I wanted you to know how much you mean to me and how happy I am to have met you. Thank you, Kim Kim. You have blessed me. You are an amazing blessing. Thank you for everything you have done for me. –Adolescent

A Bird

He studied all sorts of knowledge ranging from medicine to philosophy to religion to law, but his eagerness toward his knowledge was never fulfilled. The more he studied, the more he realized he was getting further away from the truth. So, he stayed depressed, anxious, and angry at himself all the time. One day, a traveler came into a town and heard about the young man's frustration. He said to the young man pointing at a nearby mountain, "There lives a wise man in a shabby hut on the top of that mountain. Why don't you go and see him? He might be able to help you to find what you are looking for." Then, the traveler once again raised his finger pointing at the mountain.

Suddenly he realized he might have been looking for the wrong thing in the wrong place all along. He thought he could find what he was looking for directly in books. He believed he could find it if he studied harder, worked harder, and searched harder in the external world. After all, his hard work and competitive mindset in the world brought him all the success up until then. When people pointed their fingers, he was looking at the finger, not the direction it pointed. He realized the finger is only a useful tool because of what it points us toward, and we have to look at where it points. The finger is not an object of study or purpose, but the place the finger points to is. He understood what Buddha supposedly said, "I am a finger pointing to the moon. Don't look at me; look at the moon." Buddha, Jesus, Confucius, Socrates, Gandhi, and all the other great teachers are there to teach us and show us where to find the truth. Once we find the truth, we have to detach ourselves from it to make it our own and have to abandon it until the next truth comes along. It is like a boat which takes us to cross the river. Once we arrive on the other side of the river, we have to leave it there at the bank or cut it up to use, for we no longer need it, and it is too heavy to carry with us.

He wanted to fill his emptiness with the wise man's wisdom to know the fate of all beings, to find the meaning of his life, and more important, to set him free from bondage; thus, he willingly took a journey to the mountain. After all, he was thinking, "What have I got to lose?" If he could obtain just one piece of wisdom, he thought that alone was worth traveling a thousand miles. He remembered what Confucius once said, "A journey of a thousand miles starts with a single step." Who knew it could be his first step toward his journey to self?

He had lived all of his life in a village. When he was young and free, he spent so much time playing on the mountain with his friends. Once he became an adult, he was too busy working in the city and had forgotten the existence of the mountain even though it was always right there in front of his eyes as were his childhood memories. As he was slowly climbing the mountain, he could taste fresh misty air dripping from pine trees. He listened to the swirling waters in a creek. The softness of fallen leaves and smells of the earth brought his childhood memory of being young and free. He, free of care, followed the beautiful sound of birds chirping, and there was a little bird alongside the wooden area. He carefully picked it up and put it in his pocket.

Arriving at the wise man's hut, he called out in a courtyard but no one answered. He entered a room and saw the wise man facing the wall meditating. There was hardly anything in the room and he could see how simple of a life the wise man had been living. The man heard the voice behind him and turned around to face him. The young man blurted out, "Wise man, I have a bird in my palm." The young man asked, "Is the bird in my hand alive or dead?" If the wise man said the bird was alive, he would squeeze the bird and kill him. If the wise man said that the bird was dead, he would simply open his hand and set him free. The young man smiled at the thought that the wise man was trapped. The young man asked him again in haste, "Is the bird in my hand alive or dead?" The wise man closed his eyes for a second; then he responded, "The fate of the bird is in your hand. Open your heart, young man, and let yourself live."

The moment he let go of what he had learned, what he was searching for, he realized that fate and truth were in his hands all along. He finally understood his fate and how he should live his life and the truth which would set him free. The moment the wise man said that the fate of the bird was in his hands, he realized the fate and truth that he was searching for was indeed in his hand all along. Octavio Paz writes in *The Labyrinth of Solitude* "All of us, at some moment, have had a vision of our existence, something unique, untransferable and very precious. This revelation almost always takes place during adolescence. Self-discovery is above all the realization that we are alone: it is the opening of an impalpable, transparent wall — that of our consciousness — between the world and ourselves. It is true that we sense our aloneness almost as soon as we are born, but children and adults can transcend their solitude and forget themselves in games and work. The adolescent, however, vacillates between infancy and youth, halting for a moment before the infinite richness of the world. He is astonished at the fact of his being, and this astonishment leads to reflection: as he leans over the <u>river</u> of his <u>conscousness,</u> he asks himself if the face that appears there, disfigured by the water, is his own. The singularity of his being, which is pure sensation in children, becomes a problem and a question. But the adolescent cannot forget himself — when we succeed in doing so, we are no longer an adolescent — and we cannot escape the necessity of questioning and contemplating ourselves."

The wise man felt sorry for the young man because he seemed to have so much knowledge but not only was his knowledge useless, it blinded him to see the truth he was looking for. He invited the young man into his room and decided to give him one more lesson. "Young man, you came all the way up here to see me, but as you can see, I have nothing to give you. I have a very special tea that I brew and won't you have a cup of tea with me?" The young man was red with anger and humiliation. The wise man paid no attention to him and brought a teakettle with two cups; one was an expensive and fancy porcelain cup and the other was a cheap and disposable Styrofoam cup. The young man unconsciously picked up the porcelain cup with two hands, and the wise man started pouring warm tea in his cup. His cup was overflowing, wetting his hands and pants, but the wise man kept pouring tea in his cup. The man finally screamed, "Stop! My cup is overflowing and you got me wet! Why did you do that, old man?"

The wise man smiled and said with a stern voice, "When you come to see me, your mind is overflowing just like this. No matter what I do or what I say to you, you are not able to contain anything at all. Go back to your village and first empty your cup. Then, come back to see me. Only then, are you able to contain what I say to you." He continued, "You see, I brought two different cups. You unconsciously and automatically picked an expensive and fancy cup over a less valuable one just like everybody else would. I don't blame you for wanting to have such nice things in life. In fact, I, too, chased an empty dream and wasted most of my productive life following the path others had followed instead of living a purposeful life. I thought all those material things would bring me happiness and contentment. I truly believed that was how I should live because everybody was living like that."

He said that the biggest regret was choosing to conform with society and to please everybody in it. He laughed, "To think of it, that is a lot of people to please and it is hard to be liked by everybody." He was following the crowd, doing what others were doing, and living up to other people's dreams and their expectations because he felt the social pressure and did not want social rejection. Thus, what other people say or thought about him was more important than what he thought of himself. He dreamed, just like any member of society, of being financially independent and being successful however the social norms defined it.

The young man agreed and sighed, "I also did what others did. I had what others had. After all, my dream was nothing to do with what I really wanted out of my life but how much wealth I accumulated. I thought I did not have a choice but to follow the rules and social norms established by society and to accept them as facts and as the truth."

During the Cold War, a group of Soviet Union writers were touring America to see if it still holds truth in America, "We hold these truths to be self-evident, that all men are created equal, that they are endowed by their Creator with certain unalienable Rights, that among these are Life, Liberty and the pursuit of Happiness." They found it astonishing, not because of capitalism and materialism, seeing high skyscrapers, mega shopping malls, varieties of automobiles, and webs of highways that connect all states, but what they read in newspapers and watched on TV. They were stunned to learn that all opinions from people were the same. It was like cookie cutters had molded everyone in the same way and brainwashed them all. One of the Soviet Union reporters remarked, "In our country, to get that result we have a dictatorship. We imprison people. We tear out their fingernails. We punish them severely for having their own opinions. Here you have none of that. How do you do it? What is the secret?"

When people blindly follow conformity, it becomes the institutionalized insanity supporting obsolete-social norms and dysfunctional beliefs and mentality of "we always have done it this way!" that had nothing to do with the truth. A wise man said that the moment he realized it was foolish of him, letting other people judge and define his existence, he had to ask himself why he was following followers and conforming with society. The old man said, "Young man, you have to ask yourself this question: Is the tea what you want out of your life or the expensive cup how you are spending your entire life? Find your passion and God given gift to get your tea. Living in a mansion or driving an expensive car or wearing brand named clothes are just a cup. No matter how expensive and fancy a cup you are, you are just a cup. The young man finally broke down and said, "I did not know what I was searching for before, and now I still don't know what it is, but whatever it is you have, please let me have."

As he was walking down the same path he climbed up that morning, he was pondering what it was that the wise man had that he did not. He asked himself, "How could he live a basic and simple life away from everything but seem to have everything he wanted out of life? What did I accumulate so much of that it had been preventing me from seeing the truth?" He stopped to drink spring water. He opened both hands to hold the water and drank from them. He suddenly realized that when he opened his hands and put his hands in water, he could freely feel the water and his hands being one with water. When he gripped his hands tight to hold water, he could not hold any water at all.

He wondered, "Is it what I have in the external world that holds me back from seeing what is essential in my life? My whole life, I was chasing what others were chasing and following followers. Are my hopes and dreams really my hopes and dreams? What would define my life and me? Does my existence truly matter to me and others?" Kenneth Tynan wrote, "How far should one accept the rules of the society in which one lives? To put it another way: at what point does conformity become corruption? Only by answering such questions does the conscience truly define itself." He had many questions, but no single answer echoed as the sun was descending between the valley.

Dear Kim Kim,

It's only my second day here, and you have helped me realize a lot. You have the biggest heart and I love that about you. You may not notice me a lot because I don't say much, and I never really liked making eye contact. Every time you speak in a group, I feel like you are talking only to me. You've made me think about a lot. Whether you realize it or not, you have helped me more than anyone will know. Your words are very very powerful. It may have seemed like I wasn't listening, but I heard and listened to every word.

If you don't know if you helped anyone out of the group, you helped me. I went back to my room and wrote down everything that stuck. I will keep these notes because I want to remember that I am worth it and I have a purpose even if I don't know what it is yet.

I'm only seventeen years old and I have a lot to live for. You are an amazing person ad you deserve all the good coming your way. Maybe one day I'll speak to a group like this and tell them what you told us. – Adolescent

David

Returning home, he carefully observed his surroundings with new eyes. Thousands of books that he had read on the bookshelves were whispering words he could not understand: philosophy, art, biography, religion, history, entire encyclopedias, volumes of great books, and more. None of them could set him free yet. He absentmindedly looked at the poster he hung when he was a teenager. It was the poster of the statue of David. Among many great artists, he particularly loved Vincent van Gogh and Michelangelo. It was one of his bucket list items to see Michelangelo's David at the Academia Gallery in Italy.

The story of David and Goliath is one of the most beloved stories in the Bible, so much so that it will be told over and over again as long as there is a human race on earth. Why? It is because we all are David inside of us: small, weak, unfit, rejected, and the underdog. At the same time, we are the David who is seemingly an insignificant person but later becomes a hero. On the other hand, Goliath is the strongest giant who never lost a fight, terrorizing whomever faced him. All David had was his belief in God and himself. When no one dared to challenge the giant solely based on his outward appearance, Shepard David confronted him in a single combat. With only a staff and sling, he hit the center of Goliath's forehead and killed him.

Not many of us are fortunate enough to see the real Statue of David, but people all over the world have known about David and seen it in all forms of art and in prints. A few years ago, a student from Beech High School wanted to go abroad for a year as a youth exchange student. Through my Rotary Club, my family had been hosting foreign youth exchange students for a long time and enrolled them in local high schools. That was how she found me, and I helped her to go to Germany. She came to see me right after returning home after spending a year abroad. She told me she had visited seventeen countries in Europe. Hearing she had been to Italy, the very first thing I asked her was, "Did you see Michelangelo's Statue of David?" I expected to hear her excitement. Instead, she nodded her head and paused to find words to describe what it was like. Impatiently I asked her, "Is it really like what everyone says it is? Tell me!" She said after the long pause, "I can't tell you what it was like. You just have to be there to witness what it was like." I jokingly said, "You are not much help, you know!"

Before I tell you about Michelangelo's David, I need to tell you about an eighteen feet tall single block of marble in the middle of a courtyard. It was abandoned and ruined so badly that no one else wanted it. In fact, it was a nuisance to public eyes. Leonardo Da Vinci and other great sculptors learned about it and went to see if they could make something beautiful out of nothing. Every one of them immediately turned it down because they saw many flaws in it. At a later time, Michelangelo, too, heard about an abandoned single block of marble and found the owner. If he could see it and if he liked it, he would purchase it from him. The man said, "Great sculptors like Da Vinci already saw it, and they told me it had flaws and nobody could use this block of marble. That is why I left it there. Save yourself a trip. You will not be able to use it at all." Michelangelo insisted and off he went. Standing in front of the block, his eyes were fixed on the white flawless marble at his feet. Suddenly, he saw a vision of what he could make and brought the block of marble to his workshop.

The Statue of David is a perfect man and so perfectly symmetrical that people could not accept a human being could create such a sculpture. It was so perfect that people say God must have come down on earth and created it. Giorgio Vasari wrote Michelangelo's David is the greatest masterpiece ever created by mankind, "When all was finished, it cannot be denied that this work has carried off the palm from all other statues, modern or ancient, Greek or Latin; no other artwork is equal to it in any respect, with such just proportion, beauty and excellence did Michelangelo finish it."

Hence, one day a man wanted to know how in the world Michelangelo could create such a masterpiece. So, he asked, "How were you able to create the Statue of David? It had to be the most difficult thing you have ever done." Then he waited for a profound answer. His answer shocked the man. Michelangelo said, "It was easy." "How could it be easy?" the man exclaimed looking at David right in front of his eyes. Michelangelo said, "I did not create David." He continued, "I saw David in the block of marble. Because I saw David in the block of marble, all I had to do was to chisel off what was not David. So, there came David."

When adolescents are admitted to my unit in the hospital, they come with thick charts that contain all of their medical records including their mental and behavioral history. It would seem the more I know about a patient's history, the better I am equipped to care for them, assess them, and help to heal their psychological wounds. Wrong! I used to think that way when I started working at the hospital: I read all their documents and could come up with safety and treatment plans of what I should do before I even met them for the first time. It was a huge mistake on my part. I call it a rookie mistake. If I had only known then what I know now, I would throw the chart away and burn it (literally speaking!) because we cannot treat patients solely based on their diagnosis and history written on papers when it comes to their mental and behavioral problems. I assumed and believed their diagnosis to be all facts and the truth. When I actually meet an adolescent and spend some time with him or her in my unit, I realize they are not the same kids as on papers. I created my perception based on their history and had treated them according to my distorted perception of them. We take a snapshot at that moment in their stage of lives and form educated opinions based on DSM (Diagnostic and Statistical Manual of Mental Disorders.)

I could write another book just dealing with my opinion on this matter. I am so passionate about saving young lives before it is too late by changing their way of thinking. The more and more I deal with adolescents, the stronger I believe it is possible to transform their lives to live a life worth living. According to scientists and researchers, only one percent of the world's population has a mental illness; then, we are talking about changing their behaviors, their environment, and most importantly, changing their way of thinking. I don't have to borrow what Roman emperor and Stoic philosopher Marcus Aurelius said, "Very little is needed to make a happy life; it is all within yourself, in your way of thinking. Everything we hear is an opinion, not a fact. Everything we see is a perspective, not the truth." He said that in 180 A.D. before neuroscience and all other schools of science proved that to be true thousands of years later.

I am not dismissing the importance of early diagnosis and treatment. Earlier detection and examination are essential for treatment and the quality of life. However, we as professionals examine and determine whether it is normal or abnormal behavior by looking at their symptoms and signs and how skewed it is from the norm. Then, it becomes a label and judgement — that is the way we treat them. In return, adolescents act exactly how they are labeled, judged and believed to be. Human beings are made up with heredity (genes) and social environment. Their self-image and self-worth are formed based on what they are taught and what they believe.

After all, I had good intentions wanting to know all there was to know about patients so I could pinpoint what they needed and provide that. However, I found myself treating patients the same way they were treated. I already created what kind of person he or she was and they acted the exact way my perception said they would act. If I treated them the same way they had already been treated, I had made them worse because they see themselves as unworthy. But if I treat every adolescent as though they have worth and potential, then I am able to create such an environment for them to become whoever they want to be and use their God given potential to the fullest.

Dear Kim Kim,

I just wanted to say thank you. You have inspired me in many many ways. It's been a pleasure meeting you and getting to know you. I will never forget you. You have a very special place in my heart.
Originally, I was just going to end everything as soon as I got home, but instead, I am going to begin everything. I am going to live life like I have never lived before all because of you, all thanks to the words you speak, and how you say them. —Adolescent

Two Men and an Old Farmer

What we are today comes from our thoughts of yesterday, and our present thoughts build our life of tomorrow. Our life is the creation of our mind. Gautama Buddha

There was a man living in a remote village. He lost a job and had to move to another village in search of a new job. While he was walking toward the new village, he was anxious, nervous and worried about what kind of people he would meet living in a new village. An old farmer and his young son were threshing grain with a wooden flail in their front yard. They saw a weary man walking towards them, and the old farmer stopped to help the stranger. The man swept the sweat on his forehead with the back of his hand and blew out a deep breath from his long walk. He anxiously asked the old farmer what sort of people lived in the next village. "Before I tell you that," the old farmer said, "tell me what the people were like in the village you came from." The man willingly responded, "They were the most caring and generous people you could ever meet. They treated me like a family member with kindness, respect, and love If I did not have to move in search of a new job, I would have never left them." The old farmer said, "You will find the same sort of people in the next village." The man was comforted by his words and walked hurriedly toward the next village.

That afternoon, another man approached the old farmer and asked the same question about the people in the next village. The old farmer once again asked him, "What were the people like in the village you came from?" This time the man angrily responded, "They were full of bad people: hateful, unkind, selfish, and lazy! I could not wait to get out of that village." The farmer replied, "I am sorry to tell you this, but I fear you will find the same sort of people in the next village." The man sighed heavily and walked toward the next village with a heavy heart.

Each of the two men stopped to rest in a tavern at the crossroads: one road led to a Buddhist temple in a mountain and the other to the next village. One of the men eagerly told to the other what the old farmer had described about the sort of people that lived in the village. The other man was shocked to hear the contradicting description he had received of the same village. Both men were perplexed and asked a maid at the tavern which was true.

She said, "You both are right. In essence, your thoughts have led you to the village. You have felt and made up your mind of what sort of people they are before even meeting them. You have already experienced your future before it happens." Looking at the positive man, she said, "If you think it is the best place to live, then it is." She turned to look at the negative man who foresaw the calamity in his mind and continued," If you, on the other hand, think it is the worst place to live, then you are right, too!"

You get to choose the life you live, and whether it will be heaven or hell on earth. Abraham Maslow said that if the only tool you have is a hammer, you see everything else as a nail. Looking at a colorful mosaic, you and I would see different worlds if I wore red lenses and you wore blue. I would swear I see nothing but red, and you would swear everything is blue. Which is true? Seeing is believing, right? That is precisely untrue. What you perceive is what you get out of your life, and the world you have perceived in your mind has little to do with facts or reality. In other words, how you see yourself can influence the perceptions of people around you.

Friedrich Nietzache once said, "There are no facts, only interpretations." Heaven is not a place to find but rather a choice you make by seeing with new eyes. If you change your way of thinking, not only do the things that you look at change but you also introduce yourself to a new way of living.

Almost all adolescent-patients admitted to our hospital, in one way or another, have attempted or thought of suicide or homicide toward others. The self-destructive behaviors, unsuitable living conditions, and distorted thought processes leading up to their last acts were so severe and critical that they had to be removed from their imminent dangers. They must be placed in a safe and secured environment surrounded by twenty-four-hour surveillance cameras and staff watching them around the clock.

In addition to their madness, the length of stay is from a minimum of seventy-two hours to a week or two. To make matters worse, the majority of them are minors and have no voices of their own. They end up going back to the same dysfunctional family by whom they have been sexually or physically abused and neglected or to the same environment where suicidal ideations or attempts have occurred over and over again. When neither family nor environments are safe for them to live, they are involuntarily placed by DCS (Department of Children's Services) in unfamiliar places such as residential, group homes, foster care or even back to a juvenile detention center.

As a counselor, I have been telling these kids in both group and one-on-one counseling sessions to go on living their lives no matter what has happened in the past, to forgive those who have hurt them, and all the right words to ease their pairs. To be honest with you, I do not even know myself how I would cope psychologically, physically, and emotionally if some of these traumatic events happened in my fully engaged and matured adult life.

I really don't know if it is even possible to save them from suicidal and homicidal thoughts and attempts, let alone change their behaviors in such a short period of time. The only thing I can do is to create a positive environment and the right circumstances for them to have a life changing experience and give them useful tools that stick to their hearts while they are with us during one of most vulnerable and worst moments in their lives. It is a daunting assignment what we have to do with the very limited time given, when they see that suicide is the only option they have. Someone says, "Suicide is a permanent solution to a temporary problem." I am no miracle worker. At the same time, I refuse to be a mere Band-Aid to permanently wounded hearts.

I often quote what Mark Twain said, "The two most important days in your life are the date you are born and the date you find out why." I said, "I vividly remember the first day you were admitted to our hospital. Your ankles were chained, your hands shackled, and you had the heaviest baggage on your back." Of course, I am talking about emotional baggage that they had when they came in. I continue, "Something has to happen while you are here, and that is an inside job, your way of thinking. If you are discharged with the same attitude and the same way of thinking as you first came in, you cannot expect to change your life. So, you are not willing to change yourself, but want everyone else to be changed for you? You are going back to the same environment you came from and they will not suddenly change their lives for you. You have to be the one changing your way of thinking."

Albert Einstein defined, "Insanity is doing the same thing over and over again expecting different results." Hence, it is insane to expect to solve your problems with the same thinking that you created in the first place. If you truly want to change your life, you must first change your way of thinking. You only have control over a tiny fraction of what has happened to you. Someone said that life is ten percent what happens to you and ninety percent how you react to it. The attitude and choices you are making determine your life. William James said, "The greatest discovery of my generation is that a human being can alter his life by altering his attitudes." If you truly believe that your life is worth living your belief will create the world you want to live.

In conclusion, I want to share quotes from Psychiatrist and Holocaust-survivor Viktor Frankl. "When we are no longer able to change a situation, we are challenged to change ourselves. ...Between stimulus and response there is a space. In that space is our power to choose our response. In our response lies our growth and our freedom." He added, "Everything can be taken from a man but one thing: the last of the human freedoms—to choose one's attitude in any given set of circumstances, to choose one's own way." That was the very reason why at the worst circumstance during the Holocaust losing his parents and his wife in a gas chamber, he was able to replace pain and despair with hope and human triumph that nothing could kill his spirit and take away his attitude, belief, and human freedom.

"The Man Who Thinks He Can"

by Walter D. Wintle

If you think you are beaten, you are,

If you think you dare not, you don't.

If you like to win, but you think you can't,

It is almost certain you won't.

If you think you'll lose, you're lost,

For out in the world we find,

Success begins with a fellow's will.

It's all in the state of mind.

If you think you are outclassed, you are,

You've got to think high to rise,

You've got to be sure of yourself before

You can ever win a prize.

Life's battles don't always go

To the stronger or faster man.

But soon or late the man who wins,

Is the man who thinks he can.

Kihyon,

I want to start off by saying you and everything you taught me has changed my input on life. Your story and your message had such an impact on me. I want to be like you when I grow up. I want to have your confidence. I want to have your drive to make a difference in people's lives.

I remember you talked about the girl's funeral you attended and how you said that you couldn't save them all. I want to tell you that you have saved me. Not only that, but you have made me think in such a positive way. You are the person that changed me the most during my time at Skyline. I am forever grateful. God put you in my life. You touched my heart in many ways and for that I am forever grateful for you.

My friend, keep doing what you are doing. I love ya, Kim!
Your friend, --Adolescent

A Scholar and a Monk

There once lived two young boys raised in a small village like brothers. One was a sixteen-year-old boy named Yang, and the other was one year older, named Yin. They were born from different parents but were inseparable. If you saw one, you were likely to see the other, always playing and studying together. They had learned everything they needed to learn in one classroom and could not further their education. In fact, their village was too small to contain their unlimited imagination and thirst for knowledge. Hence, both boys decided to travel to the West to quench their thirst for knowledge and hoped to find the meaning of life and of happiness.

They walked and walked tirelessly but happily in search of new knowledge. Each time they passed a new town, they sought out scholars to learn from, but when they heard one thing, they already knew ten more. All the scholars begged them to settle in the town in order to continue teaching them, but they continued their journey far and wide to the West.

Night had fallen and they had miles to go before reaching the next town. To make things worse, rain was pouring down hard; they found shelter in a cave which had been hollowed out of the earth. Yang was huffing and puffing with thirst and saw what appeared to be a gourd on the ground. He drank from it without thinking, and the water tasted so sweet and refreshing that his thirst disappeared in an instant.

The next morning Yang got up still thinking of how sweet the water was the night before and wanted to drink more. What he saw was an unimaginable and gruesome site, and he instantly threw up everything he had eaten and passed out, unconscious. Upon waking up from unconsciousness, he realized he had been to heaven and hell simultaneously. What he thought was a warm and safe shelter the night before, was in fact an old tomb littered with human skulls. The delicious water he drank was in fact from a human skull full of mildewed rainwater.

For the first time in his life, Yang had experienced the power of the human mind and began to understand that all phenomena existed and disappeared depending on how his mind chose to see it. He suddenly remembered what a teacher had meant by saying, "when a cow drinks the water, it becomes milk. When a snake drinks the same water, it becomes poison." The water itself is neither bad nor good. It is in the mind of the beholder.

He accepted that whether it was an actual cave or tomb, whether it was clean or dirty water, t did not matter because his experience was created by his mind's perception of it. He realized, "There is nothing clean and nothing dirty; all things are made by mind. The truth and knowledge we were searching for was in our minds all along." He told Yin that they could not find what they were searching for in any village because each man's truth is present in the mind. He asked Yin to abandon their journey and return to their village. Yin said that he wanted to continue his journey to the West to obtain new knowledge. Each of them promised to meet again after ten years in the village and went their separate ways.

Coming back to the village, Yang devoted himself to the Buddhism. Most Buddhist monks had affluent life styles in Buddhist Temples honored and supported by the royal family, but Yang chose to live a secular life in a village in order to bring spirituality to ordinary people living everyday life. He lived and worked with people and became their spiritual teacher. On the other hand, his friend, Yin, ended up in the West and became a great renowned scholar who accumulated so much knowledge that no persons would challenge him. In addition, he sought peace in a newly found religion—Christianity.

Ten years later, Yin finally came to visit Yang in his village. He wanted to test Yang's knowledge about life, hoping he would teach him a thing or two.

Yin asked, "What is the meaning of life in the Buddhist teachings?"

Yang responded without hesitation, "Don't commit any evils, practice the many virtues, and purify the mind."

Yin burst out laughing at Yang and said, "That is all you learned during all those years? That is so easy and simple that even a three-year-old child can say that!"

Yang nodded affirmatively, "That may be true, my friend, but can you live it?"

The moment Yin had arrived at the small village, villagers treated him like royalty and many people came to hear him speak. Yang continued "I heard you had become a world-renowned scholar and a religious leader. I am so proud of your accomplishments and your knowledge. I am certain you could recite the entire doctrines of your religion. However, knowledge in your head means nothing at all if your heart does not follow what you believe to be true! You speak Christ-like words and pray and believe in God you said, but actions, only actions like sharing a loaf of bread with a hungry fellow man sitting next to you defines what it means to be Christian."

It is a noble and hefty goal praying for the eradication of hunger off the face of the earth, but as Mahatma Gandhi said, "To give pleasure to a single heart by a single act is better than a thousand heads bowing in prayers." How often do we think about leaving a legacy so that our hopes and dreams would live through our children and someone else after we depart from this earth? Generations before us have passed on the torch to us, and now we must pass it forward to someone we face right now.

Yang was as much an intellectual and a visionary as Yin, but the difference between them was that he chose to live a secular life alongside the people of a village to plant a seed of love and spirituality so they could find it in everyday life with him. Yang confessed that in the beginning of his journey, he was like the man in a book of George Gissing written by Hery Ryecroft, "Foolishly arrogant as I was, I used to judge the worth of a person by his intellectual power and attainment. I could see no good where there was no logic, no charm where there was no learning. Now I think that one has to distinguish between the two forms of intelligence, that of the brain, and that of the heart, and I have come to regard the second as by far the more important."

How can you say you believe in God and love Him with all your heart while you are busy planting a seed of hatred and refuse to forgive those who wrong you? God says in Matthew 22:37, "Love the Lord your God with all your heart and with all your soul and with all your mind." How can you then love an invisible God while you are ignoring His children in need who are standing right in front of you?

Patients come to my hospital either empty, broken, or with a wounded heart. Seek and accept God in your life and allow Him to change you first so that He can use you as His servant to change other people and the world. The utmost important thing is to love yourself. If you have not, it is time to fall in love with yourself because you are lovable. You may not be able to look at your reflection in the mirror each morning because you don't like the person staring back at you. If you don't like who you are, what you have done, and where you are, you should not worry. You are not stuck with all those things. You can change, you can certainly grow, and you can be more than you are. I promise if, only if you love yourself and believe that your life is worth living and allow Higher Power to enter your heart, then you can finally live your God given life the way it meant to be.

Cory Booker once gave a testimony, and it has stuck in my heart ever since I heard him say, "Before you speak to me about your religion, first show it to me in how you treat other people; before you tell me how much you love your God, show me in how much you love all His children; before you preach to me of your passion for your faith, teach me about it through your compassion for your neighbors. In the end, I'm not as interested in what you have to tell or sell as I am in how you choose to live and give." You can't expect people to love you when you cannot even love yourself. You can't expect people to respect you when you can't respect yourself. You can't expect people to believe in you when you can't believe in yourself.

Yang and Yin believed in two different religions and were taught from two different schools of thoughts, but the ideologies they were searching for were the same. The book of 1 Corinthians chapter 13 says it all, 'If I speak in the tongues of men and of angels, but have not love, I am only a resounding gong or a clanging cymbal...If I have a faith that can move mountains, but have not love, I am nothing. If I give all I possess to the poor and surrender my body to the flames, but have not love, I gain nothing...And now these three remain: faith, hope and love. But the greatest of these is love."

Dear Kim Kim,

Thank you for showing me I'm worth 100%, not any less.

Thank you for cheering me up when I didn't want to be here because I was homesick.

Thank you for caring about me when I fainted.

Thank you for making me smile by calling me Princess in the morning when you wake me up! Nobody has ever called me that, not even my mom and dad.

You truly changed my life.

Much love,

--Adolescent

Mental Health Counselor

"The mystery of human existence lies not in just staying alive, but in finding something to live for." Fyodor Dostoyevsky

I wrote about all of the jobs I have previously held in Part Two: My Working Life of my book. By the time it was published in May 2014, I was to take office as a District Governor for the Rotary International a month later. Leaving the position as director at another hospital and working as a supervisor at a smaller hospital for four years had not been a dream job for me. In fact, I felt I had been demoted, but knew it was necessary to fulfill my duty as a District Governor. So, I held my head high and made the sacrifice. I accepted a job less challenging with a pay cut switching from a salary to hourly employee. This way I could manage my time better and devote myself to serving others. I had no intention of changing jobs in the middle of it. That would be a catastrophe I thought.

In truth, I was not happy with my job when I first started working there four years earlier. My reason for this was that it was intended to be a temporary fix and a stepping stone for the next big thing until I landed "the real permanent career" elsewhere. My heart just wasn't there. More than anything, I was completely exhausted physically, emotionally, and mentally, not because it required hard labor, long hours, and many challenges, but because I could not use any of the skills, life experiences, and education I had accumulated over the years; after all, it was not beneficial to anyone including myself. I often asked myself, "What am I doing here?" I did not think I was doing what I was supposed to do with my life. I told myself it was only temporary until I finished my Governorship. Nonetheless, I showed up for work with a smile on my face. I truly performed more than my job required me to do and tried my best to create a high functioning and friendly working environment with a positive attitude.

Some chase the rainbow but cannot put up with the rain. Some expect their dream jobs to fall onto their laps with their hands in their pockets. Every job I have had is a reflection of my life; thus, it has shown how I have lived my life and the influence it has made on me and the people around me. No matter how small or insignificant they were compared to others, it mattered the most to me and my family. Steve

Jobs once said, "Your work is going to fill a large part of your life, and the only way to be truly satisfied is to do what you believe is great work. And the only way to do great work is to love what you do. If you haven't found it yet, keep looking. Don't settle. As with all matters of the heart, you'll know when you find it."

So, I had not only devoted my life to work but also treated it as if everything had depended on it in order to live my life, to support my family, and most of all, to do what I was called to do; spreading God's love to anyone I meet each day. With that reason, I had refused to let my job in terms of title, position, and even money define me. It was fuel for life, and I wanted to bring joy to others and touch as many lives as possible no matter the means. As someone said about a job, "It's about one life influencing another." If not, I believed, it was not worth doing.

When I was let go from my company right after my Governorship started in July, I was devastated and dumbfounded. On my termination letter it said, "Kim's Rotary schedule conflicts with the operational needs of the department staff." My employer not only agreed to me serving as a District Governor three years earlier when I was nominated, but had also supported all of my local and international projects that required me to be absent from work three to four weeks at a time. They had supported me attending weekly Rotary meetings every Wednesday. Furthermore, I was given the highest honor bestowed to an employee for my humanitarian service from my company and from the Tennessee Hospital Association among thousands of health care employees in Tennessee.

In fact, I was embarrassed when the company used me for their PR about how one of their employees was changing the lives of others through a service organization and then encouraged employees to also volunteer to serve. That was why I was dumbfounded that I was let go right after the change of administration. I was grateful that I was a valuable employee and that the hospital wanted me to work whenever I was needed. In fact, the truth is, most right-minded employees would not give up their job for a non-paying volunteer service. So, they obviously assumed I would resign from Rotary and be available to work anytime.

However, there was no way I would resign from the

commitment and dedication I made to serve as a District Governor. That was the first priority in my life. It was a clear choice what I should do: follow my heart and trust in God as I had always done before especially during times like this. I followed through with the resignation from the hospital and continued my duty as a District Governor with no financial income.

By the end of October 2014, I finished visiting all Rotary clubs and started looking for a job. I had been visiting the Madison/Goodlettsville Rotary Club more frequently than any other clubs because its meeting place was only five minutes away from my house. The club president was the CCO (Chief Operating Officer) of Skyline Medical Center on Madison Campus. I had known her for quite some time because she and I had been working for the same hospital system but at different locations. She asked me how my job was going with my busy Rotary schedule as casual conversation during one of my official club visits.

I told her that they hired a new director a few months ago. As soon as the new director started working, she learned that I, too, was a director of another hospital, and the reason that I was working there was to do Rotary and to serve as Governor. Before she even learned of her new role, she suddenly said that the hospital could no longer support my involvement with Rotary and asked me to choose between work and Rotary. I told my Rotarian friend, "I had worked hard because I was grateful for the hospital allowing me to do Rotary. When they hired me, they knew I was to be a Governor and fully supported me until a new director came in." I added, "I need a job, but you know I just can't resign from Rotary, especially while I am serving as a District Governor. Can they really do that?"

I had enjoyed every job I had and made the best out of them, but looking back, I might not have been doing what I was meant to do with my life for all those years. I finally accepted that it happened for the reason, and it probably was the right time to find what was missing in my life. The moment I decided to move on to the next chapter in my life, I was excited and anxious about the new opportunity and wanted to do something I had never done before. This time, money was not going to be the deciding factor of whether I should spend the rest of my life doing something I was destined to do. That was the soul-searching question, but the answer came when I was least expecting it.

She immediately asked me to email her my résumé and to apply to her behavioral and mental health hospital online. I was hired just like that, and it truly has been the best job I've ever had. I had a degree in Psychology but had never worked in the field until now. At first, I could not accept my resignation, yet now I wish they could have terminated me much sooner. God was not kidding when He said that when He closed one door, He would open a better one for me.

Ever since I was a little kid, I dreamed of becoming a high school teacher. Even though I have never become one, I feel I have made a full circle by becoming a mental health counselor for adolescents. I finally understand that everything I have done in my life has prepared me to do what I am doing now for these troubled and desperate youth. Someone once said, "Every single thing that has ever happened in your life is preparing you for a moment that is yet to come. A thousand disappointments in the past cannot equal the power of one positive action right now. Let others lead small lives, but not you. Let others argue over small things, but not you. Let others cry over small hurts, but not you. Let others leave their future in someone else's hands, but not you." I love what I do, and it breaks my heart each day when I work with patients. At the same time, I thank God for giving me a last chance to make a positive influence in their young lives before their precious lives may be taken away by their own suicidal attempts.

I wonder how my life would have turned out if I stayed at my former employment and resigned from Rotary instead, for I was afraid to lose my job and worried about my uncertain financial crisis. I would not had some of the most amazing years in my life as a District Governor and would not have obtained some of the most recognizable achievements our District has ever had. Furthermore, I would have never landed my dream job. Having lived through it, I feel I was tested and rewarded abundantly because I have kept my faith.

Right now, I am enjoying and appreciating every second I have with these adolescents because it can be taken away at any moment when I am called to another purpose. If I get to finish my career as a mental health counselor, I would die a happy man. If I save one child from dying, my life, after all, is not in vain. Mahatma Gandhi said, "The best way to find yourself is to lose yourself in the service of others." It is written in Matthew 18:3 in the Bible, "Truly I tell you, unless you change and become like little children, you will never enter the kingdom of heaven." While I am helping these children, I have realized that I am the one helped. While I am loving these children, I have realized I am the one loved. While I am forgiving, and teaching these children how to live again, I have realized I am the one forgiven and taught the greatest lesson of all. "The meaning of life is to find your gift. The purpose of life is to give it away."

Everything I have learned and experienced up to this point in my life, prepared me to be the best father, uncle, brother, friend, and counselor for these children. It is my job to let them find out for themselves that they are living a life worth living. I will help them to realize what they have always had: choice, freedom, and "ability to govern and discipline oneself by the use of reason." I am committed to helping them achieve self-understanding, decision-making and coping with problems. They are destined to do something great, and each one of them has a unique gift that they are born for. It is their responsibility to use and reveal their gifts to the world.

Dear Mr. Kim Kim,

I'm going to miss you a lot. I appreciate your wise and positive words. You were the one that gave me a reason to live. I'm going to miss all your stories and positivity. I had so much fun playing "Keep It Up" with you and the group. You always made me laugh. By the way, you are doing your job well and good. If they do end up coming back, then that is O.K. That doesn't mean you didn't do your job because you did. It just means they need someone like you on a day-to-day basis. They are just getting negativity all day long, or their emotions took over. So, don't beat yourself up about it. It is not your fault; it's theirs. But I can tell you that you did your job right because I believe I'm worth over 100%, and I won't be coming back. –Adolescent

Mary's Anyway

I've always been one to take their word for it.
They say I'm ugly, so I'm ugly.
They say I'm stupid, so I'm stupid.
They say this, I believe it.
They say that, I believe it.
Anything they say, I'll believe it,
But I'm done.
I'm better than those lies.
I will finish my race, anyway.

They tell me it's all A's or nothing,
but I study hard and get a B.
I'll study hard, anyway.

They tell me I can only love myself
if what I see in the mirror is tall, blonde, and skinny.
I'll love myself anyway.

They tell me my dreams are unrealistic.
I'll dream anyway.

They tell me I laugh too much.
I'll laugh anyway.

They say I could be pretty if I only wore more makeup.
My face is beautiful, anyway.

They tell me I don't love God
because I don't always go to church.
I'll love God anyway.

They don't let me sing
because I may not be the best singer.
I'll sing anyway.

They invalidate my opinions
Because I'm "just a child."

I'll form opinions, anyway.

I pick out an outfit.
Some call me a prude, others call me a slut.
I wear what I want anyway.

I try, time after time, but it's never enough.
I'll keep trying anyway.

They speak down to me, like I should be pitied.
I'll be strong anyway.

They say I'm too sweet to fight back.
I'll fight back anyway.

You see, I'm so much more
than a name or a face or a number on a screen,
but it's ok if they don't understand that.
I'm headed for the finish line either way.
I will finish my race,
Anyway.

I wanted to thank you for everything you've done for me and everything you do for all the kids that come to Skyline. You've changed the way I see the world and made a lasting imprint on my heart.

Every time I start to feel depressed, I'll remember what you would say to me and how you would want me to live my life. You've made me realize that if someone who just met me can care about me as much as you do, I guess I must be worth fighting for. So, I'm going to fight for myself.

Thank you so, so much for the book and for taking the time to write me a note. It meant so much to me. I can't wait to read it!

I hope one day that I can be half as good a person as you. I'll never forget you.

Adolescent Mary

PART II: FAMILY

A Father's Gift to His Young Son

When I was five years old, I moved to the small Korean village of Sang Do Dong. Between the sharp peaks and pointed paths of the mountains, there was a Buddhist monastery called Mi Ryuk Ahm, and that was my home. It might be true that I had accidentally stepped into a different life, but it changed the course of my childhood and gave a new meaning to my predetermined life and pushed me into a new environment.

From time to time, a crippled middle-aged beggar in makeshift clothes came to the remote village. Later in life I learned that he had a crippling and debilitating disease called polio. As soon as the crowds of children playing in the street saw him coming, they sang humiliating songs to him while he begged for food from door to door. After begging for food, that hungry and thirsty man always climbed the steep mountain up to the Buddhist monastery to see my father. As soon as he saw the beggar, my father greeted him with kind words and a smile, and bowed before him with respect. My father held his filthy hand and brought him inside our home. My father helped him wash his hands and dust off his clothes, then would ask my mother to cook a hot meal and served him as if he were the most honorable guest.

You are probably wondering what the big deal was. After all, he just gave food to a hungry beggar. Well, it was a big deal for me. You see, my family was so poor that we ate leftovers after the daily rituals and ceremonial events at the temple; in fact, the only times I got to eat hot meals freshly prepared by my mother were on my birthday and at the start of a new year. My father refused to serve the beggar the same leftover food that we ate every day, but instead gave him what little money he had in his pocket before the man left.

One day he come to see my father, but he was out working. I felt it was the perfect moment to tell him how I felt deep inside. Before he stepped into the monastery, I pointed a finger at him and dragged him out of my house and said, "Never come back to my house again. You embarrass my family and me!" You see, my friends in the village made fun of us because they said we were friends of a filthy beggar. I was humiliated by their comments and hated being associated with a "no good, filthy beggar." I think I was five or six years old when that happened. Even today, each time I think about what I had done to him, I am overwhelmed with guilt and remorse. I have tried to comfort myself saying that I was only five years old and I did not know better, but the pain has resided in my heart and will not go away.

At the time, I did not feel sorry for what I had done to the beggar, because I thought there was nothing I could do for him. Did I have money to give him like my father? No! Did I know how to cook for him like my mother? No! I felt as though my actions were perfectly justifiable and could not find any wrongdoing on my part. That afternoon, my father, somehow, found out the beggar had come by our home and I had not done anything to help him. My father called to me from the inside of our home. When I entered the room, he was sitting down and holding a cup of water in his hand. He did not spank me for the despicable thing I had done to another human being. He did not even raise his voice. He simply said, "I understand my friend came to see me." "What? Your friend?" He was calling this unworthy beggar a friend. You should have seen how my father treated him. My father treated him like he was the most important and special person in the world. He bowed to him with full respect. In fact, I was so offended by the way he treated an unworthy beggar that it made me feel I was unworthy and unimportant. I hated the beggar even more because of it. I remember thinking, "How could my father love that man more than me, his own son?"

I worried about what other people thought of me and being judged by people I associated with. I would do anything to please them even if it caused me to do what was wrong. My father, on the other hand, did what was right in his heart even though people made fun of him for it. Furthermore, he did not give a darn about what other people thought of him as long as he did what he knew was right. These realizations I came to later in life, but back then I wrongfully believed, because of shame, pride, and prejudice that such people had no worth compared to people in high positions and those who were rich. While I sat contemplating what I would say to defend my actions, he ended the conversation by saying, "My son, you could have at least invited him in and given him a glass of water." I could see how disappointed he was just by looking at his face, now as red as a tomato. However, I still could not see any wrongdoing on my part. I remember thinking, "Why should I invite a dirty homeless beggar inside of our home and give him a cup of water?" More than anything, I was embarrassed for being the laughingstock of my friends in the village. "What will other people think of me?" That was the biggest worry in my five-year-old mind.

After I was married and had kids of my own, I wanted to be a good example and a better father for my three children. Hence, I started volunteering to help people any chance I got. No matter how difficult it was and even though no one was there to watch me, I tried to do the right thing at all costs. Decades later, I began to realize what my father taught me then. He taught me that it does not matter whether I am rich or poor. It does not matter how small or big my life is going to be. It does not matter how small an impact I am going to make. There will always be something I can do, and I should not refuse an act of kindness when I have the ability to give.

Helen Keller once said, "I am only one, but I am still one. I cannot do everything, but still I can do something. And because I cannot do everything, I will not refuse to do the something that I can do." Helen Keller was only 19 months old when she became deaf, blind and mute. If she could accomplish helping many people, and live an inspiring life, I do not have an excuse not to live a full, meaningful, and complete life as much as she did. My father had shown hospitality and compassion to a beggar who could not pay him back, and by doing so, I believe he entertained angels without knowing it.

My father passed away in 2007. One evening a few months later on, my mother and I were looking through old photo albums reminiscing about my father. When we came upon a photo of me taken in front of the Buddhist pagoda, I suddenly remembered the unquenchable question I was afraid to ask before. I was too ashamed to ask about the beggar, afraid that tragedy might have taken place for what I had done. I asked my mother in a low and uncertain voice, "Mom, you still remember what I did to the beggar, don't you? He never visited our temple again after I dragged him out of the house. Do you know what happened to him?"

My mother gave me a strange and puzzled look and seemed unaware of what I was talking about. I asked her again, "You do know the beggar who came to see father every three to four months when we lived at the temple, and I told him never to come back to my house again because I was so ashamed of him. Surely you remember that, don't you?"

I put my head down and said, "Frankly, I have never forgotten what I did to the beggar even to this day!" "You were just a child, and I don't think you were even aware of what you did to him" my mother exclaimed with a surprised voice.

She closed her eyes slightly and gathered her thoughts while playing with white paper napkins. "You had such a soft and kind heart that whenever you saw someone or even animals mistreated, you felt helpless and broke down and cried. You felt their pain deep inside, as if it were your own. In fact, your father thought you were too weak and girly so he sent you to learn Taekwondo to make you strong and make a man out of you. It didn't change you though." She said positively.

"I was not anything like that at all!" I protested.

"Sure, you were," said my mother with confidence. Continuing, she said, "Anyway, your father knew why his kind- and good-hearted son felt as though he had to treat him that way and grew sad for having his family living in poverty. We were destitute after the Korean War, but it was not just us. Everybody was poor, did you know that?"

"When you are not only young, but poor and hungry, your mind plays tricks on you. Your poor life becomes a big test, for you blindly lose your ability to see and act according to your conscience and beliefs. You are tempted to do bad things that later in life you would be remorseful and ashamed of because your basic human needs were not met. I am not making an excuse for you now, but you were just a child growing older and we should not have put you in such dreadful circumstance."

"I am truly sorry for that."

"As to what became of the man, your father met him at the grocery store in another village and fed him there. He was trying to protect you, in a way. You might not remember this, but he had two children, a daughter and a son. His daughter became a school teacher and his son a military officer. I complained and fought harshly with your father for giving them the little money we had when we could not even feed you or buy you clothes. Every new year, both of his children came to see your father, and they were able to finish their education because of your father."

Although my parents could not provide me with all of my material desires like the rich, growing up in the loving care of such wonderful parents was a rare blessing and the best gift I could ever receive from this earth. You see, no child gets to choose his or her parents and they are not able to determine the environment they are raised in.

I feel as though I turned out to be a decent man after all, and there is no doubt in my mind that my mom and dad in heaven would be proud of me. I have not done many terrible things, and neither have I committed horrible sins nor harmed others inadvertently. However, if that makes me a decent man, then why have I felt dread and regret towards my past for all these years? Someone once said, "Being a good person does not depend on your religion or status in life, your race or skin color, political views, or culture. It depends on how good you treat others." I have finally understood this simple truth at this late stage of my life. The pain and regret that I have been carrying inside for so long was not due to the wrong things I have done, but due to realizing that I'd often lacked the courage to do the right things and looked the other way. Another person once said, "The worst regret we can have in life is not the wrong things we did...but for the right things we could have done yet we never did."

As I was growing up in the Buddhist monastery, before I knew what life was all about and was able to live a full life, death was right there hovering all around me like a dark cloud. When a person passes away, Buddhists believe there is a cycle of birth and death which takes forty-nine days for one consciousness to transform into the next. It is an exceptional right for the living, with the help of a monk in a temple chanting and praying, to be guided from death towards rebirth. Through my experiences in the monastery, I had not only witnessed many funeral ceremonies in a temple but also felt similar emotions mourners had for the dead. I felt trapped, living in an environment that I could neither escape nor deny. All of these events and thoughts contributed to me believing I was a victim and unworthy. The worst feeling was that there was nothing I could do to change my circumstances except to kneel and take whatever life presented to me.

Pastor Martin Niemöller was born in Germany in 1892. Just like all other young men, he joined the military and became a cadet in the Imperial German Navy. He was a fierce supporter of Adolf Hitler's rise to power even after he became a pastor following the path of his father. As he grew closer to God, he realized that German people were blindly and madly following the dictatorship of Hitler and the actions they were taking against the Jews were horrendous and inhuman.

What is worse is that it became legal to persecute, imprison, and murder millions of Jews when Hitler and the Nazis came to power. German people mindlessly believed his idealism of their superiority over inferior Jews whom were called and labeled "Barbarians, Undesirable, Parasite, vermin, Cockroaches." In the end, the human race paid the ultimate price for not only allowing it to happen but believing it to be true. German philosopher Karl Marx wrote, "History repeats itself, the first as tragedy, then as farce." If we have not learned from it, it becomes a distant and faded memory. It is no surprise when Joseph Stalin who followed Marxism in Russia said, "The death of one man is a tragedy. The death of millions is a statistic." There are only a few thousand Holocaust survivors living today, and they are aging into the 80-90s. We have only read about them in the history books for less than a decade, and it has become a faded and distant memory to the rest of the world, but not to them.

History began to repeat itself, just twenty-years after the unthinkable Holocaust in Europe, in America. It became legal to arrest Blacks who were sitting in the wrong seat on a bus. They could not eat with other races in restaurants and were even prohibited to drink water from the same water fountain that whites drank from. That was only sixty-five years ago.

Martin Luther King, Jr. was a young unknown preacher from Montgomery. He studied Henry David Thoreau and Mahatma Gandhi. He preached to the congregation in his church about civil disobedience, nonviolent, and social injustice that Blacks faced during that time. He believed, "Whatever affects one directly, affects all indirectly. I can never be what I ought to be until you are what you ought to be. This is the interrelated structure of reality." He was a law-abiding citizen but broke the law protesting for social justice, equality, and consciousness. He was arrested and wrote a letter to his fellow clergymen in a jail about what one should do: follow the law of God that applies to all human race and disobey unjust law of segregation that man made. He wrote in "Letter from a Birmingham Jail"

My Dear Fellow Clergymen:

We should never forget that everything Adolf Hitler did in Germany was "legal" and everything the Hungarian freedom fighters did in Hungary was "illegal." It was "illegal" to aid and comfort a Jew in Hitler's Germany. Even so, I am sure that, had I lived in Germany at the time, I would have aided and comforted my Jewish brothers. If today I lived in a Communist country where certain principles dear to the Christian faith are suppressed, I would openly advocate disobeying that country's antireligious laws.

...Now, what is the difference between the two? How does one determine whether a law is just or unjust? A just law is a manmade code that squares with the moral law or the law of God. An unjust law is a code that is out of harmony with the moral law. To put it in the terms of St. Thomas Aquinas: An unjust law is a human law that is not rooted in eternal law and natural law. Any law that uplifts human personality is just. Any law that degrades human personality is unjust. All segregation statutes are unjust because segregation distorts the soul and damages the personality. It gives the segregator a false sense of superiority and the segregated a false sense of inferiority. Segregation, to use the terminology of the Jewish philosopher Martin Buber, substitutes an "I it" relationship for an "I thou" relationship and ends up relegating persons to the status of things. Hence segregation is not only politically, economically and sociologically unsound, it is morally wrong and sinful. Paul Tillich has said that sin is separation. Is not segregation an existential expression of man's tragic separation, his awful estrangement, his terrible sinfulness? Thus, it is that I can urge men to obey the 1954 decision of the Supreme Court, for it is morally right; and I can urge them to disobey segregation ordinances, for they are morally wrong.

Martin Miemoller deeply regretted not standing up for himself and what was just in the eyes of God. He felt guilt for his own antisemitism and being cowardly silent. He opposed and spoke against

Hitler's ideology of Aryan supremacy and German people's complicity and cowardice in the Holocaust. He wrote the following and it resonates more than ever even after the World War II ended and the Holocaust became the distant memory in the history book.

First, they came for the Communists

And I did not speak out

Because I was not a Communist

Then they came for the Socialists

And I did not speak out

Because I was not a Socialist

Then they came for the trade unionists

And I did not speak out

Because I was not a trade unionist

Then they came for the Jews

And I did not speak out

Because I was not a Jew

Then they came for me

And there was no one left

To speak out for me

Edward Bloor said, "History repeats itself only in that, from afar, we all seem to lead exactly the same life. We are all born; we all spend time here on earth; we all die. But up close, we have each walked down our own separate paths. We have stood at our own lonely crossroads. We have touched the lives of others at crucial points, for better or for worse. In the end, each of us has lived a unique life story, astounding and complicated, a story that could never be repeated." If we don't remember the past and don't learn from it, then why do we need the history?

The comedian and songwriter, Jana Stanfield said, "I believe that each of us is on the journey of a lifetime. I cannot do all the good that the world needs. But the world needs all the good that I do." My father did what he ought to do and did not expect anything in return. If I can help one person at a time, one family at a time, or one community at a time, my life is worth living, and I will not be living in vain. Who knows? The world can be changed because of one person, and he might be the world to the one child, the one family, or the one community that he helped. I want to erase what I did to the beggar as well as my painful memory, but the life lesson I learned from my father will stay in my heart forever. It is my duty to carry it on to my children and to the people I meet each day.

Dear Mr. Kim Kim,

or should I say the father I wish I had.
I would just like to start off by saying thank you for pushing me to not lose faith in myself, but also in helping me find my inner peace.
Although I may not really know you, I feel so connected to you...as if I were your own daughter. Since I've had the opportunity to meet you and be in your presence, I feel like that is a blessing. I've never really met someone as kind as you or so understanding and nonjudgmental. Although I may be hard-headed and stubborn sometimes, I know that you only do what is best for me.
I've also learned a lot from you and view these things as very wise. An example for me is...it's not about anyone telling me I'm worth it but knowing that I am and knowing that I am enough. You have also been

my support group in helping me find parts of myself I never knew existed and you've also help me realize to always have hope.

I also remembered when you said a few years from now I may not remember you, but I know that I will. I won't remember you as just staff but as a father to me that I've never had.

Although you may probably think you've not had an impact on me; you're right. You had an impact on my heart. And I just would like to say thank you for letting me experience what it's like to be loved by a father!

I know reading this is super long, but in closing, I would like to say thank you so much for every little thing you do and just acknowledging me like calling me your daughter, and I'd also like to say I love you!

And just thank you for being here. —Adolescent

The Aged Mother

During ancient times, there was a rule that required anyone over sixty years old to be deserted deep inside the mountains to perish, for food was scarce and people of old age were believed to be reluctant and a hindrance to society. In today's society, we cannot even imagine such a dreadful rule or tradition to have existed in the past. Believe it or not, it still exists and teaches us a great lesson. Read on!

A man had been living with his aged mother and his young son. He was diligent, honest, and extremely devoted to his mother. However, the time had come for him to abandon her. He was grief-stricken and troubled by the relentless rule of the land, but there was nothing he could do. As he lifted her to set her onto a pack carrier, he was saddened by the lightness of his mother in his arms. However, he proceeded to carry her on his back towards the mountains with his young son.

As they traveled deeper into the mountains, his mother became aware of the situation and started breaking off the tips of tree branches. He thought that she was trying to mark the trail to find her way back home, which broke his heart even deeper. He felt the gentle and smooth pressure of his mother's hand on his shoulder, and she said, "It is going to be dark soon after you abandon me, and I don't want you to be lost in the mountains. So, I am marking the trail for you and my grandson so that you can find your way home."

With teary eyes, he set his mother down with a little food and left the pack carrier with it. As he prepared to return home, he saw his son carrying the pack carrier with him. He rebuked his son sternly, "We have no use for the pack carrier anymore. Throw that away, too." His son said innocently, "Father, when you are old, I am going to use this pack carrier to carry you away. I think it is foolish to throw it away now when I will need it later!" Looking down at his fragile old mother as he listened to his son's words, he was deeply moved and could not bring himself to abandon his mother. After all, he too would be abandoned one day; at that moment, he decided to disobey the rule. They secretly brought her back home and hid her in the attic.

A few years passed, when there came a famine in the land

greater than anyone had heard of or seen before. The crops had not only failed but there was no food left in storage, let alone a single grain of seed to plow for the coming year. He told his mother of the dire situation, and she said that the problem could be easily solved if he followed her instructions. Pointing at the thatched roofs, she said, "Thresh the straw again. There must be enough grain for seed from the straw that did not fall the first time." He did just that and was able to sow and reap enough crops for the whole village.

The king was amazed, overjoyed, and wanted to give a prize to the man who had the miraculous wisdom to save his countrymen from starvation. He admitted that it was his aged mother who should be praised and asked for forgiveness for violating the king's rule and tradition. The man's courage and his aged mother's wisdom convinced the king to abolish the rule, and from that day on, the elderly were respected and lived until their natural deaths.

You might wonder what this story has to do with you and even modern-day society, for you believe such rules do not exist in this world. Do you really think so? You can hardly imagine doing that to your own mother and father. My parents lived all of their lives with me until they passed away a few years ago. There are so many memories I could begin with "Do you remember...?" related to my parents. Out of countless events that happened in my lifetime, the times I had lived with my parents from my birth until their deaths were the most memorable and the happiest of all. You might doubt "What about the times with your wife and your children? Are they not the most important persons in your life?" They absolutely are!

They have become more than the most precious and important persons in my life. They are the loves of my life and all that I am. Nevertheless, my parents were always there for all of us. They were the ones who kept us together as a family, taught us family values and gave us our moral compasses that show how a man should live. Abraham Lincoln once said, "All that I am, or ever hope to be, I owe to my angel mother." I could never repay the debts I owe to my parents. I could never love them as much as they loved me. I could never give as much as they had given me.

The feeling I have now might be due to the recent memory that I lost my father in 2007 and my mother only two years ago. I came to realize that the gifts my wife, my children, and I have received from my parents were their faith and belief in God, and their love and respect for others. I believe those things sum up everything about my parents.

Even though they were Buddhists by birth when they lived in Korea, the moment they accepted Jesus Christ as their Savior while living in America, my mother and father accepted all as God's people and treated them as such. I became a Christian because I wanted to live like my mother and father; living ordinary lives but lives that in fact mattered to anyone touched by them. Khalil Gibran wrote in a poem, "Show me your mother's face; I will tell you who you are." I want people to see my mother and father in me even now after they have passed away. It would be my great honor and attribution to my parents if people were to say to me, "You are exemplary of your mother and father."

Each of my parents inherited nothing from their parents when they were married during the Korean war but bare hands, the uncertainty of tomorrow, and devastation of war. When the Korean War broke out in 1945, only my father and two of his brothers among twelve siblings were able to escape from the communist regime of the North in the middle of a chaotic night. My father had never talked about the Korean War to any of his children, but one time, when I became old enough to understand, my father decided I should carry the family responsibility as a first-born son. He told me, "We all thought the civil war would end soon; then, we would get to go home, see our family, and pick up where we left off." He died with a broken heart because he never got to see his family since being separated from them over fifty-five years before.

Job 1:21 says, "I came naked from my mother's womb, and I will be naked when I leave. The LORD gave me what I had, and the LORD has taken it away. Praise the name of the LORD!" My mother and father lived by God's words in their daily living. When they died, my father left a twenty-dollar bill in his wallet and a large print Korean bible on his bed. My mother left her gold necklace for my daughter and some money she secretly hid under her pillow (you would not understand their mentality if you had not lived through such a horrendous war and Great Depression.)

As you can see, they did not leave us a large sum of money.

Instead, they bestowed upon us something money could not buy: their faith and belief in God, and love and respect for others. Those basic characteristics of what make a human being human and how one should live were imbedded in the minds of their grandchildren. This happened without the awareness of the children by simply living with their grandparents when they were young.

I want to tell you one funny story to demonstrate a life lesson my children learned when they were young. One evening, my father was in his room watching TV. My two boys suddenly disappeared from the dinner table while my mother and my wife were busily preparing for dinner in the kitchen. Sizzling galbi (marinated short ribs with onions, green onions, and garlic) and my kids' favorite dish, Kimchi soup, were giving out a sweet fragrance. A few minutes later, I saw one pushing and another pulling their grandfather to sit at the head of the table. They forced him to scoop a spoonful of rice in a bowl and put it in his mouth. They then started eating galbi voraciously. I don't remember ever telling my kids not to eat before their grandfather sat at the head of the table and started eating first. Somehow, they learned to respect their elders by modeling what they had seen.

I confess there were a few hard times in our lives when my wife and I felt overwhelmed, burdened, and the injustice of having to support and take care of aging parents when the times were too difficult to feed another mouth, and when they could not provide any financial support in return. Some people even thought my wife and I were unreasonable and foolish for not placing our parents in a nursing home just like most people would.

You are too young and too busy living in today's rat race to think about getting old or death knocking on your door. However, anything and everything that is born will die one day. The day that you thought would never come is waiting just around the corner. If you want to be loved, respected, and cared for when you get old, you must love, respect, and care for your own parents now while you can before it is too late. How often do you hear these golden rules?

"Treat others the way you want to be treated."

"What goes around comes around."

"You reap what you sow in this life."

All of these are saying the same thing: you will be faced and dealt with the consequences of your actions eventually, whether they are good or bad.

When my single brother moved out and lived by himself, my old mother decided to live with him to take care of him, cooking and doing laundry for him. A few times my mother fell and broke her arms and hip while he was out working. Her doctor recommended us to put her in a nursing home for rehabilitation until she got better. While she was staying in the nursing home, I learned about modern abuse from a well-dressed and successful businessman.

He was raised by both an abusive-alcoholic father and a drug-addicted mother. On the top of the toxic family environment he was reared by, he was the one who found the body of his mother who overdosed in her bedroom at the age of twenty-two one night, naked. Only a few months after her death, his father brought a woman home and introduced her to him as his stepmother, who was no better than his biological mother. His father was in and out of jails while his stepmother sexually and physically abused him for years.

He could not wait to turn eighteen. He thought that the only ticket to get away from his father, his stepmother, and the environment that always gave him nothing but troubles was to get a scholarship to go to college and to become a successful businessman. He did indeed not only become a successful businessman but married a rich woman in a much higher social class. Growing up under the negative influence of his parents, he swore both to God and to himself over and over again that he would never do to his wife and his children what his parents did to him. That was fuel for his success and what made him who he was to become.

However, sooner or later, he turned himself into his father and started drinking and abusing his wife and his two children. The statistics show that children raised by abusive parents are one and a half times more likely to become abusive parents as well. His wife begged, threatened to leave him, and even tried to put him in the best treatment center money could buy, but he reluctantly laughed at the idea and refused to accept his own demons and get help just like his father.

His old father, on the other hand, had no place to go and had no one to take care of him after he was evicted. His son went out one day and bought a wheelchair for his father, and he drove to his father's house for the last time. He told his father to sit in the brand-new wheelchair. Then, he took his father to a nursing home in another town, for he never intended to visit his father again. Arriving at the nursing home, he put his father in the wheelchair and rolled him to his room. As he got up to leave, his father looked at his son and said, "I know you are abandoning me here in this wheelchair, but let me ask you a last favor before you go." His father seemed peaceful at last, and pointing at the bed, his father asked him to lay him down on the bed instead. His father said, "I am not going to need that wheelchair anymore. Save it for yourself. Your children will need it when your time comes."

A Latin Proverb says, "Death took me by the hand and whispered, 'live, for I am coming.'" When you are given life, live while you can so that when the time comes to depart from this earth, you have nothing left to live but can welcome death. Khalil Gibran said, "For life and death are one, even as the river and the sea are one." You are the river that naturally must go back to the sea where you came from. That is all. Life and death are one!

Dear Kim Kim,

I am so glad I have met you during my stay here. I came here feeling completely powerless and now I feel better. You are so motivational to me. I really enjoy your stories. The other day you spoke about how you can't control other people's actions, you can only control yourself. I have a rough home life and I know now that I just need to stay determined and the rest will follow. I will do whatever I can to make the world a better place just like you have done. Even if I get discouraged, I will not give up. I wish the best for you, Kim Kim.
--Adolescent

A Boy Named Sean

Larry was one of first persons I had met when I moved to Hendersonville after purchasing my business. It does not matter how many years I have been living in America, fully submerged into American culture. I am still not accustomed to and find it uncomfortable to call anyone who was much older than my father "friend" and being called "buddy" by teenagers. But that was what he was, my true friend even though there was a 30-year age difference between us, one from Kentucky and me from Korea.

Oh, I'd rather have a casual conversation over a cup of coffee with him right now than writing about him and the impact he has made on my life because I had never got to thank him while he was alive. The breakfast restaurant we frequently dined was torn down, and in 2018, he also departed on September 11. Yes, the date 9/11, most Americans never forget and mourn the loss of thousands of lives, I alone on the same date, remember and mourn the loss of one person, Larry. I want to tell him in person about the letter I received a few months ago from a boy whom I would have not known if it were not for him. After all, I believe he knew all along what my mentorship with the boy would do to my heart when he asked me for the first time.

Upon graduating from high school, Larry married his high school sweetheart, Wilma, and left her in Michigan while he fought in Vietnam. He and his friend later returned to American soil. The brotherhood of these two soldiers, one from Michigan and another from Alabama was thicker than blood. Both were waiting in a bus terminal for one to ride to Detroit and the other to a small town in Decatur, Alabama. Larry got on his bus and watched through foggy windows as his friend got on his bus, but what he saw shocked him. The bus driver refused to allow him to get on the bus and civilians were spitting on his face and tearing his military uniform to pieces because he was Black and a Vietnam veteran. Larry got out of his seat and beat the living daylight out of every single civilian who spit on his friend.

He and his friend spent the night in jail. The next day Larry got out but his friend did not. He once told me that this traumatic event was worse than fighting in Vietnam. He said that there was a reason why he and his friend were fighting in Vietnam, but returning home,

Larry's friend who took bullets for him and who fought for the freedom of this country was denied the rights he deserved as a human being and treated worse than in Vietnam.

After working for 35 years as a sales manager and Vice President of a big company, Larry retired and moved to Hendersonville. He and Wilma never could have a child of their own and loved children so much that they volunteered to be mentors at elementary schools and churches. One day, Larry asked me, "Can you spend 30 minutes out of a week doing something good with me?"

I asked, "only 30 minutes out of one week?" That is nothing. What is it?" I knew he had been mentoring kids in Gene Brown Elementary School for several years and volunteering for many community services. He said, "I have a kid that needs a father figure like you in his life."

I immediately said, "No way! I can't be a mentor."

He asked, "Why not?"

I added, "You know I have a bad accent and can't read books to kids. 'Sheet of paper' sounds like 'shit of paper!' You are the one always picks on me about my Southern accent. No way!"

"Son, you don't have to read books or help him with his homework. You don't even have to take him to McDonald's or movies." You just show up once a week for 30 minutes at his school and talk about whatever you two want to talk about. That's it!"

I said, 'That is all I have to do? No reading books?" Once I was absolutely sure this mentorship didn't require reading books and all I had to do was show up once a week for 30 minutes, I agreed to do it. Well, my motive was that it was already the end of November, and if I hold on until the end of May, I can finally shut Larry up. That was my intention, not knowing it would turn out to be the biggest investment I have ever made on one individual when he seemed to be destined to fail and end up in prison just like his father and sisters.

I was asked to show up at the school library at 9 o'clock every Wednesday morning. There was a little office behind the circulation desk. I was anxious and nervous at the same time, for I had never volunteered to be a mentor for an elementary kid. I had mentored many newly hired employees in business and loved developing them to be the next leaders, but not elementary kids! "What do I do? What do I talk about? What if he or she doesn't like me and whatever I say and do, might do more harm than good?" It was like my first job interview. Hundreds of questions were going through my mind. I dressed up and even wore a tie to leave a good impression on the kid.

The side door suddenly opened without a knock, and a little boy came in with the school principal. I really should not judge a person by their outward appearance, but I instantly couldn't help but feel sorry for him when I looked at his winter jacket. He looked no more than a second or third grader: he was short and nothing but skin and bones. He was wearing a jacket that you might as well call a blanket. The sleeves of his jacket were so long that I could not see his hands and the bottom of the jacket covered his ankles. The collar of the jacket was so dirty it had turned black. It made me sad, and he did not have to say anything about his family. I knew right then.

Neither of my wife nor I would send my kids to school like that. Hair must be washed and comb, and clothes must be cleaned. We were so poor that I might wear clothes and shoes that have holes in them. But my wife and I made sure my kids would not leave our house unattended unloved. The principal said, "His name is Sean, and he is a fifth grader. Sean, this is Mr. Kim, your mentor. He will be visiting you every Wednesday morning." She added, "Well, I will leave you two alone so you can get to know each other." As soon as she left us, I began asking rapid questions as of I was interrogating a terrorist. I asked him about his family, school, hobbies, his dream, and anything that I could think of that he might be interested in talking about. He put his head down and did not look up the entire time as I interrogated him. It seemed like that was what I did.

The long needle of the clock finally reached 6. I said, "Thirty minutes is up. I will come and see you next Wednesday morning, okay?" He had not said one word, put his head down and did not look at me the entire time. He wasn't about to change his silent protest as he left me. I went to the principal's office and asked her, "Does Sean speak English? He did not say a word." She simply said, "Give him some time. He will open up to you." "Open up about what?" Now I was thinking to myself I actually interrogated this kid for whatever crime he committed. As I left her office, I dreaded going back the next Wednesday.

I did go back to see Sean but saw no reason to dress up again. I wore a t-shirt and jeans, instead. He was wearing the same dirty jacket, but this time, he raised his head and looked mostly at the wall behind me. I caught him glancing at me when I was preoccupied with my conversations to myself. The silent 30 minutes seemed like an eternity; so, I decided to call Larry the next week and tell him that I could not do it anymore. Meanwhile, I had to come up with some kind of very urgent work or family related excuse to cover that up. On my third week with him, as soon as he entered the room, he said, "I went to see my daddy on Saturday!" Wow! I was surprised that he finally spoke to me without being asked. More importantly, I learned two critical information about his family then: he had a father, and his father did not live with him. He said, "I went to Sumner County jail to see my daddy and uncle with my mommy!" That morning I also learned that his mother worked as a housekeeper in a hotel in Gallatin, and he had three older sisters. I met with Larry that week and told him I was going to see Sean until he moved on to middle school.

I showed up every Wednesday, and he never missed as well. However, I had to go to Cornwall, England for a two-week training to be a disaster first responder at the end of January. I told him in the middle of a casual conversation that I had to go to England, and I would not be here next two weeks. As soon as he heard words "I won't be here" he abruptly got up and stormed out of the door. I thought, we barely began to know each other in the past two months, and I was definitely coming back to see him; so, I could not understand his sudden behavior and did not think anything about it. In fact, I was glad that our time was cut short because that morning, because I was paged by the administrator of the hospital that the unannounced Joint Commission survey team was to visit our hospital.

After the brutal 10-day training and competition at the naval base in Cornwall, I had an extra day to spend in London. I did what a tourist normally would do and thought about Sean while I was doing so. I bought a double decker miniature bus, a coffee mug that had the England flag with London, England imprinted, and a pocketful of shillings that I could not use anymore in The States. I could exchange these at the airport but I wanted to give them to Sean as a souvenir. It gave me great pleasure just imagining how much he would like his gifts. As promised, I showed up the following week with my backpack on my lap.

I heard the footsteps. It was Sean as I expected, but he was totally shocked to see me.

He said, "I thought you didn't like me, and you never wanted to see me again. That is why you left me."

"No, Sean! I never said that. And I had to go to England. It was something I had to do." I pulled out the gifts I got for him out of my backpack and laid them in front of him.

I said, "Look at this bus and mug. These are money people in England use to buy things." He gravitated toward what he saw and played with them for a long time. When it was time for him to go back to his classroom, he thanked me for showing him and pushed the souvenirs toward me. I said, "I got this for you. It is yours, so put all that in this box." He gave me another surprised look and said, "You got this for me?" He could not believe a stranger whom he just met two months ago would go to England and think of him and buy him gifts. It really wasn't much. I probably spent twenty-five dollars for all the gifts, but he treated it like the biggest gifts he had ever received and…he gave me a hug and would not let me go. I was sad. I should be happy about making someone happy, too. But I was sad seeing that such a small thing was his biggest gift. His own father, uncle, and people whom he trusted walked out of his life so many times that he thought I was doing the same when I said I had to go to England. He thought I was making an excuse just like others to say good bye.

In the third week of May, I did say good bye to him. It was the last day of the school year and that was the last time I saw him. From hosting youth exchange students from overseas at home for several months to giving out dictionaries or speaking to students at Austin Peay State University for leadership trainings, I have frequently been actively involved with youth. But Sean was the last kid I mentored in school. I had moved on with my life, and I had forgotten about Sean until I received a twenty-page hand written letter a few months ago.

I had gone to Honduras for my yearly mission trip at the end of January. When I came home in February, there were stacks of unopened, mostly junk letters on my desk to be thrown away after my wife had already sorted out the important ones. Once I had run a Music City Half-Marathon a few years earlier benefiting both the Children's Hospital for Monroe Carell Jr. at Vanderbilt and St. Jude at Memphis, and I was overwhelmed with unsolicited advertising and promotional materials from both hospitals. There was a thick white envelop from St. Jude Children's Research Hospital in Memphis. I intended to throw it away unopened assuming it a junk mail like any others, but the sender's name on top was hand written and so was my name and my address. "That was odd" I thought, "Was it incorrectly addressed to me?" I did not know a person named Sean especially from St. Jude Hospital nor anyone living in Memphis.

I opened it mindlessly, and it was a twenty page hand written letter. The curiosity got the best of me. I did not mind whether I was the right recipient or not. I was actually mesmerized by who would write a letter in ink these days on stationary, put a stamp on it, go to the post office, and mail it. I asked myself when was the last time that I sent a hand written letter to someone and went through all those troubles. I was ashamed of myself for always taking the easy way out: using social media, emails or texts. It was like receiving an anonymous love letter from a secret admirer. I was about to find out about a guy named Sean and to whom he wrote a letter.

Surprisingly, it started with "Dear Mr. Kim," but in the first three pages I could not find anything pertaining to me. As I turned to the fourth page, he said I was his mentor and came to his school every week to see him. I vaguely remembered mentoring someone at Gene Brown Elementary School. Then, he said, "You went to England for two weeks and brought me gifts that I still have in my room." I was about to pass out because that happened fifteen years ago, and how could I ever forget that dreadful training to be a Disaster First Responder in the freezing cold winter in Cornwall? His name still did not ring a bell, but I vividly remembered a fifth-grade kid who was short and nothing but skin and bones. And, "Oh, that dirty jacket he wore all winter long!"

He went on writing chronologically how he had lived his life after graduating from high school, rather I should say what brought him this far. He played recreational soccer and football hoping to have a football scholarship as a kicker with good grades because he knew his family could not afford for him to go to college. In fact, his family wanted him to drop out of high school and carry on what his father and his uncle were in prison for: being drug dealers. They laughed at the ridiculous thought of him going to college which none of his family ever had done. He was told he would never amount to anything.

He enrolled in the University of Tennessee in Knoxville. He had no money for tuition and dormitory fees but kept his unbelievable faith and unbreakable drive to succeed in life even though he did not what his future would hold. He watched his favorite movie "Rudy" over and over again which was based on the true story of Daniel "Rudy" Ruettiger. He believed he would be the Rudy in UT. He found out UT was holding walk-on football tryouts on this particular day, and it was on Sunday. He was still skinny and half the size of the other football players, but the coach saw the raw talent, ambition, and passion in him. He thought this little kid could motivate his team from the bottom up.

He became a second-place kicker for the team and finished his undergraduate in three years because he was so driven to succeed and he knew the only way to get there was through education. He went on to graduate school at UT, but there was no scholarship available for graduate schools. He worked three jobs: his first job was at the school library so he could have some time to study, his second was at Publix Grocery Store, and his third was a janitor position at a local doctor's office. He did all that while he was in his Master's program! He was hungry for education. He had to apply for mandatory internship during the last year of school, and St. Jude Children's Hospital in Memphis was the only one that accepted him. Administrators and hospital staff loved his attitude and work ethic. More than anything else, children-patients and their families adored him, and his presence brightened up the entire room as soon as he entered. Administrators received a lot of feedback from employees and letters from patients' families stating how caring and wonderful he was to their children at the hospital while he was working for that short period of time; hence, they promised him that they would hire him as soon as he finished school. One step further, they wanted to make sure he would work for them; so, they hired him and paid full salary while he was an intern which had never happened before.

While he was working there, he met a nurse practitioner and fell in love with her. Unlike his family, she was from a prominent family; her father was a respected doctor and her mother a CEO of a non-profit organization helping underprivileged families in their community. Her family embraced him as their own son and blessed him when he asked for their daughter's hand in marriage. On the other hand, his father and uncle got out of jail when he was in college but went right back in after being arrested for doing the same thing—selling dope. Two of his sisters were involved in the family business manufacturing methamphetamine. Both were arrested and sent to the federal penitentiary for making meth in their apartment in front of a three-year-old and a six-month-old baby. His youngest sister was addicted to drugs and living on the street. My heart sank hearing what happened to his dysfunctional family, but I had no sympathy for the choices they had made when they had every right to change. They did not have to look far for an example. All they had to do was look at their own son and brother, Sean. They were blind. They might have thought that Sean was blind to the real world they live in. They laughed at his dream. The adversities he had faced were merely challenges. The obstacles he had faced were not stumbling blocks. He had used them as stepping stones to overcome.

Lastly, he wrote his wedding was to be in June in Memphis. He asked me to come as his father. I dropped the letter on the floor and it spread like a quilt. I covered my face with both hands and cried uncontrollably. "Sean asked me to be his father at his wedding! This boy I had forgotten ASKED ME to be his father! I have an American son now!" I am writing this portion of the book in the middle of a cold February. After this cold winter, spring shall not be far behind; then my American son's wedding will arrive. By the time you are reading this book, I will have already been to Sean's wedding and let me tell you how beautiful it was and how proud I was of my son Sean and his wife! Oh, how proud a father I was!

When my friend Larry asked me to mentor a boy named Sean and when I saw him for the first time, how could I have foreseen that fifteen years later his life was to turn out this way knowing his dysfunctional family tree? I am searching for the answer as to what I did to him then. To be brutally honest with you, I thought nothing of him then and completely erased him from my memory because his future seemed doomed from the start. I know the true meaning of life is to plant a tree that you never get to see. You see, Sean was not one of those seeds I was hoping to plant and make some kind of difference in his life. How ashamed I feel that I thought of someone that way!

It is written in Matthew 25 in the Bible, "For I was hungry and you gave me something to eat, I was thirsty and you gave me something to drink, I was a stranger and you invited me in, I needed clothes and you clothed me, I was sick and you looked after me, I was in prison and you came to visit me.'

"Then the righteous will answer him, 'Lord, when did we see you hungry and feed you, or thirsty and give you something to drink? When did we see you a stranger and invite you in, or needing clothes and clothe you? When did we see you sick or in prison and go to visit you?'

"The King will reply, 'Truly I tell you, whatever you did for one of the least of these brothers and sisters of mine, you did for me.'"

God advises "Not to forget to entertain strangers, for by doing so some people have entertained angels without even knowing it." Was that what I did for him, talking to a little angel without knowing it? He was an angel indeed, disguised as a poor and neglected boy. But, no, I did not do any of that. He was hungry, but I had never fed him. He was thirsty, but I had never given him something to drink. He needed clothes because his jacket was too big and too dirty for any child to wear — no wonder he was bullied and being laughed at all the time, but I had never thought of bringing him clothes. I wish there was one thing that convinces me to believe "that is why he still remembers you, and he thinks you have made a positive difference in his life even after all these years." The most shameful thing is that I can't think of anything that I have contributed giving meaning to his life as much as he thought of my place in his heart. However, I showed up every week except two weeks when I was in England for training. I did treat him the way I would treat my own son; I talked and listened the same way I did to my children. But that could not be enough reason to create everlasting ripples in his life, could it?

Oh, I wish to know what I did that was so important that it somehow helped him to change the course of his life. All the adversities he had faced were merely challenges and gave him motivation to overcome his hardships. On the night of the wedding, when there were only the three of us, I said to Sean the only words I could say, "I am sorry for not being there for you when you were going through hell all alone. You know I am a big fan of UT football and when the kicker missed the field goals, I called him all kinds of names. Who knew that boy happened to be you!" Both Sean and his new wife burst out laughing. I laughed at my own joke, too. I added, "I should have never forgotten you as much as you remembered me all these years. I am so sorry for not being there for you. I should have eased your burden, or at least I should have been there to talk to and listen to you like we did the first time we met." There was so much more I wanted to say but no more words were needed. Instead, I hugged him and squeezed him so as not to never let him go out of my life again. His newly wed wife said to me, "You were right there with him. You were the reason why he never gave up on life." That was all she said.

Suddenly I remembered a particular quote I regularly asked adolescents at work to memorize for candy bars or one of my books as a prize. I thought it was a good life lesson for all ages but especially tailored for adolescents to live by in the very beginning of their adult lives. If they did, I knew it was going to be a good journey in the end. Hence, it was worth offering my twenty-dollar books for free. It was a long quote and difficult to memorize. I was fully aware of that; in fact, many of the adolescents would not even try when they saw it written on the board, too long so it had to be too difficult, they thought. So, they automatically assumed it was an impossible thing to do. To make things worse in their minds, they felt as though were not given extra time to memorize it. Many of them simply gave up trying while in fact, they were fully capable.

In addition, they had to find a time to do it on their own during their free time. That meant they had to give up fun and lazy social times getting to know other boys and girls when their hormones were going crazy to memorize stupid, long, and difficult sentences that might not make any sense at all. I could neither judge nor blame them for not spending time on something I believed was so important and valuable to them in life. The fact of the matter was that they had not lived their full lives yet. Thus, they had no understanding of what would prepare them for events that are yet to come. Their lives were based on what they were taught by their family, peers, and environments. What did they know about life when they were only thirteen through eighteen years of age having no real-life experiences? Even though they had not experienced a full life yet, I still challenged them because every one of them were capable of reciting this quote word for word as long as they found something worth doing it for and it became important to them. If not, it is human nature that they would come up with excuses for why they couldn't. It was much easier to give up and give a perfect justification every single time when they were up against the wall. Somehow, I believed such words not only encourage us to go on living, but not to give up on life as well.

As I talked more and more about the quote during the group session, I had to reexamine my life and determine if I had been living my everyday life in such a way that adolescents would find me as a role model to follow. I hope I have been a good example to my three kids. When people see my own kids at any points in their lives and whatever they were doing right then, would people see me in them? Have I been a mirror to them and they a reflection of me? How could I say I have been a role model to my own kids, but not to these adolescents because they were my patients, not my own kids? I probably would never get to see them again until for whatever reasons they come back to my hospital. I could say to them, "Do as I say, not as I do." And I could go on and on talking about how one should live, and no one would hold me accountable or responsible for their behaviors once they left the hospital because I was saying all the right things. But, if I am not living by it, how can I expect them to live by what I teach?

This quote says, "Life goes by in the blink of an eye. It's too short to live upset, angry, resentful or ungrateful. If you look for the good, you'll find it. Choose to be happy, to be at peace. Decide that each day is going to be a great day and grab each moment and make the best of it. Refuse to let negative thoughts take root in your mind and refuse to let negative people and situations drag you down. Trust your journey and know that if you make a mistake, it's okay. See it as a lesson learned and keep moving forward. Spend less time worrying and more time being grateful for those who love you and all of life's goodness. Choose to live in joy!"

People, including myself, would not be surprised to hear he

ended up in jail just like his father and his sisters. His environment was doomed and not set up for him to succeed in life, but he did. He proved to himself that he was not going to let negative people and situations drag him down. Other people might choose to live small lives, but he decided to define his own life for himself, no matter how small his life was going to be.

We all gazed at the mighty Mississippi River silently floating down to somewhere in New Orleans. That night was only the beginning of three separate lives running together. And now I have years to make up for; fifteen years of lost time with him. I am going to enjoy every breathe, every second and every day of my life with people that I love. Sean taught me that my life has been worth living and my small, unremembered, and random act of kindness was the biggest life changer for somebody.

Dear Kim Kim,

I don't know where to start with you. You portrayed so much wisdom and your stories were so powerful, "Talk to me with your eyes, daddy!" That is something I can't forget because sometimes I feel like your daughter in that situation.
The story of your American son Sean was another big one. **We can't fix our environment, but we can definitely make a change for ourselves.**
I think that the biggest thing you said was how do you give away something you don't have? How do you give someone love when you don't even love yourself? The answer is you learn to love yourself and then help someone else.
I'm gonna miss you a lot! Keep changing people's lives, and never lose your energy and passion.
Your friend,
--Adolescent

Muddy Shoes

My family was living in East Nashville when my daughter was about to enter first grade in metropolitan public school. Wilson County was known, at that time—I hope still is for students and their families' sake, for having a good school system. My first child and the first year of school, then two younger brothers would be following suite; my wife and I had to be the best parents putting our children's education first. So, we moved to Gladeville in Wilson County. It was such a small town that you could not even find the name of the community on a local map. The bank was closed on Wednesdays (I still don't know why the only bank in the entire community closed on Wednesdays.) In addition, it was too small to have either a post office or a public library. However, we were told the schools were great, so there we moved!

We bought an old two-story house on Amber Drive in the only subdivision in Gladeville. We had an acre of land in the backyard so our kids could freely roam and play in a fenced in yard, but it was bare land, not grass. The very first thing I wanted to do after we moved in was to build a big manly deck with a gazebo. My wife, on the other hand, wanted to put in brand new carpet. "My God, she shall have whatever she wants for our dream house!" I said. It could not be our dream house unless both of us had what we wanted.

My wife was watching TV one evening. There was a mansion like O'Hara plantation house in "Gone with the Wind." A beautiful woman who looked like Scarlett was wearing a long white dress walking on new white carpet. White light from the chandelier added just enough detail to show how luxurious and rich a life she was enjoying. When it comes to remodeling or rearranging furniture around the house, I have no say whatsoever over my wife. "I am a Yes husband!" I guess that is one of the reasons why I have been married to her for over thirty-two years now.

However, I was not quite sure about her wanting to put white carpet. It looked great on TV. In fact, it was so convincing that viewers like my wife would not hesitate to put that carpet on entire floors covering the house: the kitchen and even the garage (Sorry for being sarcastic!) It should have been a good fight between rational and irrational thinking, but her emotions and pride were much stronger than my rational thinking. I had to give in. But my God, I was going to have a last word. I said, "Are you sure about this? We have three young kids, and I don't know how you are going to keep white carpet white and clean."

She seemed to have had prepared every question as if she was on trial. She said, "Our kids are not babies anymore. They are going to eat and drink only at the kitchen table. So, don't let them eat on the sofa." Ouch, she was saying it would be my fault if they ever messed up mommy's new white carpet! You guessed it. She got what she wanted, and as the title of this story foretold, her new white carpet was covered with muddy shoeprints. After all was said and done, the only regret I have now is, "Why didn't I take pictures of her white carpet covered with my son's muddy shoeprints and her shocked facial expressions." I laughed so hard that I forgot to take the perfect opportunity to say "I told you so."

I am partially responsible for my son wearing muddy shoes inside the house. Ever since I was little, I loved to play outside in the rain. I had loved rain so much that I walked and ran aimlessly in drizzling to torrential rain, mostly alone, but, I did not care. It drove my mom crazy because I caught a cold and was always sick when it could have easily been avoided. I hoped my kids would do as I say, not as I did. Now my youngest learned to imitate his father playing outside in the rain. What could I say? It was just a hard habit to break, and I couldn't help it.

I remember it was one Saturday morning. Coming home from work the night before, I had a difficult time driving in the heavy rain. The rain fell all night and continued until that morning. I sat on the sofa reading a newspaper. My wife was drinking a cup of tea at the kitchen table admiring her brand-new carpet she just put in over the weekend. We both heard the back door being opened and assumed our youngest son was going to the back deck to ride his covered tricycle. The other two were sleeping in our bed upstairs. About thirty minutes passed and I heard the door being opened and closed once more. My wife glanced at our son, and in a split second, she could not believe what she saw; so, she did a double take. It confirmed what she saw was right. He was walking on the new carpet wearing his muddy shoes! My son was playing outside in the mud, not riding his tricycle on the deck. My wife got up abruptly and sprinted to catch him, spilling some of the tea on her new carpet herself. She was screaming and chasing our son to have him take off his muddy shoes that were ruining her carpet.

I had a desktop computer in my study room, and none of my children were exposed to social media, smart phones, or even video games then. How grateful I feel now that we chose not to expose them to electronics and gadgets before they were matured, responsible, and accountable enough to use those tools wisely. Both of my sons are in the computer business (computer programmer and web designer) but if they were exposed to that early ages, I believe it would have done more harm and good. For example, alarming statistics show the dangers of technology in today's adolescents. Seventy percent of parents are totally clueless as to what their kids are doing on the internet because kids are so good at hiding their online activity. What are they hiding from parents? One in ten kids under age ten have seen pornography online. Between the ages of twelve and seventeen, one in seven children have sent naked photos, and one in four have received a "sext" (naked photo).

Instead, we played hide and seek a lot inside the house. I think my son was only four years old and probably thought it was playing time, chased by Mommy with her angry face. He was so slick and little that my wife just could not catch him. She screamed at the top of her lungs, "Take off your muddy shoes. You are ruining my carpet!" What was I doing in the middle of all the commotion—my wife chasing my son as he was painting our new carpet with muddy shoes? Nothing! I was laughing so hard I hid my face with newspapers and giggled at the scene. I'll tell you; it was something to see. Our little son was standing tall at the top of the stairs like David who defeated the Giant Goliath in the biggest battle of his life. On the other hand, my wife who was supposed to be Goliath was at the bottom of the stairs puffing and catching her breath. She definitely lost her battle, and she knew it. He said, pointing his finger at Mommy, "Mommy, I am not taking off my shoes. You change your carpet!" Then, he immediately ran to our bed and hid under the blanket which his two siblings were sleeping on, with his clothes and shoes still on!

We Koreans never wear shoes at all inside the house because it was against Korean custom. We Koreans do not have separate beds to sleep on. We eat, sit, play, sleep, and do just about everything on floor. Winter in Korea is brutally cold, and for thousands of years Koreans have had unique under- the-floor heating systems that heat entire floors called "ondol." Living in America, we did not have such a house, but my parents slept on carpeted floor and never dared to wear shoes inside the house.

Earlier I said that I was partially responsible for my son's behavior, demanding to change a carpet while refusing to take off his muddy shoes. When I came to America as a teenager, I did just that. No, I am not talking about the muddy shoes at this point. I want to leave it on one side for the moment, for I need to get into a more important matter: the stubbornness, persistence, and mentality that my son learned from me. My children are reflections of me, and I should first set a good example for them. There is an old Korean saying, "The water upstream has to be clean in order for the water downstream to be clean."

People have a culture shock when they move to a completely different, unfamiliar, and new environment. You don't have to have personally experienced it to understand what it is like living in another country. Initially you feel the euphoria of being in a new and strange place having new and exciting experiences. Everything is new and you like it. Within a short period of time, your excitement and anticipation quickly wear off and you become frustrated and overwhelmed by simple everyday life being quite different from what you are used to. As weeks turn into months and months turn into years, you struggle adjusting to your new life. You admit the honeymoon stage is finally over, and now you have to face the reality and overcome all your obstacles such as language barrier, foods, customs, people, diversity, and so on. Then, you accept, adapt, and simulate into the main culture of American society. That is pretty much what newcomers go through.

Thus, I knew I would have tremendous difficulty living in America from the moment I arrived, for I came not as an accidental tourist or a short-term youth exchange student who was to go back to his country at the end of the school year, but to live, achieve the American dream, and die with a legacy here on American soil. Disregarding everything else, how could anyone live and communicate in a new land, not knowing a word of English? Nevertheless, it was my choice to come to America even though I was only a seventeen-year-old minor, but I had no choice but to learn the language no matter how long it took.

The first wave of shock was the biggest, dealing with the language barrier in every waking moment that followed like a shadow even at night. At the same time, the second shock was immediately followed: foods. Growing up in a Buddhist monastery ever since I was young, I was not a full-fledged believer, let alone a vegetarian like devoted Buddhist monks. Eating anything other than vegetables is the quickest way to be removed from the spiritual world. For whatever reason, my house was situated inside a monastery. Believe me; I searched for the answer as to why our family was confined to live with monks when we were common folks. The only explanation I could come up with without insulting the dignity of my parents was our family might be too poor to live anywhere else but the monastery, where our distant relative was a Buddhist master of.

The eldest son of my aunt (my mother's only sister) was sent to live in the Buddhist monastery when he was a child because that was the only option they had in order to feed two other sons. It was commonly practiced and accepted during that time in Korea after the devastation of the Korean War. What could be worse, watching their children die from hunger or live on the street as orphans, or sending them to the Buddhist monastery to be fed, educated, and even become a Buddha? My parents might have been too proud or ashamed to admit that was the reason we lived in the monastery, but I will never know. However, by default, I was naturally thrown into the world of Buddhism, studying and memorizing sacred sutra (texts) and practicing meditation. I obeyed and followed the Buddhist teachings before I was even aware of and exposed to the outside world.

I was just a kid, and I believed I was born into Buddhism and destined to live in it and to become a buddha, enlightened one. What else could I know and believe when I was totally immersed in it? Hence, I never had a second guess as to why I was living in a different environment than other kids in the village. I accepted my life as it was, and I was accustomed to living within my means and lived off of food donations, which was practiced as rituality and merit. Emptiness or nothingness, whatever people call it, had become a part of my lifestyle ever since then. Even though I envied and was jealous toward those who had money and material things, (remember I was just a child) I knew from an early age on that I could not have peaceful happiness and get what I wanted out of my life if all of my life was spent obtaining and chasing material things. I appeared to have nothing but was content with living in a nonmaterial and spiritual reality.

So, I was taught as such and treated foods as sustenance which give my body strength and nourishment to maintain a healthy lifestyle. I would not eat for pleasure, habit, or out of boredom. Having said that, you would understand why I was shocked and overwhelmed with the abundance of foods that I had never tasted or seen before: hamburgers, pizza, steaks, tacos, all kinds of desserts that people eat at the end of each meal but the only time I had eaten them was on my birthday. My body just wasn't used to such diets that are mostly meat products and I even got sick quite often eating vegetables and fruits that were raised in different soil, and my body rejected them. Don't believe that your genes control your body; it is actually the environment that controls you and your body.

The third wave of shock was seeing boys and girls attending the same school and wearing all kinds of casual clothes. I attended all boys' schools after elementary school. There was no co-education, schools where both boys and girls attended. Also, students were required to wear uniforms. My face turned red with embarrassment and had to turn to look the other way, seeing what girls were showing off; they were almost naked in my young mind and disrespecting themselves. As you can tell, I could go on and on for hours and days to tell you more about culture shock, but nothing beats the one I am about to tell you about my first day in American school.

My sister took me to Gallatin High School the day after I arrived in America. Fifteen hours of time difference between Korea and Tennessee and jet lag due to the 22 hours in an airplane were no concern of hers, only my education. I could hear that echo telling my father that she would educate me in America. When she drove through the main entrance, I suddenly saw hundreds of cars in parking lots. I had never seen anything like it, not in high school! I immediately thought, "Why does this school have so many teachers and parents?" Who else could drive in high school? After school, I was in shock again.

It was students who were driving all those cars. None of the high schools in Korea have parking lcts. Do you know why there are none? It is not because they are poor. It is because you have to be over 19 to drive.

As I was adjusting to American culture, the first thing I needed was a car. Without it, I could not go anywhere or do anything living in a small town. I learned that people could take driving tests in their native languages in California. So, I went to the Driver's License Office.

I asked a lady at the front desk with broken English, "Me, take test in Korean." Just to make sure she understood what I meant, I scribbled on the palm of my hand with a finger.

She said, "In Tennessee, you can only take in English."

This time, I repeated with a hand gesture pointing West, "California, me take in Korean."

She paused a second and said a little louder and slower, "In-Tennessee-you-can- only take-in-English, Okay?"

I did not understand what she was saying, but I knew with certainty that Korean people in California could take the test in Korean. So, I could not understand why she refused to let me take the test in Korean. I thought it had to be my bad English. So, the same way she did to me, I spoke louder and slower with my finger pointing in the direction of California, "In-California, me-take-in-Korean, Okay!"

She put her head down with a disgusted look on her face and shook her head side to side; then she went to the back office. A few minutes later, she brought a young uniformed officer and pointed at me.

He said with an authoritative and no-holds-barred military voice, "In Tennessee, you can only take in English. Go home and come back when you are able to speak fluent English. Now, get out of my sight!" I heard people in the lobby giggling and laughing at the situation. I picked up the driving test book. As I was walking out, I felt something happened in there, and more importantly, inside of me that I had never felt before. When I came back to my friend's car, I became a totally different person. Even now I can remember their faces and the way they looked down on me, disgusted.

My friend asked me with a concerned face if I was okay. In return, I asked him to take me to the town square, and there was an office and stationary store. Yes, it was long before Wal Mart gobbled up all those mom and pop family businesses in the square. I bought a spiral notebook. As soon as I got home, I drew two vertical lines in the entire notebook, on the front and back of each page: first for new vocabularies and second for its pronunciation. The remaining line was to write the meaning of the word in Korean. I was determined to learn every word in the driving test book. It filled up two notebooks. To make a long story short, it took two years to understand the book word for word, and I passed the written test on my first try. It was too bad neither of those faces who gave me disgusted and smearing looks were there to witness my excitement and perseverance.

After all these years, I learned that fluency in English was not a requirement to pass the driving test. It was not relevant at all. However, their laughter and refusal to give me a test in the Korean language actually fired me up to learn English. First and foremost, I really wanted to show them "I did it in English!" The shorter the time to prove to them "I could do it and they were wrong about me" the better. I pushed myself so hard to learn English.

By going to a nonsequential place like the Driver's License Office in the beginning of my life in America, I realized that if I wanted something out of my life or wanted to achieve my American dream, I could not depend on others to do the things I ought to do. I could not leave my future in the hands of someone else and let them define how I should live my life no matter how difficult it was. I refused to blame other people or the circumstance I was in, no matter whose fault it was. I had to own it and it was I who had to do all the work because no one else was going to do it for me. Also, I learned I had to spend less time worrying about what others thought of me, and more time working on how I could change myself for the better each day and every moment in my life. The only person I could change was me, the man in the mirror. After changing myself first, it became possible to change the way I saw the world; only then, could I create the world I wanted to live in. It took years to realize the simple truth in life: nothing changes unless I change first. Only then, do the things I see change!

If I ask, "How many of us still do it?" Not many hands would go up because we are thinking, "That is silly. I don't demand to change the carpet for me while I am still wearing my muddy shoes. That is childish and immature behavior. I acted like that when I was a child, I am sure, but once I became a mature adult, I didn't do that anymore." Really? I will certainly raise both of my hands because I still have habits of doing it, consciously or not, at home, at work, or anywhere and with any persons I have relationships with.

George Bernard Shaw once said, "The reasonable man adapts himself to the world; the unreasonable one persists in trying to adapt the world to himself. Therefore, all progress depends on the unreasonable man." There is irony in his words. The reasonable (rational) man knows he should first take off his shoes and adapts himself to the environment. However, the unreasonable (emotional) man keeps hitting his head on the wall until he gets what he wants, for the environment to change for him while his still wearing his muddy shoes. The reality is he gets his head busted. Mahatma Gandhi, Martin Luther King. Jr., Malala, Abraham Lincoln, Joan of Arc, Mother Teresa, and countless others knew what they had to do to change the world and acted on it. That is why they were able to demand the world to be changed. After great men and women worked on changing themselves first, they said to the mountain, "move", and the mountain was moved!

Maya Angelou once said, "I did then what I knew how to do. Now that I know better, I do better." When we were children, we did not know better because we just did not have worthy life experiences yet: we were short-sighted, narrow minded, and made erroneous assumptions and imperfect views on things. Abraham Maslow gave us a good example of this. He said, "I suppose it is tempting, if the only tool you have is a hammer, to treat everything as if it were a nail." That was all I knew then. In 1 Corinthians Chapter 13 it says, "When I was a child, I talked like a child, I thought like a child, I reasoned like a child. When I became a man, I put childish ways behind me."

"Take off your shoes!" Only then will you have every right to demand the world to be changed. Every man has a toolbox that has everything he needs to live a life worth living. The difference between why some succeed and others fail is not that they don't have tools they need. They just don't know how to use them. Hence, learn to play the game of life, and have fun doing it. I quoted previously what George Bernard Shaw said. He also said humorously, "We don't stop playing because we grow old. We grow old because we stop playing."

Sir Isaac Newton made this remark just before his death, "I do not know how I may appear to the world; but to myself I seem to have been only like a boy playing on the sea-shore, and diverting myself by now and then finding a smoother pebble or prettier shell than ordinary, while the great ocean of truth lay all undiscovered before me."

My little wave is soon to be crushed and covered by the bigger wave right behind me to make a room for the next in an ocean. They will be too crushed and covered by the ones following, leaving an empty space for them. Does it make our lives meaningless, or precious and timeless? I don't want to waste one second of my life because it too soon will be over. So, what am I doing today to contribute to giving my life meaning? What good things do I have to give up in order to be great? It is a great start to take off my shoes first before I keep demanding the world to put new carpet in for me.

Dear Kim Kim,

Being with you these past two days, I've learned a lot. I love the way you teach things and how you relate them to real life. You have really inspired me with your stories. My favorite three stories were "The Muddy Shoes," "The Starfish," and "Two Tigers." The two tigers really motivated me. Before I met you, I used to always feed the bad tiger. I was always angry and suicidal, but you make me want to be a better person and feed my good tiger.
Even though you might think I wasn't listening, I promise I was listening. I've been touched by everything you've said and done.
When you came into my room and told me I was beautiful on the inside and out, I wanted to cry because I've never had anyone care about me like that. I didn't know or think that you, a stranger I just met, would care for me.
I want to say thank you for everything you've done, especially teaching me how to play badminton. I love and will never forget you. – Adolescent

What Is the Name of a Janitor?

Psychological Statistics is unquestionably one of the hardest graduate courses any graduate student has had to take. I put it off and put it off until I could not put it off any longer. I was working at the hospital as a director at that time and wanted to take an evening class so that I did not have any conflict or interference with my work schedule. I enrolled in a Tuesday and Thursday class at 6:45 am. Since I waited too long, it was the only available class time I could take in the spring semester; otherwise, I had to wait another year.

There were sixteen bright future researchers or Statisticians-to-be in the beginning of the semester. By the time the final came around, there were only ten of us. Yes, I was one of ten. I, somehow, had managed to stick around till the end, woohoo! Only a three hour long comprehensive final exam was standing between me and a dreadful failing grade. Professor Dr. Schmidt told us that the final counted for a whopping 70 percent of the grade, and there would be only four questions. This meant we had to get almost all correct in order to make a B or above to pass. It was an open book exam, and we could bring anything that might help us with the test including a calculator and a notebook with all kinds of cheat sheets in it. However, neither of these would help much if we did not know what to look for. In order to answer a question, we had to go through at least twenty to thirty steps.

As soon as I received my two-page final, I quickly looked through it to find the easiest question to solve first, since we only had three hours to finish. When I turned to the second page, I could not understand the last question. It not only had absolutely nothing to do with Statistics but was so bizarre and absurd that it made me laugh. Just to make sure what I was reading was no mistake, I looked around at my classmates, and they had the same confused and what-the-heck-is-that-kind-of-looks on their faces. Incidentally we all looked at Dr. Schmidt at the same time. He buried his face in newspapers which clearly indicated, "It is open book, guys. You can cheat or do whatever you want but leave me alone for the next three hours!"

The last question was, "What is the name of the janitor who cleans every Tuesday and Thursday morning?" "Are you kidding me?" I was furiously mad, "He must be freaking crazy. What do that have to do with Statistics, and why the hell that is important? As a matter of fact, who cares what her name is? She is just a cleaning lady, for God sakes!" While I was busy answering real Statistical questions, I could not help but think about the old lady who cleaned every Tuesday and Thursday morning. If he was dead serious about this question, "I am screwed." That was all I could think of while solving the other problems because no way I could pass this course without knowing the last question.

Then, I started remembering her. She was an old African American janitor. She looked over seventy-five years old: small, fragile, and stooped with an old age and a hard life. None of the students wore name tags, but I don't know how she knew our names and stopped whatever she was doing and called each of us by our first names. Now I vividly remember there was something about the way she looked at me and treated me. She called me Kim Kim with a warm and genuinely caring smile on her face, the same smile I knew I would give to my loving grandson when I had one.

Even though she always wore a blue colored apron with her name tag on it, I never saw anyone else calling her by name and neither did I. That was not worse of it. We made fun of her and laughed at her behind her back like her life did not matter, and what she was doing held no importance at all. We were in a master's program and had high hopes and dreams to become somebody who held high positions, doing important matters. One morning we had to wait in the hallway because our classroom door was locked. Seeing her mopping the hallway, one heavy set guy said, "Man, I will never be like her. Look at her. She has to clean up someone else's shit. It is so pathetic that she has to work at that old age. I am going to either own a big business or be the CEO of a multi-million-dollar company. At her age, I am going to be filthy rich and live in a mansion having people like her do all the dirty work for me. I would never be like her!"

I did not mistreat her nor did I make such verbal insults to her, but now I painfully realize what I should have done. I watched and did nothing for her when I should have had known her name and stood up for her when other students mistreated her. It was a terrible feeling that even though I was not involved in that circus making fun of her, I did nothing to stop them and worst of all, I accepted it. While I was feeling sad about the fact that I could not come up with her name, I watched 4 classmates walk out without answering the last question. Three hours later as I turned in my final exam, I found Dr. Schmidt still reading New York Times. We were the only ones left in the classroom. I sincerely felt bad and embarrassed for not knowing her name as I was thinking, what if she were my mother, and everybody treated her like she was worthless because she happened to be a janitor.

I turned in my exam without saying anything because he was still holding up the same newspapers. I started walking toward the door, but I had to say what I felt inside before it was too late. If I did not do it right then, I knew I was going to feel regret the rest of my life and live with guilt because I probably would not see her or my professor ever again. I turned around and walked toward him and said, "I am very sorry for not knowing her name. She called me by first name every time she saw me, and actually I was looking forward to seeing her smile because that was the very first thing that brightened my day when I came to class. I truly apologize for not knowing her name. She is such a sweet lady." Then, I walked away from him and suddenly heard the voice behind me saying, "Mrs. Barbara!" When I turned around, he put down his newspapers and handed my exam back to me so I could write her name. He was giving me the answer. So, I wrote her name on the last question: Mrs. Barbara.

There was an empty chair in front of his desk, and there was just two of us. He pointed the empty chair with his eyes, and that night I learned all about Mrs. Barbara. Her life story was not only more important than Statistics or all other subjects combined, but it also taught me one of greatest lessons I learned about life.

Mrs. Barbara and her husband had three boys and a girl. When their eldest child was a sixth grader, her husband had a car accident and died suddenly. She was a housewife raising her four children and never had a job. She was one poor peasant daughter of eleven from enslaved African Americans parents living in Alabama. She never went to school, always working at tobacco and cotton fields and doing all the household chores. She could not even read or write. What kind of life was she to have with her four young children? Because she was uneducated, unskilled, and wanted to go to school but couldn't, she was determined to educate her children more so than to feed them with nice meals. Knowing her situation, a friend of her told her that she could work for the school system, and her children's tuition would be waived. So, she worked as a janitor in school, cooked in the cafeteria and cleaned office buildings at night.

By working three jobs seven days a week, she made three boys become doctors: two being surgeons and one having a Ph. in education. Her daughter, on the other hand, had no interest in being a doctor. Growing up with three older brothers, she had to be a tom boy just to keep up with them, more so to survive. She was called Scout in a book "To Kill a Mockingbird." Ever since she read the book and identified herself as Scout, she craved a father and daughter relationship she was never able to have. Her father died when she was a baby, and there was no memory of him in her mind. She created the image of her father to be Atticus Finch, and Atticus Finch became not just a fictional character in a novel but a real person as well. So, ever since she was a little girl, she always wanted to be a lawyer like "Atticus Finch" standing up for what is right and following her conscience.

Her youngest son who later earned a Doctorate in Education was Professor Schmidt's roommate when they were in college in Texas for four years. That son became the President of the university where Mrs. Barbara worked as a janitor. Mrs. Barbara was living with her son and her daughter-in-law in the Presidential Mansion on the college campus. After her son became President of the university, she moved in with her son and no longer had to work. However, she missed seeing students in school. She would sit in a rocking chair in the front porch waving at students passing by and expressed silently the joy and appreciation for those students. You see, she thought all the success her children had could not be possible for if it weren't for them.

She had never forgotten where she came from and who helped her get there. She begged her son to allow her to volunteer to work as a janitor only twice a week so she could see and spend some time with students. Her son completely understood how much his mother loved students and missed them, but his being a President of that university, he hesitated to support his mother's wish and worried about what people would say. Her daughter-in-law would not have it and begged her not to do so. "Mother, I beg you. Please don't do this. Your son is the President of this University. Can you imagine what people would say if they find out his mother is working as a janitor? If you thought about your son's reputation, embarrassment, and the situation you would put him in, you would not even consider it." More than anything, her daughter-in-law worried about what other people would think of she and her husband. Her desire to see students was too strong to be ignored, and in fact, her stubbornness and her will was the only thing that kept her going all these years. She was not about to give up because of what people would think and say about the whole deal.

His mother had cataract surgery on her left eye a few weeks earlier and was not able to see clearly. Also, her legs were swollen and she was not able to stand or walk for a long period of time. So, he asked a manager of EVS (Environmental Services) to make an extra key for him, and he went to the building late at night to clean for his mother the next day. He emptied trash cans, swept and mopped the floors, and scrubbed toilets. He did not want his mother to know that he came the night before to clean for her, so he intentionally left papers and empty drinking cups in noticeable areas here and there.

One night, he heard knocking on the front entrance door. He found his wife standing there. She came to help her husband. He silently opened the door and went to a vending machine to get two cans of Dr. Pepper, her favorite drink. As a dentist, she preached and advised her patients not to drink any socas or eat candy, especially at night, and she never had sodas in her house. However, when her husband brought Dr. Pepper, it was time to make up and simply say "I am sorry!" Neither of them said anything while drinking the cold Dr. Pepper because no words were needed to explain why he had to do this for his mother, and now his wife was there to support her husband.

For the first time, he shared the most painful memory he had when he was in middle school. His teacher asked him to come with his parents for a very important parent teacher conference; so, he reluctantly agreed. His mother was cleaning at the adjacent high school where his two elder brothers were attending that afternoon. She took off her apron and put it in a plastic bag; then off she went to her son's classroom. Several of his friends saw a janitor and a teacher having a little talk with him. The next day he heard his friends talking about his mother being a janitor and making fun of him. He screamed at his friends, "I don't know her." He did not know what made him say, "My mother is a doctor, not a janitor!" He just could not bear being a janitor's son and being laughed at.

When his mother got home late that night after work, he told her, "Mom, you embarrass me. Everybody at school is laughing at me because you are a janitor. Never come to my school again!" Hearing their younger brother saying this about their mother, two older brothers flipped over the dinner table and slapped his face impulsively. "Apologize to Mom. She has done everything for us. How dare you say such a thing to Mom! Apologize to her right now!" Instead of apologizing, he stormed out of the house and went to a nearby park. Sitting on a swing set, he could not understand why he behaved such a way because he knew well how much he loved his mom. He just hated himself for being laughed at by his peers and being looked down on.

The reason his teacher wanted to meet up with his mother was that there was a magnet boarding school only available to a handful of gifted kids from the county. His teacher said his scholarship would be covered 100 percent of all expenses and it would be great opportunity for him to pursue his dream. Later he learned that his two older brothers were offered the same scholarship, but they turned it down so they both could stay home and help their mother while attending high school. Neither of his two brothers told their mother about it. They could go to any Ivy League University with their 4.0 GPA's but chose to attend community college so they could help their mother clean medical offices at night, all the while maintaining straight A's in their classes. He, on the other hand could not wait to get out and live in a place where no one knew about his mom being a janitor and how poor his family was. The next day he told his teacher he wanted to attend the magnet school which was over 200 miles away. He knew his mother could not read so he forged his mother's signature on the application and gave it to his teacher. Graduating from that school, he went on to college with a full scholarship and earned his Ph.D. in education.

When he was in college, he came home one night and went to see his eldest brother where he worked as a medical resident in a hospital. He saw his brother emptying a trashcan in a patient's room and talking to someone in the restroom. When he entered the room to surprise him, he found his mother in the restroom scrubbing a toilet. He saw his brother, who was in medical residency in that hospital, never being ashamed of having a mother who was a janitor. On his way home, he went to the same park where he ran away and hid after saying those horrible things to his mother. He cried uncontrollably and said how sorry he was and begged for forgiveness thousands of times to his mother in the car. His stubbornness and never giving up were two of the strongest traits he learned from his mother. Abraham Lincoln said, "All that I am or ever hope to be, I owe to my angel mother." He wanted to be an educator so he could teach students right from wrong and show them how one should live. He reexamined his life and did not like what he saw and how he had lived it. He could not tell a single student to live the same way he had lived, not even to his own kids if he had any in the future. From that moment on, he became a new son and a new brother.

Professor Schmidt turned off the light as we left the classroom. Neither of us had any words as we were walking down the long hallway Mrs. Barbara and her university President son cleaned. In the front of the building, there were bicycle stands. He unchained his bike and rolled down the paved road in the rain. The only thing visible was a small beaming light from his bike. I did not run to avoid the rain beating down on my body. Instead, I walked slowly so as to have my heart washed in the river of shame, renewed, and baptized by a million drops of water. Professor Schmidt could have called his wife to pick him up, but instead, he too chose to ride a bike in the rain probably with the same reasoning that I had. People who did not know him to be a distinguished Professor might think he was mad and poor riding a bike at night in the rain, as the same people saw me walking toward a dimly lit parking lot.

I understood why it was important for him to teach students how we should treat other people whom we knew nothing about and the struggles they were facing. We are not to judge them based on their appearance and positions, but to treat them with love, dignity and respect, regardless of what they did in life and who they were. Even if they were viewed as the very bottom of the hierarchy in any organization. Graduate students at this level were more likely to hold managerial positions and to become leaders: all would be fathers and mothers one day, teaching their own children how one should live by example. Some might have influential positions and power making important decisions for organizations and for society.

My father had only a sixth-grade education and I have heard him saying too many times "Whatever you do and I don't care how small it is, you have to put your name on it. Be proud of what you do because you do the best you can even if nobody watches. You will be amazed at how much you can accomplish if you don't care about who gets credit."

Thomas Carlyle once said, "The work an unknown good man has done is like a vein of water flowing hidden underground, secretly making the ground green." It became my philosophy and belief that everything I have done and every job I have had has been a portrait of myself. I tried to live my life without a speck of guilt and shame; so even if God asks me at any moment in my life, "What are you doing right now?" I want to say and show Him proudly, "I am doing this!" A friend of Charles Dickens once spoke of him, "He did each thing as if he did nothing else." He gave everything he had and wrote his name on every word he used in his entire volume of books. That is how one should live, and he should approach his job as the most important thing and make it his masterpiece. In the end, it is all about what we do for others as Martin Luther King, Jr. said, "Everybody can be great...because anybody can serve. You don't have to have a college degree to serve. You don't have to make your subject and verb agree to serve. You only need a heart full of grace. A soul generated by love. And you can be that servant."

America and the Soviet Union were in a space race after World War II. The Soviets launched Sputnik 1, the world's first satellite, in 1957. The American government, military, and civilians as a whole felt our national security was threatened and in danger, so we made a full-fledged space effort to beat the Soviets. John F. Kennedy visited NASA in 1961 to encourage and motivate employees at NASA headquarter for the first time. While touring the facility heavily escorted by bodyguards and administrators of NASA, he saw a young female janitor mopping the floor. His chest pumped up and he walked like the most powerful person in the world. Well, he was the most powerful person in the world being the President of the United States. He introduced himself to the janitor saying, "I am the President of United States. So, what do you do here at NASA?" He obviously saw what she was doing but wanted to hear how she saw herself in NASA. She said, "I'm helping put a man on the moon, sir!"

The nineteen-year-old African American girl saw no janitor in herself. That was what she was doing at that stage of her life, but her vision was much bigger than that. She wanted to define her life neither by the environment she was living under the social injustice, racial segregation, and civil rights movement, nor the neurobiological disorder called dyslexia she had inherited. It was a death sentence to a girl like her. However, she was determined to define her life by the vision of the future which she knew she could create. She saw herself being a part of something great and even if she was a janitor, she approached her job as the most important thing in NASA and did the best she could. Those who are determined only remain to act. Who knew her weakness would turn into her biggest strength? On top of being an African American in the 1960's, she had a learning disability and could not read or write; so, NASA hired her. In fact, that was the very reason why she was hired as a janitor at the first place, for NASA was highly secured and classified, they were afraid the top-secret information might be leaked. In this case, she was naturally unable to do anything with it.

Even though she could not go to school, she was determined to succeed in life and had a fascination with new computers and how they worked; so, she taught herself how to read and write. NASA had brand new IBM computers and several dozens of people with Ph.Ds. were working on them in a computer lab. She had access to the lab to clean, and late at night when there was no one in the lab, she studied the entire program by herself. A supervisor came to the lab one night to work on something and found her rewriting programs and calculating numbers that no one was able to solve. Instead of accusing her of wrong doing and firing her, he encouraged her to work on it and provided her classified information she needed to solve problems on her own. After the supervisor retired, he wrote a book about her and her accomplishments that no one knew about. He said it was not so much to do with his leadership or his team's tireless dedication and efforts to send a man on the moon. If it were not for this girl's mathematical genius and her computer programing, he said they could not have accomplished what they did. Even now, nobody knows her name, but I believe she died content with being a faceless girl who did her part contributing to "putting a man on the moon" as a janitor.

The first stone of Cologne Cathedral in Germany was laid in 1248 and the project was completed in 1380. It took 632 years to build!

When my family hosted a fifteen-year-old German youth exchange student, I learned from her about this magnificent cathedral in Cologne. Her mother was working for the German airline Lufthansa, and its headquarters were located there. An architect who had designed the cathedral had the vision. He knew he could never be able to see the completion of his work of art but was comforted by his imagination of people coming to his cathedral worshiping God and leaving the legacy for generations to come.

One day, he went to see the progress. No workmen knew who he was among the men. He asked one of workmen, "What are you doing in here?" The man answered, "I don't know what this building is for, but I was told to cut a piece of stone." He walked a little further and asked the same question to another man. He angrily said without even looking at him, "It ain't worth doing. I don't get paid enough, and I hate this job!" He was heartbroken and disappointed to hear his vision, which would take several hundreds of years and which he would never get to see, was going to be built by these unpassionate, uncaring, and visionless workmen. As he turned around to leave the place, he heard a man whistling and loving every second of what he was doing. The workman did not even notice the architect was standing there watching him. Finally, he asked the same question to the workman and also asked why he was so happy working an unappreciated and low wage job. He responded, "I am building the most beautiful cathedral for my children and their children." He knew right then, because of this workman's passion and vision of being a part of something great, his cathedral would be the most beautiful and inviting place for all people.

A few years later, he heard that the workman was very sick and dying. He went to tell him how much he was appreciated for helping to build the cathedral he designed. The workman, lying on his deathbed, called his children to leave them his last words. He asked his wife to bring his old chisel and a hammer and said to his children, "All of my life I helped to build the most beautiful cathedral with this chisel and hammer. I leave my eldest son my most prized possession, the tool that I used to cut the stone!" The legacy of this nameless workman who found purpose in his work lives on in his children and in every person's heart. When people come to see the cathedral, they are in awe of the beauty and work of art.

Leonardo da Vinci was one of the greatest painters of all time. He was not only a painter but also an inventor, architecture, scientist, musician, mathematician, engineer, and writer. He truly was one of the most diversely talented Renaissance icons. His painting of The Last Supper is the most reproduced religious painting of all time and the painting of Salvator Mundi was sold for 450.3 million in 2017 at a Christie's auction. I have only seen the reproduction of the Mona Lisa numerous times from the billboards on streets or artbooks, and I still have no words to describe what I feel inside every time I see it. Even the greatest man said in his last words: "I have offended God and mankind because my work did not reach the quality it should have." That is why Martin Luther King, Jr., once said, "If a man is called to be a street sweeper, he should sweep streets even as a Michaelangelo painted, or Beethoven composed music or Shakespeare wrote poetry. He should sweep streets so well that all the hosts of heaven and earth will pause to say, 'Here lived a great street sweeper who did his job well."

It is not that important what your job is; it is why you do it and what impact you make on yourself and others. The ultimate goal of every human being is to do great for others. You must make it a calling and masterpiece no matter what kind of job you do, as Martin Luther King said. Your job has to be a portrait of yourself, and you must make it a masterpiece because no one else is going to do it for you and do it as good as you. After all, you have been placed on this earth to discover your own path. You have all the potential to succeed in life and the power to create a world that you leave better than how you found it. Hence, success has nothing to do with your worth and accomplishments. Your worth never changes from the moment you were born until you die. No matter what you gain in life, how much you accomplish for yourself, or how small your life is going to be, your life is worth everything in God's eyes. Live your God-given life while you can because you never know when it will be taken away from you. You don't get to choose when you die; you only get to choose how you live.

Colin Powell worked as a janitor and became a four-star general and statesman. Before the first black President of the United States, Obama, there was Colin Powell who paved the road for other minorities to serve in the U.S. government. He was the first black person to serve as Secretary of State under President George W. Bush which was the highest rank position ever held by black persons. He was born in

Harlem, New York, and was the son of Jamaican immigrants. His parents were very poor and living in the projects in Harlem where gang related crimes and troubles with the law occurred daily. His parents were hard workers and honest people. Even though he had no clear direction for what he wanted out of his life, he was determined to be somebody. Right after graduating from high school, he worked as a janitor in a soda company warehouse. He did not get paid extra for working hard, being honest, and for never calling out. In fact, nobody even cared what he did and treated him like an invisible and unimportant person because he was a young black janitor. People thought he would eventually end up in jail just like many young black people in Harlem.

These people saw his appearance and judged him by his position and assumed that he would not amount to anything. Somehow, he had a different mindset. He did not know what he wanted out of his life, but he knew he would succeed in life if he never quit, continued to be patient, and do the best of his ability no matter what. So, he set the goal of being the best janitor in the entire company. Because of his determination, patience, honesty, and work ethic, he became who he is today and was able to accomplish what he wanted out of his life.

He wrote a book dealing with leadership and believes that everybody has self-worth and the potential to be leaders because leadership is learned, not inherited. Someone once said, "Leadership is communicating people's worth and potential so clearly that they are inspired to see it in themselves." At first, you must believe your own worth and potential to be great; then, you have to live it and act on what you believe. Your greatness is not defined by what you gain in life or what you accomplish for yourself. Rich Roll is an UltraMan World Champion. He said, "To me, being great means being the most actualized version of yourself; the best version of yourself. Having the balls and courage to look inside yourself and do the work to figure out what gives you a heartbeat and what gives you purpose. To find that passion inside of you. And then set in motion a series of actions that lead to a plan to help you more fully actualize that and live that. Because that is what being great is, and that is what's gonna make you happy."

People will follow great leaders who believe in themselves and have a vision to make a difference. That is it! John Quincy Adams simply added, "If your actions inspire others to dream more, learn more, do more and become more, you are a leader." Colin Powell has practiced and lived by his "13 Rules" of leadership principles, and he shared that in his book.

Rule 1: It Ain't as Bad as You Think! It Will Look Better in the Morning. Winston Churchill took a nap one or two hours daily even while bombs were falling during the War. He had confidence in himself and his people. His faith and trust in God were unchanged no matter how devastating and dire a situation they were in. General Powell believed that the dark days shall pass and life must go on; hence, he acted as if business was as usual in any circumstances.

Rule 2: Get Mad Then Get Over It. If you are not mad at things not right, you would not do anything to change it. You will not be fired up or inspired to do anything if you accept all situations as they were. Madness inspires people do something about it, and they get over it because they put all their energy and resources to change and to make it better. They channel their anger through something positive. I was so angry at their living conditions when I visited Guatemala. People looked as if they were living in a dump. I have been going back again and again using my anger to inspire and encourage me to make their lives better.

Rule 3: Avoid Having Your Ego So Close to your Position that When Your Position Falls, Your Ego Goes with It. Let's get this straight. You have been given that important and high position to serve, not to be served. More importantly, you should never forget the people who helped you to get there. Hence, every job should be a self-portrait of yourself because excellence depends on how you perform in your job and how you treat other people. Even if you are the CEO of a multi-billion-dollar business or a doctor who wears a million-dollar sign on your forehead, you should forget you are CEO in your own company and ought to forget you are a doctor in your hospital. That is what you do and you should treat others as important and valuable as you are.

Rule 4: It Can be Done. Leadership is taking a risk and making things happen. When Thomas Edison finally succeeded in inventing light bulbs after failing 999 times, a reporter asked, "Mr. Edison, how did it feel to fail 999 times?" Edison responded with a smile, "Young man, I have not failed 999 times. I have simply found 999 ways how not to create a light bulb." Every time he failed, he learned from it because he knew it could be done if he kept trying and kept learning from his mistakes.

Rule 5: Be Careful What You Choose. You May Get It. When you choose to do a certain thing, you choose not to do everything else. In that sense, every act of free will is an act of self-sacrifice because you only can do one thing and eliminate all others. You are certainly free to do whatever you choose to do, but at the same time, you are not free from the consequence of choices you make. Choose wisely. Insanity is doing the same things over and over again and expecting a different result. You know that won't work.

Rule 6: Don't Let Adverse Facts Stand in the Way of a Good Decision. Living in an informational age, there is an unlimited amount of information available at our finger tips. The small cell phone that you have in your hands has more capability than the mainframed IBM computers which sent the first man to the moon. No longer do you have to seek specialized and protected information only available for doctors, lawyers, teachers, accountant, priests, and so on. Even though there is limitless information floating around all of us, we are starving to death for wisdom. We are emotional, psychological, and social beings. When adversity and unfiltered information overload us, we think it is impossible to overcome before we even try; so, we give up. Sometimes you find yourself thinking you are the only one standing up for your beliefs while everybody else is sitting down. Sometimes you are the only one sitting down while everybody else is standing up because that is what everybody is doing, following the followers. The ultimate measure of a man is where you stand in the middle of the adversity. At the time of comfort and convenience, anybody can do what they want to do.

Rule 7: You Can't Make Someone Else's Choices. You Shouldn't Let Someone Else Make Yours. You cannot choose what happens to you, you only can choose how you respond to what happens to you. The choices you make will determine what kind of outcome you are going to have. You have to define your own life by doing things your own way. That means you have to allow others to do the same even if their choice is not same as yours. We all have different perspectives and different interpretations even if we are looking at the exact same reality. You must embrace the difference.

Rule 8: Check Small Things. A big thing did not suddenly become a big thing. What started out as small flakes, became a huge avalanche. It was the humble beginning of janitor Colin who became general Powell. People want to be President Lincoln, but they must become Honest Abe first. Pay attention to small details. They build character.

Rule 9: Share Credit. Basic human needs are not only food, water, clothing, and shelter but also recognition, a sense of worth and belonging. Not many people in America would die from hunger and homelessness these days, but we die inside not being valued and not being recognized for the contribution we made no matter how small it was. You already got the credit you deserve by accomplishing what you want to do and must recognize and share with those who helped you to get there. Standing on top of the mountain all alone without your team members is really lonely and gets boring. If you light a thousand candles with your single match, your light will never diminish! Share all of your successes and credit with others; they would follow you and help you to succeed.

Rule 10: Remain calm. Be kind. "Keep Calm and Carry On" was used as a motivational and morale boosting poster in late 1939 by the British government after the outbreak of World War II. You have to be calm and keep composure in times of difficulty because people are looking at you to lead. It is time to show your confidence and lead with compassion. No hero is born in a peaceful time. Adversity makes a man a hero and he learns to be compassionate and kind to others.

Rule 11: Have a Vision. Be Demanding. People follow a leader who has a vision and who demands them to be accountable for fulfilling their roles and responsibilities. Sam Ewing said, "Nothing is more embarrassing than watching someone do something that you said could not be done."

Rule 12: Don't take counsel of your fears or naysayers. Naysayers will always oppose your ideas and anything you do because deep inside they are afraid you might achieve the dreams they once deemed impossible. They don't want to see you proving them wrong. Fear itself is not that bad when it is faced.

"The only thing we have to fear is fear itself, "said President Franklin D. Roosevelt. Vincent Van Gogh said, "If you hear a voice within you say 'you cannot paint' then by all means paint, and that voice will be silenced." You have to face fears head on instead of avoiding them.

Rule 13: Perpetual optimism is a force multiplier. The best way to multiply your success and happiness is by sharing it with others. People want to be good, feel good, and do good. It is human nature wanting to be around optimistic people who value our well-beings. No matter how bad the situation is, they never seem to lose sight of why they are doing everything they do to make a positive impact on people's lives. That is a contagious attitude and attracts people just like them.

One of my friends is a music promoter who went through the leadership program with me a few years back. When he was in New York, promoting a benefit concert for a non-profit organization, he met Colin Powell backstage through a mutual friend. He did not know the concert he was promoting was for "America's Promise Alliance" founded by Colin Powell. His non-profit organization is dedicated to fostering character and competence in young people. My friend was so inspired by Colin Powell and his perpetual vision, that he helped to start a chapter in the county where we live.

This poor son of Jamaican immigrants started as a janitor and became a four-star general and Secretary of State serving his country. It all started when he was a janitor doing the best he could to be the best at everything he did, no matter what kind of job it was.

Ms. Barbara and Professor Schmidt…what a life lesson I learned from them in the beginning of my journey trying to find my calling! What kind of life should I live so that others are inspired to leave a giant step in someone else's heart the way these fine people did to me?

Dear Kim Kim,

You have made a huge impact on not only me but also everyone else here. During your groups, you made me think of things in a way I never thought of. However, I won't lie to you. I didn't think I was going to like

122

your groups at all because I couldn't trust anyone. It turns out, they were my favorite part of the day.

I love hearing your stories about your life in Korea and especially the story of Mrs. Barbara. My mother works at the hotel as a housekeeper, and I was so ashamed and embarrassed by having a mom as a janitor. Thank you for teaching me that her job doesn't define her worth as a human being and I know everything she is doing is for me and my three siblings. I am going to tell her how proud I am of her and how much I love her. And I am going to hug her like you hug me when I begged you. I know you are not supposed to, but I deserved it as your daughter!

--Adolescent

Happy Birthdays

Do you remember all the hype around what was dubbed by media the "Great American Eclipse" in August 2017? When the sun, moon, and Earth were aligned to create a total solar eclipse, they said it was a once in a lifetime chance to witness such an event since we won't live hundreds of years to see the next one. Watching it with special sunglasses from the fourth floor of the hospital where I worked, I had never witnessed it in my life and probably never would again; however, nothing could compare to the birth of my three children, watching them grow and living as independent thinkers and responsible doers. They are the most beautiful, unique, and special persons in my life: more than anything else, they are every reason for my being on earth.

It is said that my chance of being born was one to four hundred trillion. My mother and father were chosen to be my parents and I to my three children. I believe being a parent is the highest honor and reward, at the same time, the biggest responsibility and challenge. My three children are now grown up and clearly demonstrate in their everyday life independent thinking and are detached from parental influence and boundary. I can say my relationship with my children is more like man to man with respect and freedom to say different beliefs and opinions of their own, not like an authoritative father and obedient children.

A few years ago, my daughter gave me a more meaningful gift for Christmas than any other years. Fifty things I love about my Dad. At this stage of my life, I certainly can afford to buy anything I want. It is mistaken if you think I am filthy rich. Nothing could be further from the truth. Even though I am not a millionaire, it is an honest statement that I could buy anything I want. I do have wants, desires, and needs just like anybody else. But, what I really want I have received already: loving family, good health, brotherly friends, financially independent, the best job, and good books. I feel abundant and grateful for what I have, and I really don't want anything else that money can buy. Instead of giving material goods for my daughter's birthday, I was thinking maybe my daughter is like me, not wanting stuff for her special birthday. The following year, I wanted to tell her 28 things I am grateful for her 28th birthday. I wrote it and asked my wife to write a few things in Korean on papers and she did. Then, I laminated it and gave it to her on her birthday. Well, you can imagine how she took it! It was a gift to myself as well seeing how wonderful a woman she has become.

After eating special birthday food all prepared by her mother, I presented her with a five page letter in front of the whole family. She told me crying that it was the biggest gift she had ever received. I was happy, too. My two boys said in unison they wanted the same thing on their birthdays. My youngest son, Doun's birthday was only thirteen days away. My uncontrollable emotion was so high that I could not write 24 things in time for his 24th birthday. Instead, I decided to include what I wrote to my three children in my journal when they were young for this book. Also, I wrote twelve things I was grateful for on my wife's birthday. I include that in this book as well.

12 things I am grateful for my wife's birthday...

1. You married me so that I could love you forever with one heart.

나와 결혼해서 일편단심으로 평생을 사랑할 수있게 해준 것.

2. You have raised Ahrahm, Hannie, and Doun well and made them good men.

아람, 하니, 다운이 잘 키워주고 훌륭한 사람으로 만들어 준 것.

3. No matter how difficult situation it was, you have always smiled and lived happily.

아무리 힘든 일이 있어도 늘 웃으며 잘 살아준 것.

4. You have planted a seed of true meaning of family in me.

나에게 가족의 의미를 심어준 것.

5. You have become my best friend and lifelong companion.

가장 친한 친구이며 삶의 영원한 반려자가 되어준 것.

6. You understood me and help me to achieve what I want to do in life.

나를 이해해주고 내가 하고 싶은 것을 할수있게 도와준 것.

7. You have taught me love is not to receive but having a loving person next to me. You fulfill my happiness.

사랑은 받는 것이 아니라 사랑하는 사람이 곁에 있다는 것만으로 행복함을 느끼게 해준 것.

8. Whenever and wherever you are, you have always been my lovable wife.

언제보아도 사랑스러운 사람으로 되어준 것.

9. You have always been my strength.

나에게 힘이 되어준 것.

10. You have provided and supported your parents-in-law and your

husband's family as your own.

시부모와 남편 가족을 친부모와 형제처럼 모셔준 것.

11. You have been protecting and loving our family wholeheartedly.

온 몸으로 가족을 지키고 사랑해준 것.

12. Today we are celebrating your 53rd birthday. I am grateful and looking forward to living with you for fifty three more years in our lives together.

오늘로 당신 생일이 53살이 되지만 우리 부부 53살 더 같이 사는 것.

28 Things I Am Grateful for on my daughter's 28th Birthday...

1. When you were born, I had witnessed the miracle for the first time. From that moment on, I promised to myself I would give my life to protect and love you. You are a miracle in my life and to the world. Ever since you were born, I see miracles every day in my life. How grateful I am and how precious you are!

2. I am grateful to you for making me the proudest Dad in the whole wide world. That is huge!

3. For your being the only girl in my life, I get to love you unconditionally. I love your Mom, too, but it is conditional depending on how much she gives me for lunch money. She is too cheap!

4. I am grateful to you for being my best friend. Who would understand the struggles and obstacles I have been through and encourage me to go on no matter what? I thank you for that!

5. Because of you, I became a writer. I feel like I am getting better at it each time I write for the next book. It is not that I speak or know more English. I am becoming a better man because of your critical thinking and honest opinions.

6. I am grateful for your being a good sister for Hannie and Doun. Your two brothers adore you!

7. I am grateful for your never give up mindset no matter how difficult it is. You turn it into I can do attitude. That is why you are destined to succeed in whatever you do.

8. My legacy is not going to be measured by what I gain in life or what I have accomplished for myself. The most important thing is the relationship I have with you. Your existence in my life is all I need to smile, be happy, and get up every single time when I am knocked down again and again.

9. Not many fathers and daughters have philosophical conversations about life. I am grateful for having such a wonderful time when you were just a kid and even now as an independent thinker. That is

awesome!

10. The Fountainhead and Atlas Shrugged by Ayn Rand; A Little Life by Hanya Yanagihara; Anton Chekhov; Animal Farm by George Orwell; Fahrenheit 451 by Ray Bradbury, and many more...I would not have known these great books and authors if it weren't for you. Thank you for recommending me to read such life altering books, and I have enjoyed reading all the books you have recommended me. Please keep them coming, okay?

11. Whenever people say your daughter is just like you, that is the greatest compliment for me! You are so beautiful, lovable, and passionate about life just like your dad. As you can see, being just like your dad is not all bad!

12. I am grateful for not only learning but practicing "7 Habits of Highly Effective People" over twenty years ago when you were young. It suggested to have one on one dates with the most important person in your life and what a fun memory I have with you. We still need to do that you know!

13. When you were in 4th grade, you gave me a handmade card saying, "Thank you for marrying my mom." Later I learned there were you and only three other students out of twenty in your class that were living with both mom and dad. You were the mortar that glued our family together.

14. You can either blame me or thank me for exposing you to the world of Pink Floyd, Ollies, and alternative music. It made me happy listening to music we both like, and I hope I have bridged the generation gap through music.

15. Abraham Maslow said, "A musician must make music, an artist must paint, a poet must write, if he is to be ultimately at peace with himself." Nobody has a perfect family nor life, but I am grateful for you finding your passion and using it to make a difference.

16. Children could not pick and choose their own parents. I am grateful for being your father. God was looking down on earth looking for the best father and mother for you. I truly believe I was chosen by God to be your father. It really is the greatest honor and responsibility. I

promise I will never neglect my duty until I die.

17. I am grateful for your willingness to go to Guatemala with me and the other Rotarians to make a difference in the lives of others who could not repay you for anything you had done for them. I could see the difference it made on you. You do have a servant heart, and I am very grateful that you treat all people with dignity and kindness.

18. I am grateful for you having a great attitude at any circumstances. Even if everything is taken away from you, you choose to be happy, optimistic, and grateful.

19. While we were working together at the Skyline, I got to see you as a person. Wow, I was proud of myself, that after all, I did raise you to be such a fine woman. You know how much I like poems by Kahlil Gibran. He writes on children.

"Your children are not your children.

They are the sons and daughters of Life's longing for itself.

They come through you but not from you,

And though they are with you, yet they belong not to you.

You may give them your love but not your thoughts,

For they have their own thoughts,

You may house their bodies but not their souls,

For their souls dwell in the house of tomorrow, which you cannot visit, not even in your dreams...."

20. I accepted my duty as your loving father when you were born. I became your friend as you searched for your own identity. I hope to be a man who you look up to even after I depart from this earth.

21. I am grateful for you remembering and cherishing all those little things we have done together. "What I love about Dad" was one of biggest gifts I have received and cried many times that you remember

the times we spent together.

22. You turn twenty-eight years old today, and I am fifty-seven. I am no longer afraid of getting old or even dying because I get to see my daughter spreading her wings and flying high as I get older each year and you begin flying higher and higher. Ever since you were a little girl, I respected your opinion and let you make your own decisions even though I knew they were not rational and wise decisions for that age. But I felt it was a part of learning and growing up. Because of that, you failed some, but I have never clipped your wings to protect you and to keep you safe. You have found your place in this earth on your own, and I am grateful for you living your full life and using your God given potential.

23. I am grateful for learning one of greatest lessons of all. Having you as my daughter is not only the greatest gift in my life but also having a daughter to love is much greater than being loved by everyone.

24. Every single thing that has ever happened in your life is preparing you for your successful life that is yet to come. Yesterday and tomorrow are such small matters compared to what you are doing today, right now at this moment. I love your mentality wanting to learn, grow, and get better than yesterday so you have a better tomorrow. Your attitude is contagious, and I am grateful to you for encouraging me to keep learning and keep investing in today for tomorrow.

25. I read books to you when you were young, and even now I have been encouraging you to read books and gave you a dollar for every book you read. It was one of our favorite times to go to bookstores picking books that were short and had a lot of pictures in it so you could earn a dollar. Who knew all those very short picture books contained the most essential wisdom in life? I am grateful to you for opening my eyes to see the important things in small but different shapes.

26. There was a railroad and a train in the Parthenon. I helped you to walk on the rail and you would not let my hands go until we walked all the way to the end. I am grateful for your dependence on me and needing me when you were little. Now I am learning to let go of your hands so that you can fly freely. That is a job well done for any father.

27. I realized a man really does not become a man until he has a child.

Because he has a child, it does not mean he is a father. Fatherhood is a lifelong journey, and I am grateful for sharing our lives together as father and daughter. It is the most prestigious title and relationship a man could have.

28. Of all the things I have done, my most proud thing is being your dad. People used to say, "Your daughter is Ahrahm." Now, I am called, "You are Ahrahm's dad, Hannie's dad, and Doun's Dad." I am recognized and complimented by your name and your character. I am grateful for being shadowed by you and wherever you are, I will be right there in your heart.

This is it! Twenty-eight things I am grateful for on your 28th Birthday. First of all, I am, in a way, glad that we are NOT celebrating your 100th birthday! In that case, it is going to be a book!

Ahrahm, what else or what more can I say about your being in my life? I thought I would never get married; then, your mom changed me. I thought I was not good enough to be a father. Then, you changed me. I thought I was only one, and what could I do in this world? Once I realized my role as your father, I began to live by example and helped those in need the best I could with what I have. Thank you and thank you for being my daughter.

Happy Birthday!

From your Dad

I Am Grateful for Doun's 24th and Hannie's 25th Birthday...

Thank you for making me a better father. I believe that the best gift parents could give to their children is being husband and wife and loving each other. When I pull my car in our driveway, I let all the frustrations, anger, worries, and sadness out of my mind and body. This is our sacred home. Why am I bringing all the negative and toxic thoughts and behaviors to our home where love and happiness reside?

Because of you, I have learned to let go things I cannot control and trust in God for everything.

Sometimes I see myself through your eyes and I see what kind of Dad I have become. When your Mom and I went through the darkest and deepest times in our lives, you, too, had to experience all the adversity the same as we did. It might be my fault our family had to face that, but I am so proud of you for becoming as good of men as you are meant to be. After all, all those unavoidable circumstances and adversities have made us stronger and we get to appreciate what we have and never take anything for granted.

Dear Kim Kim,

You have been a great role model in the week that I have known you. You have shown me that I can be someone someday. You have said many wise things to me that I hope to look back on in the future. One day I would like to be a great role model to some kids like you were to me. Although I may never see you again, I will never forget you and the things you said. The things you said may have saved my life and most importantly they may have saved my heart. I now see that anything in life can be a lesson and that it may be better to look at things a little different. Even though I can't change the people around me, I want to tell them your story and the stories that you told me.

I am going to read your book "My Life in Letters" and learn what I can do to be a better me. I can't change my family or ask for another one, but I can tell/show them how much I love them by taking your stories and learning from them. I can't change my past, but I can learn from it use it to my advantage in the future.

I have learned that life is hard, but you also told me that "It goes on" and those three words can do a lot for me. I will miss you and your crazy but meaningful stories, and I hope to see you again someday...not here but just out in life or at a restaurant or something.

We may have only met a week ago, but I will forever consider you as family and friend. Speaking of family, I hope you and yours do well. I will never forget the funny things you did either. I have nothing else to say but GOODBYE KIHYON (Kim Kim).

Love.

—Adolescent

PART III:
COMMUNITY

Franklin's Little Free Library

A nation becomes what its young people read in their youth. Its ideals are fashioned then, its goals strongly determined.   James A. Michener

"Why is a dry cleaner offering free books? That is not what they do!" Some have doubtfully laughed after finding out Franklin Cleaners offers hundreds of free books, from rare and expensive signed copies of Pulitzer Prize winning authors and of Former President Jimmy Carter to local celebrities like late George Jones, Dr. Ming Wang, and Congresswoman Diane Black. However, most people who know my humble beginnings think it makes perfect sense and expect nothing less of me. Let me take you to the very beginning to answer your question, "What does reading books have to do with dry cleaning and me?" "Everything!" I exclaim.

Our family business is indeed dry cleaning, laundry, and alterations. I can say with absolute certainty that no one expects to borrow, read, and return books free and at their own convenience, at a dry cleaner. People would not go to a post office and ask for sushi! Even public libraries charge fees for lost or past due books. In fact, I have a memorable experience regarding past due library books. I found out a month before my projected college graduation that I could not graduate from MTSU because my record showed I had checked out three books two years prior to my graduation! I was held from graduating until I paid the "Late Fees" in full, totaling one hundred and ninety dollars, although I could have purchased multiple copies of those books with the total of the fine.

At Franklin Cleaners, that would never happen, for each book is absolutely and always free to the public! These books not only have sentimental value to me, but are my family treasures for generations to come, and that is why I want to share them.

I have spent over 20 years of my life in classrooms in Korea and America. My pursuit of education has cost me and my family a tremendous amount of money, although the intention for me to obtain an education was so that I could secure a safe, respectable, and well-paid job to support my entire Kim family and to make them proud. It still hurts me deeply that none of my three sisters completed high school because they had to sacrifice their young lives to find jobs immediately after graduating middle school to support our impoverished family. I began to think that my education not only cost my family a financial burden for a long time, but also cramped my younger brother and three older sisters' hopes and dreams. I made a solemn promise that all of my kids, no matter what profession they would seek, would have a college degree. I felt that it would give them a solid foundation to seek who they are and reach success in whatever way that success becomes defined, to them.

Frankly, the formal education and certificates I obtained in classrooms did greatly contribute to my accomplishments and finances, but I found that it did not contribute to providing the purpose and meaning to my life nor define who I am. I have found the most meaning in books, outside of confined classroom walls. Reading is one of the secret treasures that makes us human and has done so since the beginning of humanity, yet not everyone knows the value of what it provides for a man. The more valuable books I have, the more desire I have to share them with others.

This is why I offer books at my dry cleaner. In my heart, it has everything to do with why I do what I do, and is the reason why I have a mission statement proudly displayed in our store. We not only expect companies that touch our lives in one way or another to have a mission and vision for their companies, but more importantly, we demand them to live by their missions and deliver on their promises. We hold them accountable, and if they do not practice what they preach and fail to deliver, we go elsewhere.

It is of utmost importance to my family to stand for what we believe in no matter what kinds of jobs we have, even at one small mom and pop dry cleaner serving the Franklin community. My chosen vocation has given me the opportunity to serve, connect, inspire, make lifelong relationships. More importantly, my vocation allows me to make a difference in people's lives and in our community. What else would be greater than being called by God and being used for His purpose? That is why I love every moment in my life and feel blessed. I believe what I do matters, no matter how small. Let me show you our mission statement that we live by every day. It is such a personal matter that we even put mine and my wife' name on it.

"Our family is wholeheartedly committed to bringing ease, convenience, and joy to your life. We do our best to exceed your expectations by providing the highest quality of customer service and satisfaction. We are members of civic and charitable organizations with which we support and participate in local and international community service. Above all else, our success is measured by helping people in need and giving back to our community we have the privilege to serve. Kim and Sue."

I must tell you the pivotal moment that changed my life. I did not have the slightest idea that one small pebble could make such an enormous ripple effect later in my life. When I came to America from Korea at the age of seventeen, I could not speak a word of English. When I was first introduced to the three simple words, "How are you?" all I could do was smile back, for I had no idea what it meant. That was my first day at Gallatin High School in America. I had no friends to talk to during my entire school year, and I did not blame anyone but myself for it, "Who wants to be a friend to a foreign kid like me?"

Ever since I started working at Krystal as a janitor, which was the only job available to a guy like me, I had a dream. I watched a worker at the drive thru window taking orders from someone outside through an intercom. While I was mopping floors or taking trash out to the dumpster, I was amazed by how naturally and fluently people of all ages spoke English. "If I could speak English that well," I thought, "I could do anything in America!"

I was not a reader growing up in Korea but discovered that it provided me a new freedom in America. Reading was the easiest and cheapest way to learn English. Being foreign and unable to speak English, people called me all kinds of names "Stupid, Idiot, Dumb" and labeled me a loser. I did not know what they meant when they said, "You don't count! Your life will never amount to anything!" Even though I did not know the true meaning of these words and the way were said to me, I knew that they were not kind words. Nevertheless, I had a fire inside of me slowly burning for something. As their voices got louder, my heart was getting bigger. I did not know what it was and wanted to find that out through books.

Victor Hugo said, "To learn to read is to light a fire; every syllable that is spelled out is a spark." Oh, how true it was! Every word I learned not only lit my heart, but expanded it. Books have become a magic window connecting me to the world of all possibilities, imagination and new path I did not think existed. Books have become my best friend and the most precious gift I have ever received over and over again. Saint Augustine once said, "The world is a book, and those who don't travel read only a page." At that moment I knew that the whole world was right in front of me, and all I had to do was to open the book. It was the cheapest pleasure I accidentally ran into, and I didn't know then that it would last a lifetime. Once I discovered new findings, let go of old thinking, and changed the way I see the world, the old was crumbling down and replaced with new without me even realizing it. Oliver Wendell Homes Jr. once said, "Man's mind, stretched by a new idea, never goes back to its old dimensions." I am in the center of the universe. That is how I feel in my study room. I have over 4,000 books in my bookshelves, and all are written in only two different languages: in Korean and in English. However, I have not only visited six continents, but more proudly to say, I have books from all over that open my eyes to the world and its people who have a story to tell. I read in a book, "Stories are the basic unit of human consciousness. They are how we construct our reality." My mind is too enlarged to fit in old beliefs anymore. Reading books did that!

Franklin Cleaners is our family business, but my wife is the one running it six days a week open to close even though all our family members help her time to time. I forgot to mention my two other vocations: Adolescent Mental Health Counselor and Rotarian. I have been working in the healthcare field ever since 2001, all managerial positions until I stumbled upon this job in 2014 as a mental health counselor. Who knew everything I have done, I mean every single thing that I have done and has ever happened in my life, was preparing me to be the best mental counselor for adolescent patients who struggles with suicidal ideations or attempts?

When I started working at my hospital, there were only a handful of books available for patients. I then began thinking what a great opportunity for them to find whatever they were searching for in books the same way books opened my mind and saved me from insanity, and helped me find my identity. They are captive audiences and I did not have to do anything except make books available to them. So, I started the book project, ensuring all six units in our hospital had bookshelves. It took more than three years, but I am so happy to see each unit now have bookshelves with books that patients can read and hope to find what they have been searching for.

My Adolescent Unit has over 1,200 books ranging from Newberry Award winners to college required books such as *Don Quixote, War and peace,* and *One Hundred Years of Solitude.* These books are ones that have made a huge impact in my life. Please don't blame me for being bias because I stock books that I love. My third job is being a consultant for my Rotary Club. I have been a member of our club for the past 20 years serving all positions from Secretary to President. Once I served as District Governor, I wanted to go back to my club and be a servant. Non-Rotarian Roger was the only paid person in our club, and after he passed away a few years ago, our club was searching for someone to manage 170-member club daily function. I became that person and have happened to become the only paid Rotarian in our club. Yes, I love what I do for our club, and even if I didn't get paid a dime, I would still do it as long as I am a member and as long as I can serve as Executive Secretary. I am very grateful for being paid to do what I love to do, and since all other positions are voluntary, I use my consultant fees for all of my volunteer works and international mission trips and give scholarships on my own. At Rotary, we have a guest speaker who speaks to us each week, and we have them sign their names on books and donate them to elementary schools that we sponsor. Hence, just like Franklin Cleaners, even if there are no books, I have always found the way to have books available to people we serve.

Now let me explain how I started Franklin's Little Free Library. One day I was lazily flipping through a magazine and the title of the article and a picture of what appeared to be a one-room schoolhouse on a post in front of the house captured my interest. A man who was living in Hudson, Wisconsin built a free library to tribute to his late mother who was a school teacher and loved to read books. He called it Little Free Library for his neighbors and passersby to borrow, read, or leave books for someone else. It was a simple idea of sharing books with his neighbors and strangers when it was started in 2009. He wanted to have 2,510 Little Libraries. Why did he set a goal of 2,510? That was the number of public libraries founded by Andrew Carnegie, and he wanted to surpass that. I understand that the goal was met in

2012 by common people like me all over the world who enjoy reading books and want to share good books with others. People can find my Franklin's Little Free Library on the World Map and a charter sign is proudly displayed in my Dry Cleaners!

What else do you find in my Dry Cleaner? A good place to meet good people. Rita Rudner is a stand-up comedian and said, "A good place to meet a man is at the dry cleaner. These men usually have jobs and bathe." They are readers, too! Now you see why we have books for any readers in our dry-cleaning business. It is not a show like a lawyer's office!

I was contacted by the Managing Editor of Williamson Magazine. They were working on a feature story about Little Free Library in our community. The following is a questionnaire I was asked and my answers.

Questionnaire:

How and why did you start your tiny library?

Making reading and knowledge more accessible and normalized for everyone is a cause I will always be passionate about. I have been a member of Rotary Club since 2000. A decade ago, Little Free Library was featured in Rotarian magazine. Rotarians all over the world were advocating for the concept, building shelves, and donating books to communities around the world. I immediately wanted to start one in my neighborhood and was unfortunately denied by my homeowner's association, but I didn't give up. As a mental health counselor at Skyline Medical Center, I donated over 4,000 books to build libraries on each unit of the hospital. Then when my wife and I took ownership of Franklin Cleaners in Franklin, the very first thing we did was build a Little Free Library for our community!

Why do you think these are important to the community and different generations?

We, as members of a community, have the responsibility of

creating our culture of reading. Reading provides to us the wisdom and perception that helps us relate to one another, the appreciation of another individual's writing provides us the compassion and empathy to support each other, and sharing our own stories spreads knowledge for generations to come. This passion and quest for knowledge is what drives our community and generations from the past, present, and future!

What has been your favorite experience with your tiny little library thus far?

I am overwhelmed by the generosity of people in Franklin. People not only come to our business for their dry-cleaning needs but also to check out books and donate their own favorites so that others can also experience the joy of reading as they do! Viewing the environment of giving and sharing that it has created has been remarkable.

Why should other people participate?

It really doesn't take much effort or labor to share your books yet it can mean the world to the ones that get to read it. I came to America when I was seventeen, without knowing a word of English, and I contribute everything about where I am now to reading books. If it weren't for my love of reading, I wouldn't have become the author of eight books.

Dear Kim Kim,

You are an amazing teacher. Thanks to you I will reach the 5th chapter. Now I know that I am worth 100%. You are the reason that I am ready to become a public speaker. I even wrote a speech on your "100%" lesson. I hope that I can remember the impact you made in my life and use it to help other people. Thank you for helping me realize that I am worth so much more than I thought. I will become an eagle and stop acting like a sparrow. –Adolescent

ST's Legacy Lives on in Honduras

I am listening to Elton John's "Daniel" this morning as I am about to head to the airport. It is a ritual I have been doing, without much thought, whenever I travel overseas for mission trips.

"Daniel is traveling tonight on a plane

I can see the red tail lights heading for Spain

Oh and I can see Daniel waving goodbye

God it looks like Daniel, must be the clouds in my eyes"

Outside of my window, time stands still and it is very dark. It is only one o'clock, and the January cold is hovering around me like a blanket. The Daniel depicted in the song was a real person who came home from Vietnam. He wanted to live a normal life on his farm but could not find peace and serenity after the war; he left for Spain where he thought he could find what he was looking for because "It's the best place that he's ever seen."

I am no Daniel; in fact, I am not heading for Spain to watch bullfighting or the world-famous Spanish dance of Flamenco in Roman Theatre in Merida, either. Did you know it was built in the year 15 BC and is still being used as a theatre? One day I'd like to visit, but not this time. Instead, my mind is somewhere else: I am heading for Honduras. The name should say it all. It is where 66 percent of the population lives in extreme poverty earning less than 1.90 cents per day. Unfortunately, that is not the worst of it. It should not come as a surprise that Honduras is known for being the most violent and dangerous country on the planet.

Then, why have I been going to such a place and risking my own life, for the past six years? Ever since I have started going to Honduras, the only two hands-on projects we have ever done for each village have been installing electricity and digging wells, so they could have access to clean drinking water. It has been hard physical labor, but with basic understanding of how electricity works and by observation, anybody, really anybody can do what we do without much trouble. In addition, if anyone can tolerate 115 to 120 degrees of heat, he or she is a qualified electrician, but only in Honduras of course!

Statistics indicate that it is not the ideal place to live or even visit, but I have never felt uneasiness, threat, or danger in all these years, despite seeing armed guards even in our hotels and delivery truck drivers carrying machine guns to defend against robbers hijacking the trucks. Even thinking about landing in Tegucigalpa, rated the second most dangerous airport in the world, all the passengers cheering and clapping hands when realizing there has been a safe landing, still gives me a smile. Seeing poor but innocent families and children makes me the happiest person and eager to go back again and again because like Daniel says, "It's the best place that he's ever seen."

I was born only nine years after the Korean War broke out. The war not only brought the worst destruction and devastating poverty in recent Korean history but also deflated the economy and wiped out all resources. To think back on it now, my family was dirt poor, but we always had electricity growing up in Korea. Even though we had to skip meals often, I have never experienced the thirst of having no access to drinkable water. These people, by no fault of their own, have been living without essential electricity and water for all their lives. Oh, you should have seen their shelters and living conditions: there were no floors nor hardly any furniture, and were mostly built with corn stalks, mud, cardboard boxes, plastic bags, and anything they could find to protect them from wind and rain. They are the poorest of the poor, so much so that the poor in our standard is considered rich. Then, retrospectively should we not be happier and grateful for what we have and what has been given to us due to the simple fact that we are living in America, when these people who have literally nothing are abandoned and neglected by their own government?

Although local people have known about this village, it remained unknown to outsiders because it was isolated and hidden from the modern world. Thank God that Hondurans whom we have been working with for over fifteen years have gone out and searched for such villages for us to bring light to them so they could enjoy modern commodities and an equal chance in the playing field as others, no matter where they have been living or how poor they are. It was located on the top of the mountain covered with black lava, volcanic rocks, and unrecognizable trees only grown in tropical mountain climates. The only way to get there was by foot or on the backs of donkeys during the dry season. No outsiders would spend half a day traveling there. So, we, American volunteers, rented four-wheel drive trucks and adventured among unfamiliar territory.

A few years ago, my son visited one of the Seven Wonders of the world, Machu Picchu in Peru, and pictures of the ruined estate for the Inca emperor reminded me of the place I visited last year. Surrounded by beautiful and uncivilized nature, I saw God's creation with my eyes and wished if I were retired, I would live at a place like this with these people. We were to wire electricity to ninety houses in a village but only finished twenty-five with seven volunteers. This year I am going to the same village with fifteen other volunteers. It is the only time we have gone back to the same village to complete what we had started. As I pen this writing, I am anxious and excited to see familiar faces once more.

These people are so accustomed and immune to their circumstances that they don't know any other way but to accept their lifestyle as it is and go on living like their ancestors, grandparents and now their parents have always done. At the end of the dirt road covered with lava stones, suddenly, a two-way paved road appears. The moment our truck crosses the bridge, we were giddily exuberant at the sight of glass and modern, steel buildings, convenience stores, traffic lights, and the welcoming signs of KFC and McDonald's.

Upon reflection, the irony is that it takes us less than a twenty minute drive (10 miles) to arrive at our Hotel Rivera in Choluteca city, where we have just about everything we could want in any city in America: heated pools, cold beers, soft drinks, wi-fi, and hot and cold showers that we can take as often as we want. More importantly, there is electricity and water we can drink without worrying about whether we are going to become sick or not. Sadly, but shocking to realize, it takes no time at all from leaving the old and unprivileged to walk back into the hotel and adjust right back into the modern life we are so familiar with. While I take these luxuries for granted, this hotel seems like another world compared to the lives of those we will be assisting, lives that exist without basic human necessities, and have grown to expect their children to live the same way that they always have. On the other hand, when we have no electricity or running water for even an hour due to scheduled repair or bad winter storms, many of us treat it like an apocalypse or at least a pestering inconvenience.

To be honest, it is not the difference we make, the transformation of lives after we accomplish our mission in Honduras, the pats on our backs, recognition, or credits, that stick out the most. More than anything, I could not and still cannot erase from my mind the images of innocent children and their families living in such conditions with contentment, happiness, and appreciation for life, despite it all. It is I who has been blessed and has grown by being of service to others. Oh, what a foolish man I have been for taking for granted all those essential things in life! Now I realize that the most essential things in life are not even "things" after all. I have more than they would likely ever have, but I feel I am poorer than they are. Despite the little I saw materialistically, I witnessed contentment and happiness in everyone. That is what I am about to witness again this year in Honduras.

No matter how daunting the tasks are or how little it may seem my concern when these people live thousands of miles away, it is my duty and responsibility to perform to the best of my ability and help other human beings even in such a country. I am grateful for the opportunity given to me to do what I am called to do for my fellow human beings and my personal motto is, "If it is to be, it is up to me." I don't look around or wait for someone else or some perfect and opportune day to do what I am called to do. If it involves mankind and humanity, it matters to me, and it is my business. John Donne said, "No man is an island, entire of itself; every man is a piece of the continent, a part of the main...Any man's death diminishes me, because I am involved in mankind; and therefore, never send to know for whom the bell tolls; it tolls for thee." Their suffering is my suffering. Their pain is my pain. If I can ease their suffering and pain, then, I should, and I shall not live in vain.

This year's mission trip has more meaning to me than all others combined but please do not misunderstand my meaning. I am not degrading or minimizing the impacts we have made and the lives that have been changed thus far: everything I have done from serving food to school children in Uganda to saving lives in Haiti after an earthquake is nothing short of a miracle. All were equally important and life changing experiences to me and to the people whom I have had the privilege to help.

However, I cannot help but think that I dug many wells, and though from some wells we could draw enough water to quench one's thirst for a while, none of them were deep enough to produce fresh water for generations to come. I realize now that I had been busy giving a hungry man a fish to feed him for a day, instead of investing in teaching him how to catch fish so he could feed himself, his family, and his community for a lifetime. However, the saddest realization is that, for many, there is no creek or pond for them to catch fish, so they do not have the opportunity to learn how. That is why I hope these ongoing mission trips to the same region in Honduras will build endless rivers with abundant fish. In Matthew 13, Jesus speaks in parables perfectly, "A sower went out to sow. And as he sowed, some seeds fell along the path, and the birds came and devoured them. Other seeds fell on rocky ground, where they did not have much soil, and immediately they sprang up, since they had no depth of soil, but when the sun rose, they were scorched. And since they had no root, they withered away. Other seeds fell among thorns, and the thorns grew up and choked them. Other seeds fell on good soil and produced grain, some a hundredfold, some sixty, some thirty."

What is the difference in this year's mission trip to Honduras from any other? When I received S.T. Womeldorf's award last year, all the recipients from inception were awarded one thousand dollars to become Paul Harris Fellows by donating to the Rotary Foundation in honor of the recipient. There was no doubt that the contribution was spent towards a good cause. Instead, I, with my selfish reason, wanted the proceeds to go towards a purpose that was personal to me; I wanted to leave a legacy in young people's hearts by giving a scholarship so that the person could experience what S.T had stood for.

I met S.T.'s wife, Mary Ann, over breakfast one morning and shared my vision and passion of establishing the scholarship. She thanked me and encouraged me to carry on his legacy through young minds to be a light where there is darkness, to be hope where there is despair, and to be love where there is hatred. Most young people are not given such an opportunity to have and to witness such a life changing experience. Jesus said, "It is not the healthy who need a doctor but the sick. I have come not to call the righteous, but sinners."

No knowledge or books could teach them how one should live other than to let them see with their own eyes and let them have the personal experience of helping people in need.

Martin Luther King, Jr. once said, "Darkness cannot drive out darkness; only light can do that. Hate cannot drive out hate; only love can do that." S.T died ten years ago and those of us who knew him have been carrying his torch and keeping it lit brighter than ever. As time goes by, the memory of him is fading away and he has become a man in the past: unfamiliar and unknown.

Hence, I not only decided to give a scholarship to one of my co-workers at the hospital this year who has a servant heart, but I also made a commitment to take a young person to an international mission trip each year. She does not know yet that she is about to embark on a journey that will change her life.

Let me explain how it was all started three years ago. Our Adolescent Unit at Skyline Madison Campus is really like a big family with which we get to share just about any and all family matters, from unexpected deaths of loved ones to sadness to all celebrations and congratulations. We offer each other not only our shoulders and hugs more than anything, but advice, too. We are present for one another because we care.

Nurse Pam has a teenager daughter Carol, and even though I have never met her, I started caring for her as her God father, as Pam said I was. I was truly interested in her life after hearing about her emotional turbulence during the death of her best friend and her growing desire to help other people. Well, it is my profession as an adolescent mental health counselor to inspire and empower adolescents to live a life worth living, so, I told Pam that if Carol was interested in going on a mission trip, I would not only take her but would pay all of her expenses as well.

Like many adolescents, she was consumed by unexpected events and circumstances out of her control, that left her unable to come on the mission trip with me. Nevertheless, I decided to honor her with a Paul Harris Fellow instead. Here is the letter I read in front of the special ceremony held at Skyline hospital for her.

Dear Carol,

Kahlil Gibran wrote, "Show me your mother's face, and I will tell you who you are." If you have met or have had the pleasure of working with Pam, R.N. on the Adolescent Unit, you would instantly recognize the character of her daughter, Carol.

Ever since I started working alongside her mother Pam, caring for adolescent patients facing the most difficult trials and tribulations of their lives, I have been seeking the higher meaning of why, of all people, I have been blessed to enter their lives and they into mine, during these dire and urgent times.

Carol's contagiously positive and inspirational attitude has renewed my own motivation to make a difference in the lives of patients and their families. Carol has reminded me that, "It is better to light a single candle than to sit and curse the darkness," and encouraged me to believe in, fight for, and never give up on each patient that arrives at our hospital. Therefore, that is why Carol deserves to be today's recipient of one of the most prestigious awards from the humanitarian service organization, Rotary International.

Hence, I have made a one-thousand-dollar contribution to the Rotary Foundation in her name, and this contribution will help communities create safe and positive environments where children can thrive without living in fear of being bullied. Her contribution will also supply vaccines to protect children in other countries from polio for their entire lives.

By receiving this award, she is standing with notables such as Mother Theresa, Nelson Mandela, Pope John Paul II, Prince Charles, and U.S. President Jimmy Carter.

Thank you for living your God given life the way it is meant to be lived. Thank you for your encouragement and most of all, for being a wonderful daughter and friend of all of us on the Adolescent Unit. We love you so much!

Once I learned from Pam that Carol was not able to attend this year's mission trip, I started to look for who I would take instead. The

S.T. Scholarship would cover air fare for one person, and I saved enough money to pay all other expenses for whomever I take. One day I was working with my co-worker Stacia and asked her if she wanted to go on a mission trip to Honduras with me. She jumped to say yes without even thinking about it. I frequently showed picture slides to my patients of the mission trips I had attended on six continents, during my two-hour groups on the weekends. She had seen the presentation numerous times and voiced that she had always wanted to do something like that. Her "once in a life time opportunity" came true and I am now able to meet her with her parents at 2:00 am at the Nashville Airport. I am sure her parents might have experienced some doubt about who would offer such things to their daughter and wanted to ensure that their loving daughter would come home safely.

I am grateful and glad that the idea of taking an adolescent on the mission trip blossomed into the matured and strong willed Stacia going to Honduras. It does not take much skill to do what we do, but it is essential for volunteers to tolerate 120-degree heat and work their ass off from the moment we land! At this time, let me explain what type of a person she is by showing the letter I wrote last year.

Dear Stacia,

Miracles happen every day at the Skyline Adolescent Unit. Between their arrival to our unit and by the time they leave, I have witnessed miracles. You are leaving giant footprints in their hearts. They stay with us only for a short while and disappear as if nothing has happened, but I know that their lives from that moment on will not be the same because of you, and they don't even know it.

It is easy to forget and take it for granted because I get to see the difference you make to them when I work with you regularly. I don't say often enough how grateful I am and what an asset you are to our team. It truly is a privilege working with you and being your partner at the gym and being a cheerleader for adolescents.

I learn as much from you as the adolescents do and realize I am becoming a better person each and every day as I listen to you talk and watch how you act. The reason why adolescents are inspired and

149

willing to change their ways of thinking and their behaviors is because you talk the talk and walk the walk.

"Thought of the Day" is not only for adolescents; it is for all of us to act and live by. I believe that the only way we can truly make a difference in their lives is by our actions and by living by example. They can see whether we are real or faking it.

Albert Schweitzer once said, "What we do with our lives individually is not what determines whether we are a success. What determines our success is how we affect the lives of others." It has been a wonderful journey ever since I began to work with you, and most of all, thank you for being my friend even though I am twice your age!!

I am now sitting in front of Gate #3 in Tegucigalpa Airport waiting for the Delta airline to take me to Atlanta en route to Nashville. It was a little rough landing when arriving here but I remember the pilot that reassured all passengers he had twenty-five years of experience, before we took off in Atlanta seven days earlier, and I am hoping the same pilot will take us home. I pull out my fully charged iPhone from my back pack and slowly begin preparing myself for another long journey. This time, I am going home, but still I am listening the same song as I did when I left home.

Do you still feel the pain of the scars that won't heal

Your eyes have died but you see more than I

Daniel you're a star in the face of the sky...

My wife told me last night on the phone that Nashville was expecting a few inches of snow and was very cold. It has been unbearably hot here (120-degree Fahrenheit) from sunrise to sunset. When I land in Nashville this afternoon, it is going to be unbearably cold (16 degrees Fahrenheit!) Oh, man, please don't think I am a complainer or anything but come on. That is too much for one day, I thought.

T-shirts, very thin pants, and slippers with no socks on, is what I am comfortably wearing right now because it is just right for this kind of temperature. Then, suddenly I felt a sharp pain in my right index finger and I began looking down at my hands. After wiring 56 homes and dearly holding onto a steering wheel for the nearly three-hour drive to Tegucigalpa, my hands are too numb to clench my fists and it's hard to grip anything. These hands are attached to my weary body but look nothing like the ones I had seven days ago: soft and tan-free. I have been often accused of having womanlike hands that do not appear to have experienced hard work or physical labors in my entire life. Today, these hands look like those of a construction worker: rough, bruised, and bandaged. And I am so proud of it.

All in all, when I look around at the faces of our teams, they are all quiet, but I can read joy, satisfaction, and unexplainable contentment. I could read their commitment for this worthy project, and as I am already committed to coming back next year, so are they. Yes, we can't wait till next year to start all over again in another village. I am happy to say the mission is accomplished!

Dear Kim Kim,

First, I want to start off by telling you that you have helped me through a lot that was going on in my head and in my life. You have helped me realize that I deserve so much better, and you have made a major impact on my life. I never thought that somebody like you would want to help change someone's life like mine because I always thought I was unworthy. But then I thought that you do this because you love me and these other kids that are here at Skyline. I want you to know that I really do appreciate you for working with me and being patient with me. I know that you and the other staff members probably didn't know how you guys were going to get in to help, because I always have my defense mode up, and I don't really trust a lot of people. But I had to tell myself that you and the other staff are here to help me, not to hurt me. So, what I did was let y'all in and learned to trust again, and it feels so great. Y'all have helped me so much.

I love you so much Kim Kim and thank you for everything. I also want you to personally know that you are like a dad to me. I am going to miss you coming into my room to have all those conversations with me. Those conversations really did help me start to believe in myself and they helped me start to change into the better me.

I love you so much, Dad!

--Adolescent

Help Wanted Ad

Norman Douglas once said, "You can tell the ideals of a nation by its advertisements." I was in Korea visiting my family a few years ago. A TV in a living room was on even though there was no one around to watch it. I don't like to leave the lights and TV on when no one is around. While I was looking for a remote to turn the TV off, I happened to see a TV commercial playing. t was one of my most unexpected aha moments that came from nowhere and hit me like a train. I could not believe I had forgotten this important lesson in life up until then. I was thinking, "Wow, how could I miss that all of these years knowing that everything is built upon relationships and especially relationships with people being the most important matter in life?" One thirty-second commercial showed me how I had shamefully lived in America up till then and was influenced by the vastly different idealism between the west (where I live now) and east (my forgotten past in Korea.)

It was a smartphone commercial most people were familiar with. A young female reporter was walking down with a Buddhist monk in a forest totally immersed in their surroundings and conversations. The phone in her purse was showing text messages asking her how the interview was going with the monk. She turned off her cell, but she never missed taking all the important messages while she was giving all of her attention to the monk.

In America I had watched the commercial advertising the same smartphone a hundred times. Many people as early as six or seven years of age to old grandparents who would not know what to do without it would certainly disagree with me on this, but a smartphone is one of the most convenient, useful, and necessary tools that we want but not need. However, the commercial portrays it as a "must have" if you want to be a vital and successful member of modern society. If not, you chose to become a caveman, alienated and ignorant! It was brilliantly done converting wants to needs.

Unlike the commercial I watched in Korea, the same smartphone advertisement was showing people checking the stock market index, and a businessman at the airport lounge watching Netflix movies. A man was in Las Vegas for a trade show and met a businessman at the bar. They exchanged business cards, and he immediately excused himself to a restroom. Using his brand-new smartphone, he learned all about the man: where he works, where he lives, his educational background and work experiences, and even his favorite movies and the name of his pet posted on Facebook. He texted his boss in New York saying he met one of their biggest clients and the man just became his best friend.

We unconsciously have been watching such advertisements so much that we don't even realize we are brainwashed, and they are imbedded in our subconscious mind so deep that our feelings and emotions make irrational decisions. It is like our quality of life depends on the quality of the emotions we have; hence, we are easily bought by whatever they are selling, whether we need it or not. In fact, wants are turned into needs, and we don't even know the difference anymore. I hope by now you understand why it was an important life lesson for me. One showed a human relationship such a You and I, and the other showed a material relationship, I and It. People cannot be treated as animals, machines, a non-entity, or as something we can pawn to exchange goods for personal gains.

Most people know Andrew Carnegie was the wealthiest man and owned Carnegie Steel, the largest steel corporation in the world. Consequently, he was one of most powerful men in the 19th century. For centuries to come, people would remember him and carry on his legacy, not as once the wealthiest and powerful, but more importantly, as a man who dedicated his life to philanthropic endeavors and influenced those who had great wealth to have social responsibility and to use their assets to make a difference in the lives of others. If we understand his humble beginning and what he had to persevere to reach his dream, we would know how he became what he was and why he was destined to succeed in life after all.

He immigrated to America at the age of thirteen from Scotland. Being a poor son of a handloom weaver, he had little formal education. Arriving in the land of opportunity, he started working at a factory earning $1.20 a week; then became a telegraph messenger that worked at railroad. He never lost his desire to learn and grow. He became an avid reader and learner all of his life. No matter how small and trifling the job was, he did every job as he did nothing else. He gave his all as he stumbled, for he believed his struggles and failures were only the building block for the next greater thing.

After accomplishing everything he wanted to do, he was looking for ways to leave a legacy of how he became a successful and influential person so that people could learn essential knowledge and be as successful as he was. Napoleon Hill was an unknown young reporter for a small magazine. He, too, had a difficult childhood growing up like Carnegie: born in a one-room cabin near an Appalachian town in Virginia and lost his mother when he was only nine years of age. When he was asked to interview Carnegie to find the secret for success for the magazine, he was poor and living with his brother sleeping on a sofa, not having a clear vision of what he wanted to do with his life.

He interviewed Andrew Carnegie in Carnegie's office, and Carnegie invited Napoleon to his house that afternoon so he could tell him more about how one should live in abundance spiritually. After the interview, he just knew that the young reporter was the right man he was searching for all along. So, he gave the young man only sixty seconds to answer a question. He said, "Young man, I am going to ask you one question, and it is going to be the most important question you have ever been asked." Then, looking at his eyes straight, Carnegie asked, "Would you spend the rest of your life chasing an idea for which you would probably receive no compensation whatsoever for at least twenty years?" How could anyone decide the most important matter in his life in a second whether it was worth spending his entire life or not without serious considerations and time well spent on it? Should he not consider pro and con, benefit and drawback, and all such dilemmas?

Later in life, Napoleon Hill said that interviewing Carnegie and then spending years to find answers to the simple formula for success was the turning point of his life. He credited Carnegie for writing his book *Think and Grow Rich* which has been one of best self-help books of all time. I know now why Napoleon did not hesitate to say yes even if he was not to receive any compensations for it. Because it was worth doing it. He'd rather have failed in pursuing something he was called to do than succeeded in something he was not called to do.

I had to face a similar situation when I worked at the Cock of the Walk Restaurant. At first, I started working as a dishwasher, busboy, cook, and later became a waiter. When I was a senior in college, I was contemplating what I should do after graduating college. I was making good money as a waiter. It was a famous themed-dinner restaurant. Even though I made good money with less working hours, it was hardly my vocation or career. So, I was going to quit the restaurant and find something like a nine to five, white collar job if I could. Somehow, the owner Mr. Jackson found out that I was thinking about leaving, and he flew in from Jackson, MS. He said, "Kim, I know you are making good money as a waiter, but waiting tables is not a career. I have been watching you over the years and you need a career." Then, he offered me an assistant manager position with weekly pay of three-hundred dollars. That was a huge pay cut from making over $100 a night, working only 4 to 5 hours waiting tables. It was an easy job and easy money while in school.

I was not going to easily give up that easy job and easy life. Instead, he was asking me to work over sixty hours a week: every weekend and six days a week with much less money. Is he crazy offering such a job or am I crazy and willing to take the job? He gave me a day to think about it because he had to go back to Jackson. Without consulting with my wife and without hesitation, I said yes and thanked him for giving me the opportunity to prove what I was capable of. I thanked him for overworking me and giving me less pay! Why did I take the job? I was looking for an opportunity for someone to give me a chance to prove what I could do and what I was made of. I wrote of my experience at the Cock of the Walk Restaurant in my previous book, but it was the biggest challenge I had ever faced. I failed and made so many mistakes because I had never run an over 600 seating capacity with 80 employee business as a general manager. However, Mr. Jackson not only had never lost faith and trust in me but gave me full authority to lead a multi-million-dollar business. I could lose his business because I did not know anything about running a multi-million-dollar business, and I had hundreds of families depending on me. Somehow, I had never, ever thought of losing the business. Never! Like I said, I failed too many times to count, but I had never seen myself a failure. As Mr. Jackson trusted in me, I trusted my entire team from non-English speaking Mexican cooks to college student waiters. They outperformed way more than what was expected and did many tasks without being asked. I think all I had done was to create such an environment that any member of the team felt it was up to them, and they were encouraged to find their talents and use them to benefit others. I feel bad that my employees had to face unnecessary, difficult and challenging times when they were with me but those trial and errors truly had prepared me to be a better businessman, leader, and after all, a better person.

Most people wanted comfort and easy lives, and I was no exception. In fact, my parents were living with us all of their lives and I had to support them in addition to raising three young children. I did not know how I was to break away the bondage and cycle living from hand to mouth in those days. Many times, I did not know week to week where the money was coming from to pay rent and get food for my family. I even had dangerous and tempting thoughts of doing anything that would give me a rich quick opportunity even if it meant to lie a little, cheat a little, and sell myself short. Everybody was doing it, right? However, as long as I had a clear conscience, I just couldn't. I just could not knowingly do anything that caused me to feel ashamed and regretful. Conventional and rational thought was not to take Mr. Jackson's offer, especially when I was facing one of the most financially difficult times and the lowest point in my life. If I alone chose to live such a way, no one but myself was to blame. However, how could I as a son, father, and husband have the family go through difficulty due to my selfish or noble reason? The thing that led me to the right path was the story of Booker T. Washington and George Washington Carver which I learned when I was taking a Black Psychology course. I could say they saved me from falling into degradation and disgrace.

Of course, I had read about Booker T. Washington in the history book and when he was being featured in Black History Month in February as the great educator and civil rights leader. What I did not know was that his struggle and perseverance for education and the relationship with one person-General Samuel Armstrong had changed the course of his life. He wrote an autobiographical essay *The Struggle for an Education* in his book *Up from Slavery*. When I read it for the first time a few decades ago, his words resonate in me profoundly then and even louder now. His chosen words are alive and from within. No one could tell the way he did unless they had painfully experienced it. After all, he expected human nature and its environment to change for the better for all people: oppressors and oppressed. Many people struggled and faced harsh environments as much as he did during that time, but not everyone had the same outlook on life. He said, "I shall allow no man to belittle my soul by making me hate him." What makes one have a successful and purposeful life while others do not? I want to include his entire essay in my book. I confess that readers might not get much benefit from reading my book, but his essay *The Struggle for an Education* is alone worthwhile reading. My hope is that it may change you the way it did to me.

Dear Kim Kim,

You impacted me on a very deep and personal level…more than anyone else in here. You are more yourself than anyone I have ever met. You made me laugh but also made me think about things. You really made me think about my worth although I don't fully know my worth yet. You opened a door that I won't ever let be closed. I don't really know you, but I have loads of love for you in my heart. You make me see the world with fresh eyes and have an open heart. I really have never met someone like you. Every story you told us was so easy and simple to understand, and that is why it resonated with me in so many different ways that I will apply them to my life. –Adolescent

Booker T. Washington: The Struggle for an Education

ONE day, while at work in the coal-mine, I happened to overhear two miners talking about a great school for coloured people somewhere in Virginia. This was the first time that I had ever heard anything about any kind of school or college that was more pretentious than the little coloured school in our town.

In the darkness of the mine I noiselessly crept as close as I could to the two men who were talking. I heard one tell the other that not only was the school established for the members of my race, but that opportunities were provided by which poor but worthy students could work out all or a part of the cost of board, and at the same time be taught some trade or industry.

As they went on describing the school, it seemed to me that it must be the greatest place on earth, and not even Heaven presented more attractions for me at that time than did the Hampton Normal and Agricultural Institute in Virginia, about which these men were talking. I resolved at once to go to that school, although I had no idea where it was, or how many miles away, or how I was going to reach it; I remembered only that I was on fire constantly with one ambition, and that was to go to Hampton. This thought was with me day and night.

After hearing of the Hampton Institute, I continued to work for a few months longer in the coal-mine. While at work there, I heard of a vacant position in the household of General Lewis Ruffner, the owner of the salt-furnace and coal-mine. Mrs. Viola Ruffner, the wife of General Ruffner, was a "Yankee" woman from Vermont. Mrs. Ruffner had a reputation all through the vicinity for being very strict with her servants, and especially with the boys who tried to serve her. Few of them had remained with her more than two or three weeks. They all left with the same excuse: she was too strict. I decided, however, that I would rather try Mrs. Ruffner's house than remain in the coal-mine, and so my mother applied to her for the vacant position. I was hired at a salary of $5 per month.

I had heard so much about Mrs. Ruffner's severity that I was almost afraid to see her, and trembled when I went into her presence. I had not lived with her many weeks, however, before I began to understand her. I soon began to learn that, first of all, she wanted everything kept clean about her, that she wanted things done promptly and systematically, and that at the bottom of everything she wanted absolute honesty and frankness. Nothing must be sloven or slipshod; every door, every fence, must be kept in repair.

I cannot now recall how long I lived with Mrs. Ruffner before going to Hampton, but I think it must have been a year and a half. At any rate, I here repeat what I have said more than once before, that the lessons that I learned in the home of Mrs. Ruffner were as valuable to me as any education I have ever gotten anywhere since. Even to this day I never see bits of paper scattered around a house or in the street that I do not want to pick them up at once. I never see a filthy yard that I do not want to clean it, a paling off of a fence that I do not want to put it on, an unpainted or unwhitewashed house that I do not want to paint or whitewash it, or a button off one's clothes, or a grease-spot on them or on a floor, that I do not want to call attention to it.

From fearing Mrs. Ruffner I soon learned to look upon her as one of my best friends. When she found that she could trust me she did so implicitly. During the one or two winters that at I was with her she gave me an opportunity to go to school for an hour in the day during a portion of the winter months, but most of my studying was done at night, sometimes alone, sometimes under some one whom I could hire to teach me. Mrs. Ruffner always encouraged and sympathized with me in all my efforts to get an education. It was while living with her that I began to get together my first library. I secured a dry-goods box, knocked out one side of it, put some shelves in it, and began putting into it every kind of book that I could get my hands upon, and called it my "library."

Notwithstanding my success at Mrs. Ruffner's I did not give up the idea of going to the Hampton Institute. In the fall of 1872 I determined to make an effort to get there, although, as I have stated, I had no definite idea of the direction in which Hampton was, or of what it would cost to go there. I do not think that any one thoroughly sympathized with me in my ambition to go to Hampton unless it was my mother, and she was troubled with a grave fear that I was starting out on a "wild-goose chase." At any rate, I got only a half-hearted consent from her that I might start. The small amount of money that I had earned had been consumed by my stepfather and the remainder of the family, with the exception of a very few dollars, and so I had very little with which to buy clothes and pay my traveling expenses. My brother John helped me all that he could, but of course that was not a great deal, for his work was in the coal-mine, where he did not earn much, an most of what he did earn went in the direction of paying the household expenses.

Perhaps the thing that touched and pleased me most in connection with my starting for Hampton was the interest that many of the older coloured people took in the matter. They had spent the best days of their lives in slavery, and hardly expected to live to see the time when they would see a member of their race leave home to attend a boarding-school. Some of these older people would give me a nickel, others a quarter, or a handkerchief.

Finally the great day came, and I started for Hampton. I had only a small, cheap satchel that contained what few articles of clothing I could get. My mother at the time was rather weak and broken in health. I hardly expected to see her again, and thus our parting was all the more sad. She, however, was very brave through it all. At that time there were no through trains connecting that part of West Virginia with eastern Virginia. Trains ran only a portion of the way, and the remainder of the distance was travelled by stage-coaches.

The distance from Malden to Hampton is about five hundred miles. I had not been away from home many hours before it began to grow painfully evident that I did not have enough money to pay my fare to Hampton. One experience I shall long remember. I had been traveling over the mountains most of the afternoon in an old-fashioned stage-coach, when, late in the evening, the coach stopped for the night at a common, unpainted house called a hotel. All the other passengers except myself were whites. In my ignorance I supposed that the little hotel existed for the purpose of accommodating the passengers who travelled on the stage-coach. The difference that the colour of one's skin would make I had not thought anything about. After all the other passengers had been shown rooms and were getting ready for supper, I shyly presented myself before the man at the desk. It is true I had practically no money in my pocket with which to pay for bed or food, but I had hoped in some way to beg my way into the good graces of the landlord, for at that season in the mountains of Virginia the weather was cold, and I wanted to get indoors for the night. Without asking as to whether I had any money, the man at the desk firmly refused to even consider the matter of providing me with food or lodging. This was my first experience in finding out what the colour of my skin meant. In some way I managed to keep warm by walking about, and so got through the night. My whole soul was so bent upon reaching Hampton that I did not have time to cherish any bitterness toward the hotel-keeper.

By walking, begging rides both in wagons and in the cars, in some way, after a number of days, I reached the city of Richmond, Virginia, about eighty-two miles from Hampton. When I reached there, tired, hungry, and dirty, it was late in the night. I had never been in a large city, and this rather added to my misery. When I reached Richmond, I was completely out of money. I had not a single acquaintance in the place, and, being unused to city ways, I did not know where to go. I applied at several places for lodging, but they all wanted money, and that was what I did not have. Knowing nothing else better to do, I walked the streets. In doing this I passed by many food-stands where fried chicken and half-moon apple pies were piled high and made to present a most tempting appearance. At that time it seemed to me that I would have promised all that I expected to possess in the future to have gotten hold of one of those chicken legs or one of those pies. But I could not get either of these, nor anything else to eat.

I must have walked the streets till after midnight. At last I became so exhausted that I could walk no longer. I was tired, I was hungry, I was everything but discouraged. Just about the time when I reached extreme physical exhaustion, I came upon a portion of a street where the board sidewalk was considerably elevated. I waited for a few minutes, till I was sure that no passers-by could see me, and then crept under the sidewalk and lay for the night upon the ground, with my satchel of clothing for a pillow. Nearly all night I could hear the tramp of feet over my head. The next morning I found myself somewhat refreshed, but I was extremely hungry, because it had been a long time since I had had sufficient food. As soon as it became light enough for me to see my surroundings I noticed that I was near a large ship, and that this ship seemed to be unloading a cargo of pig iron. I went at once to the vessel and asked the captain to permit me to help unload the

162

vessel in order to get money for food. The captain, a white man, who seemed to be kind-hearted, consented. I worked long enough to earn money for my breakfast, and it seems to me, as I remember it now, to have been about the best breakfast that I have ever eaten.

My work pleased the captain so well that he told me if I desired I could continue working for a small amount per day. This I was very glad to do. I continued working on this vessel for a number of days. After buying food with the small wages I received there was not much left to add to the amount I must get to pay my way to Hampton. In order to economize in every way possible, so as to be sure to reach Hampton in a reasonable time, I continued to sleep under the same sidewalk that gave me shelter the first night I was in Richmond. Many years after that the coloured citizens of Richmond very kindly tendered me a reception, at which there must have been two thousand people present. This reception was held not far from the spot where I slept the first night I spent in that city, and I must confess that my mind was more upon the sidewalk that first gave me shelter than upon the reception, agreeable and cordial as it was.

I had saved what I considered enough money with which to reach Hampton, I thanked the captain of the vessel for his kindness, and started again. Without any unusual occurrence I reached Hampton, with a surplus of exactly fifty cents with which to begin my education. To me it had been a long, eventful journey; but the first sight of the large, three-story, brick school building seemed to have rewarded me for all that I had undergone in order to reach the place. If the people who gave the money to provide that building could appreciate the influence the sight of it had upon me, as well as upon thousands of other youths, they would feel all the more encouraged to make such gifts. It seemed to me to be the largest and most beautiful building I had ever seen. The sight of it seemed to give me new life. I felt that a new kind of existence had now begun — that life would now have a new meaning. I felt that I had reached the promised land, and I resolved to let no obstacle prevent me from putting forth the highest effort to fit myself to accomplish the most good in the world.

As soon as possible after reaching the grounds of the Hampton Institute, I presented myself before the head teacher for assignment to a class. Having been so long without proper food, a bath, and change of clothing, I did not, of course, make a very favourable impression upon her, and I could see at once that there were doubts in her mind about the wisdom of admitting me as a student. I felt that I could hardly blame her if she got the idea that I was a worthless loafer or tramp. For some time she did not refuse to admit me, neither did she decide in my favour, and I continued to linger about her, and to impress her in all the ways I could with my worthiness. In the meantime I saw her admitting other students, and that added greatly to my discomfort, for I felt, deep down in my heart, that I could do as well as they, if I could only get a chance to show what was in me.

After some hours had passed, the head teacher said to me: "The adjoining recitation-room needs sweeping. Take the broom and sweep it."

It occurred to me at once that here was my chance. Never did I receive an order with more delight. I knew that I could sweep, for Mrs. Ruffner had thoroughly taught me how to do that when I lived with her.

I swept the recitation-room three times. Then I got a dusting-cloth and I dusted it four times. All the woodwork around the walls, every bench, table, and desk, I went over four times with my dusting-cloth. Besides, every piece of furniture had been moved and every closet and corner in the room had been thoroughly cleaned. I had the feeling that in a large measure my future depended upon the impression I made upon the teacher in the cleaning of that room. When I was through, I reported to the head teacher. She was a "Yankee" woman who knew just where to look for dirt. She went into the room and inspected the floor and closets; then she took her handkerchief and rubbed it on the woodwork about the walls, and over the table and benches. When she was unable to find one bit of dirt on the floor, or a particle of dust on any of the furniture, she quietly remarked, "I guess you will do to enter this institution."

I was one of the happiest souls on earth. The sweeping of that room was my college examination, and never did any youth pass an examination for entrance into Harvard or Yale that gave him more genuine satisfaction. I have passed several examinations since then, but I have always felt that this was the best one I ever passed.

I have spoken of my own experience in entering the Hampton Institute.

Perhaps few, if any, had anything like the same experience that I had, but about that same period there were hundreds who found their way to Hampton and other institutions after experiencing something of the same difficulties that I went through. The young men and women were determined to secure an education at any cost.

The sweeping of the recitation-room in the manner that I did it seems to have paved the way for me to get through Hampton. Miss Mary F. Mackie, the head teacher, offered me a position as janitor. This, of course, I gladly accepted, because it was a place where I could work out nearly all the cost of my board. The work was hard and taxing, but I stuck to it. I had a large number of rooms to care for, and had to work late into the night, while at the same time I had to rise by four o'clock in the morning, in order to build the fires and have a little time in which to prepare my lessons. In all my career at Hampton, and ever since I have been out in the world, Miss Mary F. Mackie, the head teacher to whom I have referred, proved one of my strongest and most helpful friends. Her advice and encouragement were always helpful and strengthening to me in the darkest hour.

I have spoken of the impression that was made upon me by the buildings and general appearance of the Hampton Institute, but I have not spoken of that which made the greatest and most lasting impression upon me, and that was a great man — the noblest, rarest human being that it has ever been my privilege to meet. I refer to the late General Samuel C. Armstrong.

It has been my fortune to meet personally many of what are called great characters, both in Europe and America, but I do not hesitate to say that I never met any man who, in my estimation, was the equal of General Armstrong. Fresh from the degrading influences of the slave plantation and the coal-mines, it was a rare privilege for me to be permitted to come into direct contact with such a character as General Armstrong. I shall always remember that the first time I went into his presence he made the impression upon me of being a perfect man: I was made to feel that there was something about him that was superhuman. It was my privilege to know the General personally from the time I entered Hampton till he died, and the more I saw of him the greater he grew in my estimation. One might have removed from Hampton all the buildings, class-rooms, teachers, and industries, and given the men and women there the opportunity of coming into daily contact with General Armstrong, and that alone would have been a liberal education. The older I grow, the more I am convinced that there is no education which one can get from and costly apparatus that is equal to that which can be gotten from contact with great men and women. Instead of studying books so constantly, how I wish that our schools and colleges might learn to study men and things!

General Armstrong spent two of the last six months of his life in my home at Tuskegee. At that time he was paralyzed to the extent that he had lost control of his body and voice in a very large degree. Notwithstanding his affliction, he worked almost constantly night and day for the cause to which he had given his life. I never saw a man who so completely lost sight of himself. I do not believe he ever had a selfish thought. He was just as happy in trying to assist some other institution in the South as he was when working for Hampton. Although he fought the Southern white man in the Civil War, I never heard him utter a bitter word against him afterward. On the other hand, he was constantly seeking to find ways by which he could be of service to the Southern whites.

It would be difficult to describe the hold that he had upon the students at Hampton, or the faith they had in him. In fact, he was worshipped by his students. It never occurred to me that General Armstrong could fail in anything that he undertook. There is almost no request that he could have made that would not have been complied with. When he was a guest at my home in Alabama, and was so badly paralyzed that he had to be wheeled about in an invalid's chair, I recall that one of the General's former students had occasion to push his chair up a long, steep hill that taxed his strength to the utmost. When the top of the hill was reached, the former pupil, with a glow of happiness on his face, exclaimed, "I am so glad that I have been permitted to do something that was real hard for the General before he dies!" While I was a student at Hampton, the dormitories became so crowded that it was impossible to find room for all who wanted to be admitted. In order to help remedy the difficulty, the General conceived the plan of putting up tents to be used as rooms. As soon as it became known that General Armstrong would be pleased if some of the older students would live in the tents during the winter, nearly every student in school volunteered to go.

I was one of the volunteers. The winter that we spent in those tents was an intensely cold one, and we suffered severely — how much I am sure General Armstrong never knew, because we made no complaints. It was enough for us to know that we were pleasing General Armstrong, and that we were making it possible for an additional number of students to secure an education. More than once, during a cold night, when a stiff gale would be blowing, our tent was lifted bodily, and we would find ourselves in the open air. The General would usually pay a visit to the tents early in the morning, and his earnest, cheerful, encouraging voice would dispel any feeling of despondency.

I have spoken of my admiration for General Armstrong, and yet he was but a type of that Christlike body of men and women who went into the Negro schools at the close of the war by the hundreds to assist in lifting up my race. The history the world fails to show a higher, purer, and more unselfish class of men and women than those who found their way into those Negro schools.

Life at Hampton was a constant revelation to me; was constantly taking me into a new world. The matter of having meals at regular hours, of eating on a tablecloth, using a napkin, the use of the bath-tub and of the tooth-brush, as well as the use of sheets upon the bed, were all new to me.

I sometimes feel that almost the most valuable lesson I got at the Hampton Institute was in the use and value of the bath. I learned there for the first time some of its value, not only in keeping the body healthy, but in inspiring self-respect and promoting virtue. In all my travels in the South and elsewhere since leaving Hampton I have always in some way sought my daily bath. To get it sometimes when I have been the guest of my own people in a single-roomed cabin has not always been easy to do, except by slipping away to some stream in the woods. I have always tried to teach my people that some provision for bathing should be a part of every house.

For some time, while a student at Hampton, I possessed but a single pair of socks, but when I had worn these till they became soiled, I would wash them at night and hang them by the fire to dry, so that I might wear them again the next morning.

The charge for my board at Hampton was ten dollars per month. I was expected to pay a part of this in cash and to work out the remainder. To meet this cash payment, as I have stated, I had just fifty cents when I reached the institution. Aside from a very few dollars that my brother John was able to send me once in a while, I had no money with which to pay my board. I was determined from the first to make my work as janitor so valuable that my services would be indispensable. This I succeeded in doing to such an extent that I was soon informed that I would be allowed the full cost of my board in return for my work. The cost of tuition was seventy dollars a year. This, of course, was wholly beyond my ability to provide. If I had been compelled to pay the seventy dollars for tuition, in addition to providing for my board, I would have been compelled to leave the Hampton school. General Armstrong, however, very kindly got Mr. S. Griffitts Morgan, of New Bedford, Mass., to defray the cost of my tuition during the whole time that I was at Hampton. After I finished the course at Hampton and had entered upon my lifework at Tuskegee, I had the pleasure of visiting Mr. Morgan several times.

After having been for a while at Hampton, I found myself in difficulty because I did not have books and clothing. Usually, however, I got around the trouble about books by borrowing from those who were more fortunate than myself. As for clothes, when I reached Hampton I had practically nothing. Everything that I possessed was in a small hand satchel. My anxiety about clothing increased because General Armstrong made a personal inspection of the young men in ranks, to see that their clothes were clean. Shoes had to be polished, there must be no buttons off the clothing, and no grease-spots. To wear one suit of clothes continually, while at work and in the schoolroom, and at the same time keep it clean, was rather a hard problem for me to solve. In some way I managed to get on till the teachers learned that I was in earnest and meant to succeed, and then some of them were kind enough to see that I was partly supplied with second-hand clothing that had been sent in barrels from the North. These barrels proved a blessing to hundreds of poor but deserving students. Without them I question whether I should ever have gotten through Hampton.

When I first went to Hampton I do not recall that I had ever slept in a bed that had two sheets on it. In those days there were not many buildings there, and the room was very precious. There were seven other boys in the same room with me; most of them, however, students who had been there for some time. The sheets were quite a puzzle to me. The first night I slept under both of them, and the second night I slept on top of both of them; but by watching the other boys I learned my lesson in this, and have been trying to follow it ever since and to teach it to others.

I was among the youngest of the students who were in Hampton at that time. Most of the students were men and women — some as old as forty years of age. As I now recall the scene of my first year, I do not believe that one often has the opportunity of coming into contact with three or four hundred men and women who were so tremendously in earnest as these men and women were. Every hour was occupied in study or work. Nearly all had had enough actual contact with the world to teach them the need for education. Many of the older ones were, of course, too old to master the text-books very thoroughly, and it was often sad to watch their struggles; but they made up in earnest much of what they lacked in books. Many of them were as poor as I was, and, besides having to wrestle with their books, they had to struggle with poverty which prevented them from having the necessities of life. Many of them had aged parents who were dependent upon them, and some of them were men who had wives whose support in some way they had to provide for.

The great and prevailing idea that seemed to take possession of every one was to prepare himself to lift up the people at his home. No one seemed to think of himself. And the officers and teachers, what a rare set of human beings they were! They worked for the students night and day, in season and out of season. They seemed happy only when they were helping the students in some manner. Whenever it is written — and I hope it will be — the part that the Yankee teachers played in the education of the Negroes immediately after the war will make one of the most thrilling parts of the history of this country. The time is not far distant when the whole South will appreciate this service in a way that it has not yet been able to do.

Hampton Institute President Samuel C. Armstrong knew what it took Booker to be admitted to his school and what he had to sacrifice and endure to fulfill his desire for education. He hired Booker to be a teacher at his college and mentored him. Through his personal relationship with Booker, he knew Booker could be a great leader and saw what Booker was capable of. So, he asked Booker to be the first President of the new Tuskegee Institute in Alabama, college for black training future teachers. He was only twenty-five years old and had a vision, "Leading to return to the plantation districts and show the people there how to put new energy and new ideas into farming as well as into the intellectual and moral and religious life of the people."

George Washington Carver

Another person had an unquenchable desire for learning like Booker Washington. The only way to live a better and free life in slavery was to break away from the bondage within himself that chained his soul and his people no matter how cruel the environment, how much injustice and inequality he faced, and the amount violence directed toward him. His name was George Washington Carver. He walked nine miles each way to school and left home for good at the age of twelve to attend high school. Finishing high school, he applied to Highland College and officially was accepted. When he showed up, he was not allowed to enroll because he was black. The school could tell he was an excellent student on the application papers, but his name alone could not tell them whether he was white or black. He went home with a broken heart. But his desire for education was too strong to be silenced. He applied again and again to any colleges that would accept him as black and was able to enroll in Simpson College, which accepted students regardless of race.

He had a passion for arts, but when he transferred to Iowa State, he suddenly changed his major from art to agriculture. He had a higher goal for the betterment of mankind, and he thought that art was exactly what he was being called to do. The reason why he changed his passion from art to agriculture was that he found his place and knew what he had to do for his people. The Dean of Agriculture at Iowa State recalled,

> "I remember when I first met you, you said you wanted to get an agricultural education so you could help your race. I had never known anything more beautiful than that said by a student. I know that taste you have for painting and the success you have made along that line, and I said, 'Why not push your studies along that line to some extent?' When you replied that that would be of no value to your colored brethren, that also was magnificent."

His response summed up how he wanted to devote his life, "Art would not do my people as much good." He found there was something much greater than his personal gain and was willing to devote his entire life to it. Once he realized his place among his people, he was able to tolerate all suffering and discrimination that came with being a black man. He went on to become the first African American faculty member at Iowa State College. He finally received the fruits of his hard work and was living a comfortable life. Dr. Booker T. Washington had never forgotten where he came from and what he had to do to improve the lives of African Americans. Learning about George Washington Carver, faculty at Iowa State College, he wrote him a letter to bring him to the Tuskegee Institute in the Deep South.

"I cannot offer you money, position, or fame. The first two you have. The last, from the position you now occupy, you will no doubt achieve. These things I now ask you to give up. I offer you in their place: work...hard, hard work, the task of bringing a people from degradation, poverty, and waste to full manhood. Your department exists only on paper and your laboratory will have to be in your head."

Carver was thinking, "I have worked so hard to be where I am, enduring all hardship and sufferings. I alone did that without anybody's help. Am I willing to give up a comfortable life having money, position, and fame? For who and what purpose?" When he reexamined his purpose in life and what he was set out to do in the beginning, he realized the reason he got into agriculture, botany, and horticulture was to help people out of misery. Even if he had already achieved all of those things in his young life that most people admired and desired spending the entirety of their lives, he wanted more out of his life: he could not be settled and content as long as he could help a person or a underprivileged class from socioeconomic bondage. He packed his belongings and moved to Tuskegee Institute, Alabama where he would be regarded as a second-class citizen. With the support of Washington at Tuskegee, he taught and developed agricultural advancement and discoveries for the poor black farmers in mind, and all in all, he had helped both oppressors and oppressed to live better lives and helped them to live in unity. And as a result, he helped to tear down invisible social barriers for generations to come.

He gave up having money, position, and fame when he became a faculty member at Tuskegee Institute. If he had patented all his discoveries for himself, no doubt he would have accumulated insurmountable wealth and fame. However, his goal was, "It is not the style of clothes one wears, neither the kind of automobile one drives, nor the amount of money one has in the bank, that counts. These mean nothing. It is simply service that measures success." His servant heart has made an everlasting difference in people and his legacy would be never forgotten. He had become the richest man in his heart.

Sir Ernest Shackleton

Sir Ernest Shackleton in England was about to set out on one of his expeditions to the South Pole. He put on the newspapers to recruit men, "Men wanted for hazardous journey to the South Pole. Small wages, bitter cold, long months of complete darkness, constant danger. Safe return doubtful. Honor and recognition in case of success." He could simply say, "It will be a journey to Hell with no return!" So many people wanted to be a part of his expedition that newspapers reported, "It seemed as though all the men of Great Britain were determined to accompany him."

Shackleton's Ad-Men Wanted for Hazardous Journey was run in the newspaper in 1900 in England. This is today's ad in America which shows a complete opposite side of the ad.

Newspaper Ad: No education or experiences needed.

Annual income of $100,000 with signing bonus.

Best health insurance and company match 100% of your contribution to 401k.

Work only 30 hours a week at home.

A week of paid vacation every month.

No drug test required.

Anyone who applies will be hired immediately.

The above ad was run for several months and people did not respond enthusiastically and eventually the company had to close down the business. It seemed like a perfect job that everybody would apply for. The company was selling illegal drugs and child pornography. So many caring and responsible people did not dare to work for such a company even if they would live a comfortable life.

In the beginning of this chapter, I said that we could tell people's beliefs and its nation's ideals by its advertisements. Generally speaking, most people seek comfort, security, and safety in life. It seems a no brainer what most people would choose between Shackleton's ad in 1900 and today's ad in America. At the same time, it is in our genes to leave this world a better place than what we found it regardless of danger or recognition. Life really is a daring adventure or nothing at all. In that case, we should not and cannot be afraid to live and die for the worthy cause that only a few of us get to live for. Vincent van Gogh wrote, "The fishermen know that the sea is dangerous and the storm terrible, but they have never found these dangers sufficient reason for remaining ashore." Unless we see everything as "I and YOU" instead of an "I and IT" relationship with other human beings, we cannot truly say our lives matter and treat others as the most important and most unique persons.

God did not create men and women to show how powerful and how strong He was. He did not create us to slave, subdue, or toy around with us. He loves us so much that he has created us in the image of Himself and died for our sins so that we could have a never-ending and loving relationship with Him. So, men must treat each other in such a way that we are all God's children.

Life Lessons from Diane and Dave

Before you speak to me about your religion, first show it to me in how you treat other people; before you tell me how much you love your God, show me in how much you love all His children; before you preach to me of your passion for your faith, teach me about it through your compassion for your neighbors. In the end, I'm not as interested in what you have to tell or sell as I am in how you choose to live and give.
Cory Booker

I lived the first seventeen years of my young life in South Korea and have lived the rest as a naturalized American citizen of the United States. From birth until the day I left Korea, I lived under military dictatorship. I was born one year after Army General Park Chung-hee had rose to power after the military coup d'état of 1961 when he declared himself to be the President of South Korea. Ironically, I left Korea one year after he was assassinated by his closest friend and the head of intelligence agency, in 1979.

Under dictator Park's regime, the governing body of Korea had desired rapid economic growth and industrialization in order to garner support and ultimately, the hearts of the wartorn Korean people. At the same time, conglomerates wanted the prosperity and power that would come from supporting the hierarchical government system and saving the deflated economy after the Korean War. The hierarchical military government's exercise of power became enmeshed with select corporate conglomerates, like bread and butter. Ultimately, Korea became one of the first developed and most technologically advanced countries in the world; However, the consequence was a vastly extensive gap between those who had riches and those who did not, and the corruptions that led to this cast a dark shadow on Korea's social morality. It was nearly impossible for those that were already without, to move up the ladder of success. Social statuses were already established and fixed, and this was protected by the small circle of elite yet invisible hands of Korea's governing body. You were "in" or you were "out" and it took a miracle to change that.

I don't know just how much has changed in my native country today, but I know that my experiences had greatly shaped my perceptions of the world as I became a young man. The United States has not been ruled by dictators and its citizens live in an open and free society. Under the Constitution, we have the freedom to create the nation we want to live in. Despite this, I reached the United States with a view that in this world existed only two groups: a tiny group of the elite, and then those like me, that would always find glass ceilings that we could never climb past or tear through.

Furthermore, I was raised and taught by the philosophies of Confucianism, which has influenced Korean culture for thousands of years, still today. Confucianism teaches that the supreme goal of man is to live by moral values and by filial piety, being good to your parents; only when you bring a good name to your family and ancestors do you experience harmony. The family is a fundamental unit, man's priority, and the bridge that connects a man to his society. If the family is divided, then the nation is divided. This means that consequently, your personal failure and success is determined and judged by your family as a unit and your contribution to it, instead of your individual gains such as fame, social status, and wealth. If you attain any of these, then the honor goes to your family name, not you as an individual.

Hence, it was deeply embedded in my heart and soul to accept my place in the Kim family as a firstborn son that must do everything possible to take care of my family. I treated this responsibility as my only purpose in life. The negative impact of this was that I could not see myself being or doing anything beyond that. I did not view myself as having an identity or motivation of my own, outside of my family unit. I did not see my own capabilities, potential, and leadership skills nor that I, too, am morally responsible and accountable for other people and the community we all live in. It took a very long time for me to realize that I am not only a part of my family, but I also belong and connect to much greater things.

Truth be told, I spent most of my youthful years feeling as though there were no place that I could truly call home, in neither Korea nor the United States. I experienced a sense of alienation and loss, a deeply rooted fear that there would always be powerful, authoritarian hands that would control our lives— hands that did not believe I deserved success, and they would prevent me from achieving it. However, my life in the United States carved away at this perception of the world that I had developed, right before my eyes.

When I first arrived in the United States, my first home was in Gallatin, Tennessee. This was where I obtained my first job in America, employed at Krystal in Gallatin and Hendersonville, first as a janitor, then eventually as a manager. Eventually, our lives took us to a small community called Gladeville, just outside of Mt. Juliet, where we lived while I was managing at the Cock of the Walk restaurant in Nashville. This journey brought my wife and I to purchasing a restaurant in Hendersonville on June 1, 2000. Our home was almost an hour commute from the restaurant, so we packed the little that we had, and my parents, three children, my wife, and I moved to Hendersonville, just a stone's throw from the restaurant. We opened this restaurant and gave it our own name, Oriental Coast. We were enchanted by reaching this goal of owning our first business. My wife and I felt like millionaires! This was our first taste of what I heard described as the American Dream.

By this time, I had never met State Representative Diane Black nor her husband Dr. David Black but had heard of them quite frequently in our community. Our local newspapers often detailed their involvement within the community, and I heard of them frequently through the Hendersonville Area Chamber of Commerce, where I became actively involved in promoting my business. However, from time to time, when any of my children were recognized for good grades or other achievements in school, I found their pictures in newspaper clippings. These newspaper clippings were sent from Diane Black. I did not think she had any knowledge of my family's existence in Sumner County since we had never met, yet I rejoiced when I received her genuinely kind handwritten letters about her pride for my children's academic achievements. Ironically, they are still in my scrapbooks from my children's early years, to this day. Despite this, there was also the indoctrinated part of myself that thought that this was a politician, and this was a political motion, attempting to garner my support for office. It wasn't possible that this person cared about how children, much less my own, performed academically!

That is when Diane and her spouse, David Black began dining at my restaurant. It was always during the evenings and they were always together. I noticed something distinctive about them from the very first time I saw either of them. Whenever Diane Black came to the restaurant, she carried an energy like she was still in her office, serving people from all walks of life; people would stop by her table to speak with her to bring her their problems and concerns. Instead of requesting privacy or declining to speak, as she very well had the right to do, each time, she would push her plate to the side, make direct eye contact, and talk to them like they were the most important person in the building.

No matter or concern brought to her was too small. She would walk to their tables to meet their families and even hold their children like her own. While these are likely small and trifle deeds that she does not notice about herself, these are the actions that left the most impressive influence on me: I hoped to become a person like her: a faithful servant to God and His people.

During this time, there was also a kind young man that regularly dined at my restaurant. He introduced himself as Steve, only providing his first name. Even now when he comes to mind, a warm and good-natured feeling hovers over me, for his smile never left his face and he only radiated positivity and an air of humility. I fondly remember one evening when he asked to show my wife and I something, and in the back of his truck outside, was a five-gallon bucket full of fish that he had caught at the Old Hickory Dam. He asked me to pick out the fish that I wanted, and my wife made Korean fish soup with them the following day. Our whole family had a feast. One evening, I saw Steve in our lobby and walked up to say hello. He was waiting for someone, and it turned out that "someone" was Diane and Dave. I had no idea that Steve was their son! This was one of the many moments where I have realized how approachable this family is, and one of the many moments where I discovered that my preconceived notions of others, especially politicians and those with power, was completely wrong. This was a family just like mine.

Every time Diane and David Black came to my restaurant, I made a point to speak to them because even a brief conversation with them and seeing the way they conducted themselves made me feel ten-feet-tall inside. There was something revitalizing about just speaking with them. Now, as I look back on these times, I realize that as I got to know them personally and learned more about their community involvement and their loyal commitment to making our world a better place for our grandchildren and future generations, they were planting seeds within my heart. They spoke about helping others with a genuine passion and love that made me increasingly curious about their service work and volunteerism.

Until this point, I had thought that I had already been living a decent life. I was married to a faithful and devoted wife, had three wonderful, blossoming children, and I, myself had loving parents. I had not committed profound wrongdoings nor intentionally harmed others. Frankly, I thought that I had reached the pinnacle of my life, owning my own business. Growing up in Korea and witnessing the grueling battles of achieving social mobility, I thought that I had already achieved the token image of the American dream as a first-generation immigrant and could not exceed this, much more. However, once I met Diane and David Black, I quickly realized that there was so much more that I yearned for, and as our friendship grew in strength and depth, they also helped me realize that even an ordinary man like me could do the extraordinary and that I, too, could make a difference. By the time they extended an invite into the Rotary Club, an internationally recognized service organization, I was already enthralled.

Now, I will share two of the staple moments where Diane and Dave helped shape me into a better version of myself, by merely being themselves. One of the events that profoundly changed me, happened during the year of my induction into Rotary Club. This was the year that Diane Black shattered the glass ceiling by being the very first woman who joined this sector of the previously male-only Rotary Club. No woman prior had been permitted to join the most prestigious service organization since its founding in 1905. This is hard to accept or believe, today, thanks to women like Diane Black. Not only was Diane the first female, but Diane and David were the first married couple that became members of the same club, and they both served as Presidents of the Club.

While I have frequently discussed the importance of Rotary in my life, including in my previous books, I must note that Diane Black paved the way for people like me, from all different backgrounds and walks of life, to join and serve our community. I became the first Asian to join the Hendersonville Rotary Club in our history, then club President, then Rotary International Governor, and it is all thanks to women like Diane that illuminated the way. Today, anyone could join a service organization regardless of gender, race, religion, nationality, or even wealth, with the only true requirement of having a servant heart and passion to make a difference.

The next event where my friendship with Diane and David profoundly affected me, happened after I had to file Chapter 7 bankruptcy, ultimately losing everything that I owned, including my restaurant business and house. There had been many times that I had confronted large obstacles, yet quickly persevered because I had my family to take care of. They pushed and motivated me to move forward. However, when I filed bankruptcy, I felt utterly defeated. I had invested every penny I had and earned towards my business and our home. Every one of those pennies were built and fought for by my wife and I, through blood, sweat and tears. I was married with three small children depending on me, yet seemingly overnight, I lost the entire business and was on the verge of eviction from our home because I could not make our house payments. The sense of security and pride I had felt, left me in an instant. As a father to my children, a husband to my wife, a son to my parents, and a brother to my siblings, I had brought failure and dishonor to my family and we were now doomed to become homeless. I did not know what to do.

I still vividly remember, like it was just yesterday, the day that Dave put his arm around my shoulder and asked me if there was any way that he and Diane could be supportive of me, after learning about my bankruptcy. I can still vividly remember the sincerity in this gesture that almost made me cry, on the spot. I was defeated, a man in despair. At that moment, Dave withdrew a silver dime from his pocket and shared with me some of the adversities that he and Diane had to face. Both grew up with very humble beginnings. At twelve years of age, Dave worked at the car wash of a local gas station, earning one silver dime for each car that he washed, to support his family and his dreams. Diane grew up living in public housing and in poverty, with hopes of studying to become a nurse. Before me stood the leader of Aegis Sciences Corp, an internationally recognized organization, where I'd frequently visited this man, yet it all began with one silver dime, at a time.

As I continued to listen to the adversities that they had both overcome, individually and together, I became revitalized with the realization that no adversity is too large to ever equate to just giving up. During one of the most difficult points of my life, I realized that I had imagined myself living in a pond, and within that pond, I was comfortable, safe, and secure. I wasn't even aware that this pond led to a vast, open sea, but when life forced me to leave this pond, it was not an end—it was merely a means to a new beginning with limitless possibilities. I was only able to realize this when I realized that I live for so much more than the narrow world I saw myself in, and came to realize that I myself could help create the world I wanted to live in, that I am connected to so much more.

My point is that often, having even two solid friends can make all the difference. At one of my very lowest points, Dave pushed me to realize that I was much more than I thought of myself, and I could do more than I thought I could. He helped me break down the imaginary barriers and limitations that I battled with, by showing me that I, myself had created them. He helped me redefine the meaning of success, and once I changed my limited view of what success means to me, my life flourished. In time, I came to understand what Danny Thomas says, "All of us are born for a reason, but all of us don't discover why. Success in life has nothing to do with what you gain in life or accomplish for yourself. It is what we do for others."

You see, in the corner of David's office of his laboratory, sits the seabag that he brought home with him after serving in the Vietnam War as a young Marine. The seabag was all that he had owned then, and it still sits in his office as a daily reminder of his humble beginning. Several years later, he published a book detailing his life story with Diane, and in it he wrote, "Hard work and determination- the old-fashioned American way we could overcome our circumstances." This is a statement he truly embodies. Frankly, Diane and Dave have encouraged me, cheered for me, and have showed me time and time again that they believe that I, too, can overcome adversity, but they have largely inspired me by merely being themselves. They embody both a type of humility that I once thought impossible and an unshakeable drive to move forward, and I can truly say that everything they do is with the intention to have the means to help and lift others.

By joining Rotary, I have rediscovered my place on Earth. There are over 1.2 million Rotarians in over 200 countries living by the motto of "Service Above Self," and I am inspired and motivated by all of them. It is through Rotary that I have not only seen the American dream come alive, but I have also had the opportunity to travel across six continents, carrying on the torch with like-minded people, all united to make a better community, country, and world. I have met great men and women from all walks of life, from national Presidents, to the former Secretary-General of the United Nations, to Ban Ki-moon. I cherish the young mother's infant whom I was able to provide the polio vaccine in Africa, and I will always remember the Haitian earthquake, and the sixteen-year-old that survived the loss of her entire family and the amputation of her right leg. If it were not Rotary, I could not have this purpose-driven life that is now full of meaning. However, most importantly, I could not have Rotarian friends like Diane and Dave who have exemplified how I should and must live.

Today, Sumner County has been my home for a long time, and I have now known Diane and David Black for over twenty years. They inspired me, believed in me, and accepted my family and I as their own. Even a good seed cannot grow unless it is planted in a right soil and right environment to blossom fully. I always remember what W.

Clement Stone said about the importance of environment and friends we make. He said, "Be careful the environment you choose for it will shape you; be careful the friends you choose for you will become like them." If you could meet my friends, you would see the kind of man I have finally become.

In conclusion, I need not say anymore when Roosevelt perfectly summed up in a paragraph what I wanted to say all along about Diane and Dave. He wrote, "It is not the critic who counts; not the man who points out how the strong man stumbles, or where the doer of deeds could have done them better. The credit belongs to the man who is actually in the arena, whose face is marred by dust and sweat and blood; who strives valiantly; who errs, who comes short again and again, because there is no effort without error and shortcoming; but who does actually strive to do the deeds; who knows great enthusiasms, the great devotions; who spends himself in a worthy cause; who at the best knows in the end the triumph of high achievement, and who at the worst, if he fails, at least fails while daring greatly, so that his place shall never be with those cold and timid souls who neither know victory nor defeat."

I thought it would be an easy feat to write about my dear friends, Diane and Dave, but I quickly determined that it is the hardest. So few words could express what these years of friendship has meant to me. I want you both to know that the two of you have walked beside me during my journey of discovering what I am meant to do in this world. Thank you for believing in me. Thank you for showing me that my dreams do come true.

Service Above Self

Each of us is born into a family. An individual can choose to live anywhere in the world, but most of us stay in the community where we were born, grow up, go to school, raise a family, and spend the rest of our lives working in the same environment; and then we probably die there in the familiar soil. Because family is the natural and basic building block of society, it indeed takes an entire community to raise a child to be a good member of the society. Hence, community not only gives meaningful social connections and relationships but often determines the path of our lives as well.

It is not often easy to differentiate between a community and a society, but it is important to mention that a community refers to a group of individuals who share their values, interests, and common attitudes living together in a specific geographic location. On the other hand, a society is made up many different communities that are bound together by laws, customs, and tradition. Humans cannot exist without both a community and a society.

Abraham Maslow proposed the hierarchy of human needs. According to his theory, even if the basic physiological needs are met such as food and shelter, humans cannot live without their four other needs being met: safety (personal security, employment) love and belonging (friendship, intimate relationships, family, sense of connection,) esteem (respect, self-esteem, status, recognition, strength, freedom,) and self-actualization (achieving one's full potential.) We are wired to live with others and have a strong need to belong and to build social relationships. Through our sense of belonging, we feel cared for and valued because we are an important part of something greater than ourselves. Most of all, we find meaning and purpose in our lives through the connections we make in our communities. One argues, "Belonging can also be referred to as connectedness. Humans have a profound need to connect with others and gain acceptance into social groups. When relationships deteriorate or when social bonds are broken, people have been found to suffer from depressive symptoms. Having a greater sense of belonging has been linked to lower levels of loneliness and depression."

We can see how the community plays an important part in our

lives and why it is vital for each of us to engage and participate. The story I am about to share happened when I was little and it made such an impact on me about finding my place in our community and doing my part to make a better community for all. The story is about a Christian-pharmacist who had given me an unescapable journey in my life yet, which neither she nor myself knew then the impact she made on me.

There was an orphanage in the front of my elementary school, and there, my earliest memory of her was permanently engraved in my heart. My friends and I used to call the orphanage "a crazy house." These children were abandoned by their families and society because they were mentally challenged children.

A female pharmacist whom my family had known came to this orphanage once a month with her friends and later I learned they were Rotarians. I remember her drawing water from a public well and bringing it into the house. She bathed them with cloths and fed them. The indescribable beauty of her smile and her silent demeanor left in me an everlasting memory of "Service Above Self" and what Rotary Club was all about. I said to myself, "When I grow up, I want to join Rotary Club and be just like her." I did not even know what Rotary was but wanted to be a part of it because of her.

After I finished my education and had a business going in America, I started volunteering for non-profit organizations. As much as I was involved in my community and volunteered for the United Way, Red Cross, and CASA (Court Appointed Special Advocates for children), something was missing inside. It was that I had not yet become a member of Rotary Club. At that time, I was participating in a Leadership program in Donelson/Hermitage. When I saw one of the alumni wearing a Rotary pin, I was excited because I would finally be able to join. So, I asked him, "I'd like to join your Rotary Club. Would you invite me?" He never did. Every time I saw someone wearing a yellow Rotary emblem, I asked for an invitation. I even looked for the Rotary Club in the phone book. It was not listed. After years of denial, I thought, "They are right. I guess I am not good enough to be a Rotarian."

When I gave up hope to become a member of Rotary Club, an old man wearing a Rotary lapel pin came to my business with a folded newspaper in his hand and demanded to see the owner. Pointing at the newspaper article he said, "What is wrong with this article?" There were not many minorities like me in Sumner County, and the newspaper thought my life story was unique and interesting: growing up in the Buddhist monastery, coming to American at 17 knowing no English, marrying a woman I've never met through arranged marriage, and now owning a successful business.

At first, I was offended by his remark because people had told me how wonderful the story was. Then he added, "There was no mention of the Rotary Club in your article. I will come next Wednesday morning at seven to pick you up, and I would like to invite you to the Rotary Club." Do you know what I told him? I said, "What took you guys so long?"

When he asked me to join, I do not think he knew the difference he had made in my life. By simply asking me to join, he gave me a life changing opportunity to do things that I couldn't have dreamed possible. Did he know then that this young man he asked to join would be a club president, a District Governor one day, and he would be the fourth Korean American District Governor in North America since 1905?

He believed that Rotary has a culture in which ordinary men and women can find their own passions and do extraordinary things that they did not think they could. He simply wanted to share the spirit of Rotary uniting all walks of life and to leave an extraordinary legacy. He asked potential or prospective members to join because he believed Rotary could turn ordinary men and women into community leaders and leave an extraordinary legacy. Rotary is like an ocean. We take all different waters and unite into one.

From time to time, I wonder whom I would have become if he did not ask me to join the Rotary club in 2000. Would people ask a guy like me to join? Would I still be waiting to be asked to join, even today? Ever since I joined Rotary Club in 2000, I have traveled to many countries on six continents and met many people who have different religions, cultures, social status, and races. What I have learned is no matter how different we are and how far we live apart, we are truly one big family connected by love and service.

Mother Teresa once said, "I alone cannot change the world, but I can cast a stone across the waters to create many ripples." No matter how small your candle is and no matter how small of an impact you are going to make in this world, each of us must light up our own candle because "It is better to light a single candle than to sit and curse the darkness." When we belong together, we are giving other people a life changing opportunity to serve others and ultimately to reach self-fulfillment. Everybody is not only obligated to help people in need, but it is our duty and our responsibility to leave the world a better place than we found it.

In one of my published books, I wrote about Malala Yousafzai from Pakistan who was the youngest recipient awarded the Nobel Peace Prize in 2014. The title of her book says it all, "I Am Malala: The Girl Who Stood Up for Education and Was Shot by the Taliban." All she wanted was to go to school and play, but the Taliban banned all girls from attending school. Her family received many threats of assassination from the Taliban, but her Rotarian father taught her to speak up for her right to get an education and go to school. One girl's actions against the rules has inspired the dreams of hundreds of thousands of girls, and she has become a beacon of hope and encouragement.

There have been many polio volunteers who have been injured and shot because it was against the rules of that land to immunize children. Should we not educate girls nor save children from polio because the rules in the land say so? We have to light up our single candle where there is darkness and give hope where there is despair.

"We have always done it that way," is the most commonly used excuse to not challenge ourselves or to safeguard ourselves against unfamiliarity and intrusion. It is the easiest way out, for we do not have to do anything. We ignore and never give a second thought about changing what is safe, accepted, and has been practiced for years. It must have served its best purpose if it has lasted this long, and most of all, we have no power to change it, right? I urge you to look into your own life to examine what prevents you to do what you are called to do. If the rules are not relevant and effective anymore, set new and inspiring rules for the generations to come. All great life changing inventions, revolutions, or movements are started with one man's idea and his own belief to make a better world for mankind. He did not think about what it would do for himself alone.

I will conclude this chapter with a quote by a Holocaust survivor from Elie Wiesel's Night. "I swore never to be silent whenever and wherever human beings endure suffering and humiliation. We must always take sides. Neutrality helps the oppressor, never the victim. Silence encourages the tormentor, never the tormented."

Kim!

I haven't known you for very long, but I can honestly say that you have changed my life! When you talk about self-worth and loving ourselves, it puts everything into a different perspective for me. You've taught me that no matter how much bad I've done or how little I think I've accomplished; I am worth 100%. There will never be another me. I truly believe God brought you into my life for this short amount of time to teach me exactly what I needed, which was to realize how much I am worth and how loved I am. I can't wait to read one of your books! Thank you and much love!
--Adolescent

Welcome Letter to a New Member

When I served as District Governor in 2014, I had visited 205 clubs, traveling 18,182 miles. While traveling, I could not attend my own club. After I finished my term, I made a promise that I would go back to my local club and serve as an ordinary member, not as Past President nor as Past District Governor. Serving people and my community did not need such titles or positions. Thankfully I was asked to serve as a Club Secretary, and that position involves all daily aspects of club business. I have been serving that position since 2015, and I have loved it dearly. Also, I remember what it was like being a new member. So, I volunteered to write all new members a letter for five months to explain what Rotary is all about and what it means to be a Rotarian. The following five letters are what I have been mailing to all new members, and I believe it shows a little glimpse of Rotary, what it stands for, and what we Rotarians are asked to do.

Dear our newest Rotarian,

It truly is a great pleasure welcoming you, and congratulations for being a member of the finest Rotary Club in the world! I am looking forward to getting to know you and volunteering together to make a difference in local and international communities.

Poet Tagore said, "I slept and dreamt that life was joy. I awoke and saw that life was service. I acted and behold, service was joy." Who knew joining a Rotary Club would make such an impact in our lives and those we serve!

In the next five months, you will receive a monthly letter from me each month. Having been a Rotarian for over twenty years, I realize the more we know about Rotary, the more we love Rotary and everything we have done in the name of Rotary ever since Rotary was founded in 1905.

Service Above Self is more than just a motto as Rotarians. Anybody can say that. It is our actions that define Rotarians. Hence, we get out of it what we put into it. It is our duty and responsibility to leave the world better than we found it.

You may be the newest Rotarian when you joined among over

1.2 million Rotarians in the world, but people will know, judge, and believe in Rotary because of you. Now you have become the face of Rotary. Congratulations!

Truly Yours in Rotary Service

Kim Kim District Governor 2014-2015

My First Letter to the Newest Member,

When you first visited Hendersonville Rotary Club as a guest, you heard over one-hundred and seventy-five members enthusiastically, proudly, and shamelessly screaming in unison, "The finest Rotary Club in the world!" while reciting the 4 Way Test that Rotarians live by every day. You wondered, "What is it about Rotary that have members so passionate about making a difference and what brings them together from all walks of life in such high esteem for the betterment of others?"

When I first joined the Hendersonville Rotary Club more than twenty years ago, I did not have the slightest idea what it meant to be a member of a service organization that unites business and professional people to provide humanitarian services, encourage high ethical standards in all vocations, and help build goodwill and peace in the world ever since it was founded by one man, Paul Harris, in 1905.

Looking back, joining Rotary was not only the turning point in my life, but it has also been one of the best decisions I have ever made for my personal, professional and community life because it has allowed ordinary men like you and me to do extraordinary things together that we could not even dream possible alone. Hence, it is the greatest feeling that we are being used for a higher purpose to carry the ideals and principles of "Service Above Self" to every corner of the universe. Yes, I am proud of being a Rotarian because Rotary has changed my life and has given me a new purpose in life: I will remain a passionate Rotarian as long as I am able to serve and until my last breath on earth. At the same time, I am very excited to serve our community and to do good in the world with fellow Rotarians like you hand in hand.

The moment you join Rotary, you become the face of 1.2 million Rotarians because of your servant heart and your occupation as an opportunity to serve local and international communities. The community will know and judge Rotary by your actions, and the future of Rotary is truly in your hands.

Wow, that is a lot to swallow as the newest member when you know so little about what you are getting into, right? The more you know about Rotary and what we do, the more you come to love Rotary and believe, "One Profits Most Who Serves Best." It becomes your way of life. When he was nineteen years of age, Fellow Rotarian Dr. Kent Keith wrote "The Paradoxical Commandments" for high school student leaders. He came to Nashville for the Zone Institute and gave me the signed copy of his book, *"The Case for Servant Leadership."* He argues, "Becoming part of something larger than yourself is about joining with others in a team, an organization, a movement, a cause, a religion that makes a difference bigger than any of us can make as individuals." I believe the power, position, wealth, fame, and social status that we have does not define who we are. It is what we do for others in that power and position, with that wealth and fame, that defines who we are. I want to be a fire starter who has a servant's heart. I will keep the flame alive and will carry my torch to the darkest places on earth so they can see the light through me. Is that not the very reason we join Rotary Club and remain as Rotarians?

It is true that anyone can join Rotary Clubs to serve, but only a few have become lifelong Rotarians, for it takes belief, commitment, dedication, and a servant heart. A Rotarian explains what it means to be a Rotarian:

To Be A Rotarian	
To be young is to swim in pools you did not dig; *To be young* is to dance to music you did not write; *To be young* is to sit under trees you did not plant; *To be young* is to seek benefits from a city you did not build;	*To be a Rotarian* is to dig pools in which you will not swim. *To be a Rotarian* is to write music to which you will not dance. *To be a Rotarian* is to plant trees under which you will not sit. *To be a Rotarian* is to build a city and a community from which you will not benefit.

Rotary is about making a difference in the lives of others through friendship and service. While we are serving others, we find ourselves and our own gifts: we become better persons and we leave our community better than when we found it. They say the meaning of life is to find your gifts, and the purpose of life is to give them away. It's no accident that we have found both in Rotary, and we realize what a privilege it is to be Rotarians! Past Rotary International Vice President Lou Piconi once said, "I hope I'll never fail a child, if I can help somehow, I want to be as generous as my resources will allow. And when my life on earth is done, it will be my final plea: Let someone, somewhere think or say...you made a difference to me."

Once again, I welcome you to the finest Rotary Club in the world and can't wait to get to know you and to work together to better our community.

The Second Letter to a New Member,

Rotarian Pat Lebkuecher wrote the history of the Rotary Club of Hendersonville in 2009, celebrating forty years of service. She wrote, "The Hendersonville Rotary Club was started by a small group of professional and businessmen during the same year that Hendersonville was incorporated as a city." This small group of dedicated leaders in our community foresaw the need of an international service organization that would enrich the lives of members through fellowship and networking, bridge continents to embrace humanity, and make a difference through hands on service projects that benefit local and international communities. They believed in Rotary's Motto "Service Above Self" and wanted to create international understanding and goodwill between the peoples of the world. Past Rotary International President Carl Miller summed up what Rotary was about at the Rotary Convention in 1963, six years before our club was chartered. He said, "International understanding will not be created in the stratosphere of politics, but in the minds of neighbors, among business associates, and through the local media of communication and education."

For almost five decades, our club has done just that. A club of twenty-two charter members has grown to be one of the finest clubs in our District with over one- hundred- ninety members. When Cultural anthropologist Margaret Mead said, "Never doubt that a small group of thoughtful committed citizens can change the world; indeed, it's the only thing that ever has," I undoubtedly believe she was referring to our club and Rotarians.

Hence, it is not an overstatement that the history of Hendersonville is the history of our Club. The development and prosperity of our community and the quality of life we sometimes take for granted are due to the accomplishments of our club and dedicated Rotarians who have been involved in every facet of our community. I have never met Rotarian Robert Ellis, but every time I drive by Ellis Middle School and see the Rotary emblem in front of the school, it reminds me of the Rotary club's past. In fact, many public buildings are named after fellow Rotarians whom I have had the privilege of knowing personally from R.J "Hank" Thompson Sumner County Archives Building—he was my Rotary Buddy for several years, to the Bob and Connie Barker Animal Control Facility—when he was a club president whom named me to be his successor so I could be a club president two years later.

As for tomorrow, we Rotarians are sowing seeds for the future. Though we may not be around to enjoy the fruit of the trees we plant today, our children and our community will, and that is enough reason to be Rotarians. For example, our club was the first organization that initiated to raise funds of $25,000 to build a new library. To commemorate Rotary's 100th anniversary, our club raised $100,000 to build the Rotary fountain and beautified the Memorial Park to dedicate fallen soldiers. For more than a few decades, our club has given over $26,000 for scholarships each year. From mentoring students in local elementary schools to going to Guatemala for dental, medical, and vision trips, our club has given financial support to many non-profit organizations that align with the object of Rotary, and which depend on Rotary to carry out their mission. Our members have also been volunteering for such organizations.

Christmas for Kids is one such organization Rotarians have given financial support and volunteered to aid. This not-for-profit-organization, for example, has been providing one-hundred-fifty under privileged elementary students with the gift of spirit and love during the holiday seasons who could not have Christmas otherwise. One year, I decided to volunteer for the entire event instead of chaperoning a student to Wal Mart for about a half hour or so in the afternoon. Martina McBride and dozens of music artists donated their tour buses along with drivers for this event. I, along with four other Rotarians, went to Portland Elementary School to pick five students there. We brought them to First Baptist Church in Hendersonville and gave them one of the most memorable Christmas parties with music, foods, and pictures with Mrs. Claus. That afternoon, along with several dozen tour buses, we arrived at Walmart and helped students buy their Christmas gifts.

My designated student was a 3rd grade girl. She already had a list written down of what she wanted to buy for her parents and three siblings. It took less than thirty minutes to spend one-hundred-forty dollars for her family yet none of them were for herself. I told her, "You have only ten dollars left, and it is for your Christmas. I want you to buy something for yourself." She said, "My family did not have Christmas last year and if I don't get gifts for my family, we will not have Christmas again this year!" Well, I have been known as a rule breaker time to time. I was not supposed to give any money to a kid, but I just could not let that happened to this kid not having a gift for herself. So, I whispered to her, "I have twenty dollars, and now you have thirty dollars total to buy your own gift." She said, "You do that for me?" It took another 30 more minutes just to buy her unexpected gift, and I could not believe twenty dollars could buy that much happiness to this girl and me.

She and I were the first two individuals to get back on our bus and we waited for the rest. The school principal had told parents in advance to pick up their children by 9 pm. When we arrived in front of the school, all the parents were waiting for our arrival except for the parents of my student. Ten o'clock came and went but there was no sign of her parents. By ten-thirty, a white Buick with dents on the driver side entered the parking lot and a man stepped out, intoxicated and barely walking straight. The little girl ran to her father and started telling him what she got for her family with utter excitement, "Dad, I got you a winter jacket and a fire truck for Sean, and......" However, he hurriedly dumped her gifts in the trunk and said "Get in the car. We are late!" As the taillights of the car disappeared from my sight, I stood in disbelief. I was angry at myself and felt empty inside. I said to myself, "Why am I doing this? Her father did not even care. No matter what I do, it would not make any difference!" For that moment I regretted not staying at home with my three children and my wife during the holidays. I was visibly upset and made my mind up that I would never do this again. Yet on the contrary to my awful feelings, the bus driver was whistling and got on the bus. Then, he played a song I had never heard before but needed to hear.

It was Martina McBride's "Anyway." She sang her heart out to my own disappointed heart and lifted my soul:

You can spend your whole life building'
Somethin' from nothin'
One storm can come and blow it all away
Build it anyway
......

This world's gone crazy and it's hard to believe
That tomorrow will be better than today
Believe it anyway

......

You can pour your soul out singing
A song you believe in
That tomorrow they'll forget you ever sang
Sing it anyway
Yeah, sing it anyway
I sing, I dream, I love
Anyway

The driver explained that he had been doing this for twelve years and left Los Angeles three days ago to be here with children, adding that he was going home to New Orleans to spend the holiday with his family right after this. You see, he did not care about being recognized by many or receiving any awards for what he had done for the past twelve years. He did not even care about receiving credit. Here I was being upset with a father's disregard and questioning why I even volunteered when nobody seemed to care. I felt embarrassed while listening to the song. When I got home past midnight, I woke my three kids up and gave them big hugs with teary eyes, and I silently thanked them for letting me spend time with that little girl whom I might never see again.

A few years later, I happened to read the local newspaper on December 21, 2012 about my fellow Rotarian Andrew Finney's testimony and understood why he became a Rotarian and what made him who he is today despite life difficulties growing up. He is the pharmacist who owns Perkins Drugs and Gift Shoppe in Gallatin. He is the Past President of Gallatin Rotary Club and the very first thing people notice about him is his genuine big smile, caring heart and passion for Rotary. He wrote:

> "I was about 7 years old and my family had just moved to Sumner County. I was at a new elementary school (Beech) with a new teacher and new classmates to try and befriend. My family was going through an extremely difficult time because

my father was out of work due to back surgery/recovery. I had no clue how hard this time was on my parents, which is a tribute to their faith and strength. One afternoon after school I was met by a large bus with very friendly people, police, and my parents' blessing. A few students and I spent the next three hours having a wonderful time just before Christmas break. We went to eat and then came to the front entrance of a large retail store which I had been in many times looking at the many toys I would love to have. As we entered, they told me I could pick some things for Christmas for me and my family. An hour so later I emerged with some Christmas gifts, but to this day I can still remember the awe with which I held my first remote control red sports car. I was on top of the world. As an adult, I later realized that this group so generous of time and money for some children whose family needed a little help was the Rotary Club. This is why I am a Rotarian today and why I look forward to taking children shopping with our club each year, early in the morning, a Saturday before Christmas."

Every person has a story to tell no matter how large or small they feel their life is. What is your "Do it Anyway" story? People would say it is foolish to plant trees under the shade we never get to sit under. So many things we do are out of the goodness of our hearts rather than to be remembered, and so many random acts of kindness are made without minding whom receives the credit. The good we do today stands the chance of being forgotten by nightfall, yet we do good anyway. We have been in the journey of wiping polio off the face of earth since 1985. We have made a commitment to the children of the world that we will not stop until we accomplish a polio free world. Each day is challenging working to eradicate polio from millions of children in the world. People and other organizations have said it cannot be done in the history of mankind yet we are only 1 percent away from reaching that milestone. Mother Teresa said, "You see, in the final analysis, it is between you and God; it was never between you and them anyway." Do you believe in Rotary's motto, "Service Above Self" and live by "the Four Way Test" each day? If it is to be, it is up to you and me. Yes, we will do it anyway!

My Third Letter to a New Member

"The most beautiful things in the world cannot be seen or touched. They are felt with the heart." The Little Prince

Those who have either known me through the years or read any of my books have no trouble testifying to how much I enjoy reading. It appears to them that books are the only things that bring me happiness, life lessons, and serenity because they find me spending most of my leisure time reading classics such as *The Little Prince* by Saint-Exupery, *To Kill a Mockingbird* by Harper Lee, and *War and Peace* by Leo Tolstoy.

Those are my most cited and beloved books of all time. In fact, I will go so far as to say that as long as I have my favorite books, I could live on an uninhabited island and find peace in my mind or see the light in my heart. Furthermore, I can easily fall in love with such a companion who likes what I like and could carry conversations endlessly. No wonder I love like-minded people and treat them as my family members even if I've never met them before!

Ever since I started being involved in my community, I have seen, felt, and understood the simple secret in life, "And now here is my secret, a very simple secret; it is only with the heart that one can see rightly, what is essential is invisible to the eye," said the Little Prince. Why do volunteers have no second thoughts when donating their hard earned money to non-profit organizations to do good in the world and to help those in need in our community? Even though continents and oceans separate us, we feel their pain in our hearts, their struggles become our own struggles, and most of all, their happiness is our own happiness. Why do volunteers travel thousands of miles at our own expense and sacrifice valuable time to save disaster victims whom we had no relations with or to help rebuild communities in which we will never live? It is because money is priceless when touching some one's heart and giving dignity and love when they have lost everything by a disaster that was no fault of their own. Paul Harris said in 1912, "It can be done. How? Through service...We must experience the emotion that makes heart service possible." *The Little Prince* showed me that the way to find true happiness was by seeing with the heart and

199

experiencing it through service.

In the midst of searching for my own identity and for the meaning and purpose of my life, I accidently stumbled upon a book, *To Kill the Mockingbird*, and that book made all the difference in my life. An awakening and realization came so sudden and unexpectedly that I could not believe that I did not see it this way before.

The story takes us to the one of the darkest and ugliest eras in our history—the Great Depression and the racial segregation of the Jim Crow laws. I learned from Atticus Finch that the worst sin a man could commit was being a bystander of his own life and doing nothing when he was called to do what was right and to stand up for what he believed in. His townspeople said that he should not defend a black man, and he himself knew there was no chance of winning the case, let alone making a dent in the racial injustice polarizing the entire nation. How can one man do that? His six-year-old daughter Scout asks,

"'If you shouldn't be defendin' him, then why are you doin' it?

"'Atticus, are we going to win it?'"

"'No, honey.'"

"'Then why-'"

He responds, "'Simply because we were licked a hundred years before we started is no reason for us not to try to win.'"

Before you became a volunteer, you were a son or a daughter. Some of you might be parents or uncles. Some of you are community leaders, employers, soccer coaches, and in fact, have been playing many other roles at the same time. However, by adding another role as a volunteer, your circle of influence is no longer limited to your own family but your community at large. Your new role as a volunteer will be judged by how one should live and care for the community, and people will look up to you for guidance, leadership, and moral values. Atticus says, "'...If I didn't take this case, Scout, then I couldn't hold up my head in town, I couldn't even tell you or Jem not to do something again.'" His belief in justice was not only significant to himself or Tom Robinson, the accused, but more importantly to his two young children-the next generation and his community to break the cycle of injustice and discrimination.

He realized that no one but himself could do it. So, he firmly said, "'Every lawyer gets at least one case in his lifetime that affects him personally. This one's mine.'" This is the heart of a volunteer. When volunteers see such issues, we do not blame or rely on others to solve them. We own it and follow through with it until the end, no matter what. That is why you joined a volunteer organization in the first place. We make a difference and that will be the reason why we stay in it for life.

I do not want it to sound like I am too sentimental, but at this age (believe me I am not that old!), I confess I am finally practicing the life I should have lived from the beginning, "I came naked from my mother's womb, and I will be naked when I leave." I am slowly letting go of everything I have accumulated in this life and am living out its remainder in the way it is meant to be lived until He calls me home. You may call it a bucket list. What is the one thing that you have pushed to the back of your mind despite a little voice inside of you yearning, "I ought to, I ought to," but have either avoided or put off for a day that might not ever come? In my case, t is conquering major Russian literature from Alexander Pushkin and Anton Chekhov to Fyodor Dostoyevsky's *The Brothers Karamazov* and Leo Tolstoy's *War and Peace*. They have been slow reads and very difficult to digest but wow, they have awakened my soul and rekindled my love for literature once again.

It is my second time reading *War and Peace*, and this time, I have come to understand what English novelist E.M. Forster meant when he said, "A book is a mirror, if an ass peers into it, you can't expect an apostle to peer out." When I was busy chasing my faulty dream that accumulating wealth and climbing to higher social status at all costs was of utmost importance in my life, my heart was too tamed to see the truth, and I paid the high price dearly. That is why I did not see the first time when Leo Tolstoy said, "To live only so as not to do evil and not to have to repent is not enough. I lived like that. I lived for myself and ruined my life. To live for others, only now have I understood all the happiness of life."

I realized that the serenity I was desperately searching for could be found from within me the moment when I finally let go and started living for others. Martin Luther King. Jr. once said, "Our lives begin to end the day we become silent about things that matter." People would not be invited to join the service organization if people did not have a servant heart. It is my hope that people will find happiness, life lessons, and serenity in serving others and pay it forward to anyone you touch.

My Fourth Letter to a New Member

"A journey of a thousand miles begins with a single step." Confucius's principles were embedded in Korean tradition, culture, belief, and even daily life for over 2,000 years. I had taken many essential things in life for granted like the air we breathe, water we drink, and principles embedded in my heart without being grateful. Growing up in Korea, I heard it too often to understand the true meaning of it until a Rotarian shared his Rotary moments with me.

In fact, your journey had begun the day you joined your Rotary Club. Along the way, you had to walk alone and even doubted if your Rotary journey was a worthwhile effort. But among many occasions, you have been walking with fellow Rotarians side by side on unfamiliar and less traveled roads and shoulder to shoulder with non-Rotarians to do good in the world. They have become your friends, and you have been comforted that it has been a worthwhile journey after all. Through your humanitarian service to others, you have witnessed and experienced firsthand the life-changing moments every day; so you have become "the change you want to see in the world," as Gandhi once said.

Now it is your duty as a Rotarian to take your club and members to the same level as you are: a passionate, dedicated, and servant hearted Rotarian for life. Not only that, it is your responsibility to create an environment so that each and every Rotarian will find their passions and calling in Rotary so they can use their God given talents to make a difference in a world. May Lou Retton was 14 years old and 4 feet 9-inch-tall when she won a1984 Olympic gold medal. She said passionately, "Each of us has a fire in our hearts for something. It's our goal in life to find it and keep it lit."

Hence, it is our greatest gift of all that you and I, like minded people, are invited to join such a purpose-driven service organization that we can spread our individual fire onto the world and keep it lit together to change the world. Rotary has offered each Rotarian the opportunity to serve, fellowship to share, and purpose in life for over one hundred-sixteen years. Past RI President Crawford McCullough said, "If we can make real Rotarians out of 25 percent of our membership, we will have the most powerful organization in the world." Can you imagine what we can accomplish if you can convert members to 100 percent fully pledged Rotarians? We have been saying proudly there are 1.2 million strong and dedicated members for decades. However, I am ashamed to admit it is a very small number of people compared to the world population of 7.6 billion according to the United Nations. Our club is 165 members, the second largest club in our District. But it is too small compared to over 54,000 people living in our community. Yes, I am proud of our District for having over 3,400 members, but it is too small compared to 6.6 million people in Tennessee. No matter where we live, I can say with certainty that Rotary clubs in any Districts in the world are not even 1 percent of the population of the community we serve.

That is the reason why you hold a critical key as a new member of your club. This year will be not only the best year yet, but it also will be one of your finest moments in your Rotary life. You would meet many wonderful people who you couldn't have met otherwise and would be invited into their personal lives. Also, I know you would leave a legacy so that Rotarians would measure their success by you. You have begun your journey of a thousand miles with the end in mind. You already know how it is going to turn out. He who has seen the end and knows where he is going, it remains only to act.

It is going to be a challenging year for you as a new member, and you should be glad you are the one that lead your club and members through the challenges because it is going to be worth it! Author and motivational speaker Jon Gordon said of great leadership. "I've realized that great leadership is really a *transfer of belief*. Great leaders share their belief, vision, purpose and passion with others and in the process, they inspire others to believe, act and impact. Great leaders are positively contagious and they instill confidence and belief in others."

As you know, Vocational Service is the second Avenues of Service, and all membership is based upon classification. Classifications are simply determined to "recognize the worthiness of all useful occupations" so that we can use our full potentials and talents to serve and make better communities. Your belief in the motto "Service Above Self" will have members of all different vocations inspired and empowered to serve and impact their own communities. Author Jim

Collins argues about good-to-great business leaders in his book, "Good to Great" why some companies become great and others stay being good and never make the leap. I think his arguments apply to even volunteer-service organizations like Rotary. He said it is not vision or strategy as some might think. Instead, great leaders, '...first got the right people on the bus, the wrong people off the bus, and the right people in the right seat—and then they figured out where to drive it." They live by their belief and purpose, and then followers follow because of shared belief and they finally find their own purpose while working together.

In conclusion, I'd like to continue Jon Gordon's statement about great leaders, "To lead others in a powerful way you must invite them on your bus, share your vision for the road ahead and then encourage, empower and inspire them to drive their own bus. In the process, instead of having just one bus that you drive, you create a fleet of buses and bus drivers, all moving in the same positive direction. When you create a fleet of buses and empower people to drive their own bus, you generate an amazing amount of power and momentum that becomes an unstoppable force. This is what great leadership is all about."

My Fifth Letter to a New Member

When I drive alone, whether it is a five-minute drive to a nearby market or five hours on the Interstate, I always listen to audiobooks. I want to feel like that time is well invested rather than wasted on the road. On this particular day, I turned on the radio instead, and happened to fall upon NPR (National Public Radio) interviewing Malala and her father, Ziauddin Yousafzaik. You most likely know the story of this 19-year-old Pakistani girl that has captivated millions of people around the world and has become a beacon of hope and inspiration, already. The title of her book says it all, *I Am Malala; The Girl Who Stood Up for Education and Was Shot by the Taliban*. Time magazine featured her as one of "The 100 Most Influential People in the World" and at the age of seventeen, she became the youngest-ever Nobel prize recipient.

However, one intriguing fact that few people know about her is that she is a daughter of a Rotarian. In 2014, the January issue of Rotarian magazine simply put, "Malala is one of us." Rotarian father Ziauddin is an educator and activist who has spoken out for women's rights to education and empowerment even when the Taliban banned all girls from attending school in Pakistan. Despite many threats of assassination from the Taliban, he taught his daughter to speak up for her rights to receive an education and to attend school.

His response when asked about what he had done to raise such a brave and extraordinary girl that is unafraid to speak her mind, even against the Taliban, still echoes in my heart. "Malala is an average girl… You should not ask me what I have done. Rather you ask me, what I did not do. I did not clip her wings to fly. I did not stop her from flying." Malala has a Rotarian father who acts upon what he believes in, and it is by no surprise that Malala is much like her father. Malala's father wanted to create an environment where his daughter could, before all else, be a woman that could spread her wings to fly wherever her dreams would take her. With that freedom, she has impacted the world and generations to come. The environment Malala's father sought for his daughter is in Rotary.

How often have we heard that it takes a village to raise a child? Rotary has been involved in youth service ever since Rotary was founded. As a matter of fact, our very first grant was given to disabled children, which later became Easter Seals, founded by a Rotarian in 1919. Hence, Rotary is no different from any other organization whether they are for profit or not-for-profit: they all produce products. However, unlike others, we are in the business of producing the most important product of mankind: world community service, including youth service. Our motto, Service Above Self and 4 Way Test are not just lip service for Rotarians. We live by it in our personal lives and demonstrate the highest of moral and ethical standards in our vocation and professional lives. Other than Rotary, where else can we create such an environment where we can build such passionate, dedicated, and committed men and women?

Ralph Waldo Emerson said, "The true test of a civilization is not the census, nor the size of the cities, nor the crops, but the kind of man the country produces." We produce outstanding young men and women through RYLA (Rotary Youth Leadership Awards), youth exchange program, Interact, Rotaract, Rotary Scholars, and Rotary Alumni. I believe we not only reveal the true measure of men, but we expose men to the ideals of service. Isn't that one of the reasons why we joined Rotary, to become a better person so our children would follow the example we set for them? The dream of Malala's father was, "'I dream of a time when we will go back to Swat, our dream valley, and I will ask Malala to join our Rotary Club.'" Being a Rotarian, he not only knew that Rotary has shaped his life, but the value it can teach young men and women like Malala.

However, we cannot fully promote the good we do if we do not invite more young people to be a part of making significant impacts on our communities. Often before we even ask why young people don't join Rotary, we have already made excuses for them: they are too busy with their careers, too busy raising families, it is too expensive to join Rotary, and other various reasons we may come up with for them. Nothing could be further from the truth. I was one of the youngest members when I joined my Rotary Club, although I was already thirty-nine years old. I often wish I had joined Rotary much younger and wonder what more I would have accomplished if I had started my Rotary journey with Interact in high school, then Rotaract in college, and finally Rotary as a young person. I can assure you I would have been a better person much sooner and could have avoided many years searching for the purpose in my life, as I am now certain that I have made a bigger difference through Rotary.

The four magic words of I-Am-A-Rotarian, say everything about me, and it has truly become the most extraordinary part of and made the biggest difference in my life and my family's life. I started living by principles by which Rotarians ought to live even if no one is watching or how small it is. I learned to seek neither approval nor consent for following my passions, regardless of whether I would receive credit or recognition. Rotary has opened doors that I could not even dream possible. It has been a match made in heaven, and I am very grateful for the opportunity given to me. I am proud to say my family is Rotary, and Rotary is my family, inseparably. Thus, it is our duty to spread and promote these gifts to our next generations to see what they will make of them.

In the book of David McCullough's The Wright Brothers, Wilbur Wright said, "If I were giving a young man advice as to how he might succeed in life, I would say to him, pick out a good father and mother, and begin life in Ohio." Rotary is the ideal service organization for young people to join because we offer the opportunity to serve, personal growth, leadership development, world citizenship, and friendship. Most of all, Rotarians are ordinary fathers and mothers who come from all walks of life, doing extraordinary works. There are so many Rotarians who exemplify Service Above Self, and there are famous Rotarians in every Rotary Club in the world: Sam Walton (founder of Wal-Mart), Orville Wright (co-inventor of the first airplane), John F. Kennedy (President), Chung Yul Kim (Prime Minister of Korea), Thomas Mann (German novelist & 1929 Nobel prize recipient for literature), Sir Winston Churchill (Prime Minister of England), Diane Feinstein (U.S. Senator,) Holly Compton (1927 Nobel Prize recipient for physics), Joyce C. Hall (Founder of Hallmark Cards), Neil Armstrong (Astronaut and first man to walk on the moon), Jean Sibelius (Finland composer), Emmanuel "Manny" Pacquiao (world champion professional boxer and Politician of Philippines). The list is endless.

French philosopher Jean-Jacques Rousseau says in his essay, "It matters little to me whether my pupil be designed for the army, the pulpit, or the bar. Nature has destined us to the offices of human life antecedent to our destination concerning society. To live is the profession I would teach him. When I have done with him, it is true he will be neither a soldier, a lawyer, nor a divine. Let him first be a man; Fortune may remove him from on rank to another as she pleases, he will be always found in his place."

The many Rotarians listed above were not world famous or the most influential Rotarians when they joined their Rotary clubs. Rotary has a unique culture and environment where ordinary people can find their passions and callings in. Then, they live to reveal the true measure of men and expose themselves to the ideals of service in their vocations. Other than Rotary, where else can we create such an environment where we can build such passionate, dedicated, and committed men and women?

This is my last letter to you. When I wrote you my first letter four months ago, you were the newest member in the world—it was true at that time! By the time you receive my fifth and last letter, you have transformed yourself into a true Rotarian by participating in service projects or sharing fellowships with fellow Rotarians. It has been my pleasure knowing you in letters, and I look forward to serving our community with you.

The History of the Rotary Club of Hendersonville in 2009 by Pat Lebkuecher

Kim Kim (2008-09), possibly the first Korean-American Rotary president in the United States, presided over the Hendersonville Club during the 40th anniversary year. When he took the gavel, preparations for our 40th year celebration were already underway.

Kim's enthusiasm is infectious and has inspired many Rotarians to become more involved in the Club. Shortly after assuming office he began promoting the ambitious goal of having 100 percent of the members becoming Paul Harris Fellows. On December 3, Bill Sinks recognized eleven new Paul Harris Fellows and acknowledged several major donors who have contributed many thousands of dollars. By February of his presidential year, twelve new Paul Harris Fellows had joined the ranks of the PHF membership, giving the Club a total of 69 Paul Harris Fellows, counting 30 sustaining members. Kim Kim announced that by July 2008, the Hendersonville Rotary Club had contributed $174,000 and was responsible for supporting the immunization of 60,000 children against the ravages of polio. Surely one of President Kim's legacies will be his commitment to bringing members into the Paul Harris Fellowship.

The fifth annual 5K run, sponsored by Rotary and held in July 2008, had the biggest ever field of runners with 166 finishing the race. The event raised $4,585 to support Club charities. Rotarian Dennis Greeno reported that he was blacklisted as a —spammer‖ by Bellsouth.net because of the large number of race applications he emailed to hundreds of runners. (Nice move, Dennis!)

The Festival by the Lake had a great turnout in 2008 and the Club raised more than $21,000 in that event. Again, Michael Clark knocked himself out organizing the Festival, and scores of Rotarians met all the challenges of hosting this popular community event. Among those who stepped up to the plate in leadership positions were Don Ames, Julie White, Brenda Payne, Pam Tidwell, Bethel Coleman, Wally Nicoll, Sandra Bobo, Rose Bruce, V. Moore, Matt Corcoran, Rand McFarlin, Scott Hanning, Eric Jackson, and David Barbuto. Dozens of other Rotarians collected tickets, monitored the Kids Zone, or worked in the other venues which needed supervision or a Rotary presence.

The Days of Wine and Roses party in 2009 was beautiful, thanks to Fran Marcou, Julie White, Sandra Bobo, Rose Bruce, Bob Dulany, Chris

Hughes, Ken Jones, Jennifer Flanagan, Bill Sinks, Bethel Coleman, Paul Belcher, and the indomitable Brenda Payne. Don Clausen and Bill Myers documented the event with their photographs.

The Club's continuing generosity was demonstrated by a check for $3,500 to Christmas for Kids, an annual event intended to insure that the community's least fortunate children enjoy a happy Christmas. Christmas for Kids is ably led by Rotarian Debbie Lamberson. In addition to providing financial support to Christmas for Kids, many Rotarians turned out to chaperone more than 400 needy children for their whirlwind shopping spree at the Hendersonville Super Wal-Mart.

In support of a goal to increase literacy, the Club furnished 2,200 dictionaries to give to each third grade child in Sumner County during the 2008-09 year. This ambitious project was spearheaded by Joe Beaver and Kent Cochran. Kent successfully solicited a $1,500 grant from the Memorial Foundation to support the Dictionary Project, and he and Norman Tripp were charged with responsibility for delivering the dictionaries to the schools. The Club received hundreds of thank-you letters from parents and children who received the gift. The Literacy Committee asked Dollar General Corporation, Memorial Foundation and GAP to join us in the effort to perpetuate the Dictionary project for the County for the 2009-2010 school year. To date the Committee has commitments from the Dollar General Corporation and the Memorial Foundation for next year.

In yet another promotion of increased literacy, the Club contributed $1,000 to Books from Birth. Meanwhile, Rotarian Karen Mitchell reported that the Club has contributed a total of $56,650 over the years toward scholarships for Volunteer State Community College students.

One of the loveliest and most enjoyable social events in the Club's history was provided by Captain Burkett Nelson on a series of evenings in July-August of 2008. Burkett offered to treat every Club member to a sunset cruise on Old Hickory Lake on his ship, Vagabum. The weather was perfect, the boat was fabulous, the host and first mate could not have been more gracious, and the fellowship was outstanding. With the Club growing so rapidly that it has become difficult to remember everyone's name, the cruise gave members a wonderful opportunity to get to know their fellow Rotarians.

The Christmas party at David McKenzie's spectacular home was another highlight of the Rotary social year. The food and drinks, catered by Donna Cornelius and Karen See, were fabulous and David and his wife, Beverly, were perfect hosts.

Cheryl Sesler served well as the first woman Sergeant-At-Arms and Mary Anna Womeldorf, the first woman Chaplain and ever thoughtful of others, reminded members of those who were experiencing difficulties as she led the Club in the weekly prayer.

The color graphics by Rose Bruce gave the weekly Bulletins a classy new look during the 2008-09 year.

In April 2009, the Club hosted five young Argentine professionals participating in a Rotary Group Study Exchange (GSE) program. Rotary hosts included David and Diane Black, Brenda and Jim Payne, Robin Williams, and Bill and Erin Taylor. Rotarians Bruce Pershke, Bob Barker, Todd Batson, David Resha, Ken Warren, and Don Ward helped in transporting the group to and from Hendersonville; and Grace Guthrie and Bethel Coleman accompanied the group on their whirlwind tour of Mammoth Cave in Kentucky. Rotarian Kaye Ireland arranged for a tour of Rock Castle and worked with Brenda Payne to host a wine and cheese reception for the visitors. Rip Lebkuecher coordinated the GSE project.

A visit from Rotary International President Dong Kurn Lee in April 2009 was a one-of-a-kind event for the Club. President Elect Robin Williams invited Lee and was thrilled when the R.I. President accepted her invitation. Club members had opportunity to hear Lee's remarks at a breakfast meeting held at Blue Grass Yacht & Country Club.

Meanwhile, the Club sponsored another outstanding foreign student for the 2008-09 academic year, Frank Chung from Taiwan. S.T. and Mary Anna Womeldorf, Janet and David Carr, and Todd and Andrea Odum were Frank's hosts while he attended Hendersonville High School.

The Club's 40th year was full of successes. As the anniversary approached, preparations were underway for a joyful celebration of four decades of service to this community. Tireless Rae Collier led the effort to produce yet another outstanding tabloid showcasing the accomplishments, history, and contributions of this Club. Rod Lilly, Sandra Bobo, Keith Dennen, Kaye Palmer and Dale Flowers joined in the effort as an editorial committee. Photographer Bill Myers provided the pictures and talented Gayla Zoz worked on editing the publication to be distributed by the Hendersonville Star News. Pam Tidwell, Rae Collier, Phil Kile and Todd Odum made up the committee planning the 40th Anniversary Celebration.

Rotary's effort to fight cancer in the annual Relay for Life was led by Jim Harrison, Fred Rogers and Frank Freels. All was going well. Volunteers were lining up to work the Rotary booth. Money was coming in. Then, on the night of the Relay, strong storms blew in and ruined the evening! Not willing to accept defeat by bad luck with the weather, the valiant Relay leadership team re-scheduled this important event for July. Rotarians will again be ready to participate in this fight against the killer cancer. Also coming in July of the 41st Rotary year will be the annual Rotary Fun Run. Dennis Greeno, Frank Freels, Todd Batson, Oliver Barry and Allen Curtis have been laying plans and will lead the way in this fundraiser, which helps to fund our charitable contributions to the community. Threats have circulated that Oliver Barry will appear at a Rotary meeting in spandex if more Club members do not get behind this event.

The unexpected death on May 19, 2009 of former President and outstanding Rotarian, S.T. Womeldorf, brought an outpouring of grief, but also an outpouring of love, appreciation and awe for a man whose life will always inspire those who knew him.

Two morning programs, both presented by Club Rotarians, stand out during the 2008-09 year. Connie Sue Davenport, well known newspaper columnist and expert antique appraiser, presented a program in which she explained how she evaluates an object, then demonstrated her knowledge by appraising some interesting pieces brought in by Club members. Another unforgettable program, presented by Barbara Brennan, featured Dale Flowers strumming a guitar as he talked about his heart transplant and the feelings of love and gratitude he has for the family of the young boy whose heart he received. Rotarians were moved by Dale's presentation and were reminded of the importance of certifying willingness to be an organ donor upon their death.

President- Elect Robin Williams, Secretary Buddy Shaw, Treasurer Michael Grubbs, Michael Clark, J.D. Dordal, Rip Lebkuecher, Jane Wheatcraft, David Black, Dennis Greeno and John Cross served as members of the Board of Directors for the 2008-09 year.

Looking Back

The 2008 Summer Olympics in Beijing wowed us and Michael Phelps' swimming skills netted him a record eight gold medals. The historic election of Barack Obama gave the nation its first African-American President. In January 2009, Bill Gates, wearing a Rotary hat, spoke to the Rotary International Assembly and pledged $255 million in addition to his original donation of $100 million. Gates challenged Rotary International to match the $200 million grant by the middle of the year 2012, making it time for Rotarians to step up to the plate and become Paul Harris Fellows. General Motors, an American icon, declared bankruptcy on June 1, 2009. The world population in July 2008 was 6,706,993,000, more than three billion persons more than when the Club began in 1969.

PART IV: THOUGHT OF THE DAY

Why I Wrote "Thought of the Day"

I believe it has been at least four years or more since we started the Thought of the Day for inpatient-adolescents at our hospital to memorize each day for prizes (candy bars, signed copies of my books, or other unique gifts I collected from traveling to six continents.) We have been using quotes from great minds and even from unknown authors which we thought would be beneficial to adolescents.

Then, one afternoon while I was talking about the Thought of the Day, I was unexpectedly asked by a quiet sixteen-year-old-girl who was adopted by a white family when she was a baby from Haiti, "Kim, what is your philosophy about life? You told me you were born in Korea, raised in a Buddhist temple, and came to America at a young age. Now here you are. I want to know your thoughts on life and what you can tell adolescents like us who are drifting at sea without purpose and lost in the shuffle." She added, "I am not disregarding the works of Shakespeare, Henry David Thoreau, or Marcus Aurelius you frequently quoted. I really don't want to hear what these famous people said, for one click away, I can learn everything about them. Besides, you are an old man now (thank God she was smiling when she said that), and you should have been living your life based on something you truly believe in, your own philosophy. What is it?"

I could not think of any other exclamations than "Ouchy!" and "Wow!" It was like thunder waking me up with a roar in the middle of the night, and I was the only one who could hear and was struck by it. Even though I authored several essay books containing my thoughts and beliefs on how people should live and I certainly could quote them left and right, I've never either been asked such a question until then nor thought of writing quotes for them to recite.

I had been living my life based on my personal beliefs, and my beliefs were influenced and shaped by my environment and other peoples' opinions and their beliefs. I am open to everything, and at the same time, trying to form my own opinions, that are independent from opinions of others. Hence, my beliefs change constantly except the core values as Martin Luther King, jr. puts it, "If a man has not discovered something that he will die for, he is not fit to live" kind of values.

217

Every single person has a different personality which creates their own personal reality. That is why we see things as we are, not as what they are because we can only see things through our own lenses. The reason why I did not want to write my own thoughts for them to memorize was that it was one thing to share my thoughts, beliefs, and life experiences with them in a group, but more important, it was another matter to ask them to memorize my own personal beliefs, whether it is the wisest and the truest of all or not: it still is my personal interpretations of the things that have happened in my life and the environment we are in.

Nevertheless, I carefully wrote a dozen quotes for them and have been using it ever since a little girl had challenged me (by the way, she wrote me a letter last summer, saying she was in college and doing well. A picture taken of her rowing a canoe in a river said it all.)

There are so called "frequent flyer" adolescent patients who come back to our facility over and over again. What I often hear firsthand from them was "I still remember your quotes!" As they recited them in the front of me, I gave them a faked smile hiding my disappointment and my failure underneath. My initial thought in my head was "If you truly have lived by any of these quotes you still remember, you should not be here, for you would be busy living!" However, I had to comfort myself, "After all, all we did plant a seed in them, and it is a matter of time when we get to see these adolescents turn into beautiful flowers after a brutal winter. That time would come!"

As I received many good comments not only from adolescents and their parents, but also my co-workers saying how powerful the Thought of the Day was even for them, I contemplated quite some time whether I should write more of my own thoughts for adolescents or continue to use quotes from other great minds whom should be their role models. Whether my intention of writing sixty Thought of the Day was a worthwhile effort or not, the dice was cast, and arrows were sent forth from an archer. Now, it solely lies on adolescents to believe these thoughts would initiate and inspire them to reexamine their lives and guide them to live a life worth living.

In spite of everything, I still feel what I have done seems like killing an ant with a sledgehammer or burning a barn to kill a bug. From the beginning, I knew it was overkill and redundant having sixty Thought of the Days for adolescents who are to stay in an acute hospital only for seventy-two hours to the longest-two weeks for suicidal ideations or attempts. It is the lowest and darkest point in their lives, and during this short stay with us at the hospital, I am hoping that one quote will stick in their hearts and give them a reason to go on living as Robert Frost did to me when I was an adolescent. He wrote, "In three words, I can sum up everything I've learned about life. It goes on." Over forty plus years, I still remember the words, and I decided to write my personal words so that it might save one adolescent. I believe in the power of words and who knows, some adolescents may find something worth memorizing in my words and those words just might save them from dying.

In Ecclesiastes 12:9-10 it is written, "Not only was the Teacher wise, but also he imparted knowledge to the people. He pondered and searched out and set in order many proverbs. The Teacher searched to find just the right words, and what he wrote was upright and true." As I pen these sixty thoughts, I don't know if I could deliver that to every adolescent. However, this is what I promise: I might not be a wise man but always would be a student to learn and to share what I learned with young people. I pondered and searched for the right words. My mission is to inspire and empower adolescents to reach within to find their purpose and transform them to live a life worth living. It is my hope that sixty thoughts would be the message lingering on even after they are discharged and be their guiding lights for the rest of their lives. We are always one thought or one action away from living or dying. After all, is it not, "A tale told by an idiot, full of sound and fury, signifying nothing" a quote of Shakespeare's Macbeth or Abraham Maslow's, "If all you have is a hammer, everything looks like a nail?"

Dear Kim Kim,

When I first came here, I felt like a nobody until you gave me a reason to believe I was someone. I don't think you know you actually make a difference in people and their lives, Kim Kim.

I have found myself because of you. Your stories have taught me that I am alive and want to live because you gave me a reason to love myself and to love other people, too.

You change the world. You might not see it, but you do every single day. I am going to say I remember a guy in a hospital that told me stories of his life, and he changed my life. His name was Kim Kim.

Your stories to me mean that no matter what you are going through, there is always a reason for something to happen in your life that was purposely meant to happen. I understand the "Thought Of The Day" because I want to be the best I can be. Thank you, Kim Kim, for this journey for as long as I've been here and for helping me find myself. – Adolescent

A Letter to Adolescent Counselors,

   With no particular reason, I decided to write more on the "Thought of the Day" as I am not only witnessing, but personally experiencing the unprecedented circumstances the world is facing. In many cases, an individual lives on his own island; not directly affected by catastrophe such as disease, disasters, or wars happening on the other side of the walls so to speak, but it is nothing like COVID-19 which we have been facing since late February 2020.

   What does that have to do with writing sixty Thought of the Day? During this difficult time, I decided to do two things. First, I decided that I will do my part to be a solution to the problem rather than adding additional burdens to the society. John F. Kennedy delivered a speech at his 1961 presidential inauguration to the nation, "My fellow Americans, ask not what your country can do for you, ask what you can do for your country." I may be the only one, but I must do my part as a member of this great society. Second is that I want to invest in myself during times like these. The essence of life depends on how we respond to things that happen. I believe all of us have the ability to choose positivity and personal fulfillment in circumstances where people choose madness and blindly follow others who are blind.

   What you see are my thoughts and beliefs that I hope may stimulate or inspire adolescents to reexamine their own lives while at Skyline. My original thoughts are not new or original in the slightest. You would see my thoughts and beliefs are influenced by a diverse array of individuals from Jesus to Buddha, Shakespeare to Tagore, Plato to Confucius, and T.S. Eliot to Tolstoy. Dr. Billiyar said he was curious about our Thought of the Day for a few years now because the adolescents quite frequently and proudly have recited them in front of him during their consultations. Even if it were with good intention, words can be interpreted in completely different ways and could potentially do harm than good. Hence, I asked Dr. Billiyar to look over all the sixty TOTD carefully to find any words which might cause any harm to adolescents as you recall "the pen is mightier than the sword." He kept it for three weeks and gave me valuable suggestions and made a few personal changes.

   I am confident this would be a good resource for counselors, and you are not required to use any of them if it does not fit into your scheme. On the other hand, if you believe adolescents would find some value and meaning in these aforementioned TOTD, I want you to pat yourself on the back because I gather inspiration and admiration from you as well as your groups. If not, it is my fault for having a lack of knowledge and wisdom, and I will continue to push myself to be a better person than yesterday. I always welcome any of your feedback, and you are also welcome to change some or the entire text. You can even throw them away if you think it would not help their journey in life. I can handle criticism, and in fact, you speak better than I do! Hahaha.

The end of knowledge is virtuous action and the beginning of ignorance. Let us keep challenging them so they can find their hidden potential, worth, and their place in this world.

Dear Kim Kim,

First of all, thank you for caring so much more than your job requires. It means a tremendous amount to me and the dozens of kids you have had the opportunity to inspire.
You are an amazing man and counselor, so full of wonderful lessons, stories, passion, and joy. I have already learned so much from you that I will carry with me through life, in only two days. You have made such an incredible impact on me and my choices in two short days. I just wanted to say thank you so much for caring, teaching, and loving us. – Adolescent

Thought of the Day 1 Wow, what a beautiful life it was!

Everything that is born will die one day, but you make a choice of how you live in the space between birth and death. Most people choose to live in comfort and safety, avoiding challenge, obstacles, and pain at all costs. They don't get to live a life worth living. Me? I'd rather live life to the fullest, facing all obstacles head on, having thoroughly used up all the potential God has given me. Only then can I arrive at death, completely worn out and proudly yelling, "Wow, what a beautiful life it was!"

Thought of the Day 2   Unlimited Life

Your life on earth is short and limited, but there are no limitations of what you can accomplish or who you can become. You are only limited by your own beliefs, passions, and your imagination. Believe your life is worth living and change the way you see the world; then you can create the world you want to see. Have passion in life and pursue what fuels your heart because no one else is going to do it for you. Finally, imagine that anything is possible: who you are, where you are, and what you want out of your life is only limited by the limits of who you think you are.

Thought of the Day 3 Transformation into a butterfly

The caterpillar thinks it's at the end of its life when it is only the beginning of the most beautiful and unique transformation into a butterfly. Your life is no different. Your struggles, hardships, and suffering seem to never end because you are going through the deepest, darkest moments in your life right now; yet at the end of this journey, you are destined to be something as special and beautiful as a butterfly that no other beauty can touch or compare. If you persevere and never give up, by just being you, you will become the most beautiful

223

human being in your own way.

Thought of the Day 4 Your life is worth 100 percent

You have been placed on this earth to discover your own path. You have all the potential to succeed in life and the power to create a world that you leave better than how you found it. Hence, success has nothing to do with your worth and accomplishments. Your worth never changes from the moment you were born until you die. No matter what you gain in life, how much you accomplish for yourself, or how small your life is going to be, your life is worth 100 percent. Live your God-given life while you can because you never know when it will be taken away from you. You don't get to choose when to die; you only get to choose how to live.

Thought of the Day 5 Discover the true meaning of your life

Martin Luther King, Jr., once said, "Our lives begin to end the day we become silent about things that matter." The things that matter most are not seen by your eyes nor scream for your attention. You have to see it with your heart and choose to make it urgent and important to you. Otherwise, you only exist without ever truly living in this world. Do you really want to discover at the end of your life that you had never lived?

Thought of the Day 6 Do the most important matter

Someone once said, "Every act of will is an act of self-limitation. To desire action is to desire limitation. In that sense, every act is an act of self-sacrifice. When you choose anything, you reject everything else."

In other words, when you choose to do a certain thing, you choose not to do everything else. What you decide to do at this moment must become the most important matter in your life. If not, then why are you doing it?

Thought of the Day 7 Advice to Adolescents

What advice can I give to an adolescent who believes his or her life is not worth living, has lost all hope, and is giving up? I would like to ask them, "What do you know about life? You have not lived your full life yet and haven't used any of your God given potential. So, how can you say your life is not worth living, you are hopeless, and you are destined to fail, when you are created in the perfect image of God and God resides in you?" All the struggles and obstacles you are facing right now is preparing you for your successful future that is yet to come. Life is meant to be lived no matter what. You can never, ever turn your back on life no matter how difficult it is. It is your job to find your passion in life and keep it lit to brighten up this world.

Thought of the Day 8 A prisoner or a pioneer

Free will is defined as the ability to think, choose, and act voluntarily, not influenced by external conditions, past experiences, or even fate. You are the author of your own books. You take your own actions and create your own destiny. It doesn't do any good reading the previous chapter over and over again, merely hoping to live a bright future. You have to let go of the bad chapters to move on to create a brand new one. You have to declare you are no longer a prisoner of the past. You are the pioneer of tomorrow, by creating your future today.

Thought of the Day 9 You have every tool you need

You already have every tool you need in your toolbox to live your life, but you have not learned how to use them yet. Everything that you need is already within you. Life is about molding and renovating yourself by using your talents in new ways and seeing life with new eyes. What you did yesterday or where you are going tomorrow are not important compared to what you are doing with your time today. Your actions today should be contributing meaning to your life. What have you done today to better yourself? What are you doing today to mold a life worth living tomorrow? If you are not living a life worth living, shouldn't you be in the process of changing it, right now?

Thought of the Day 10 Journey to my authentic self

The most important journey in my life is the journey to my innermost, authentic self. That is to rediscover who I was meant to be. As time goes on, I begin to lose sight of that authentic self. I was created in the image of God and despite how much can change, this remains the same. Oh, what have I done during this sojourn on Earth? Have I lived the life I wanted to live while I am alive? Or have I turned into a total stranger? At the end of this journey, after all the trials and tribulations, may I be the man I was meant to be.

Thought of the Day 11 I am chosen by God

I was created in God's own image. It doesn't matter how other people see me through their distorted lenses, if they reject me for being different, or label me as a failure. The truth is that I must see and accept myself as the one God sees. I am chosen by God, and I must live my life the way God wants me to live. In His eyes, I am the most unique and precious child, and there is no other person like me on this earth.

Thought of the Day 12 Right here, right now

You are one of a kind, distinct and unique. Your existence in this present time and space is all you have. However, you choose to live it, you will not get a second chance at life. Know that you are a gift from

God, and what you do with your life on earth is your gift to God. Despite this limited time and space, nobody else will touch, connect, and influence the same as you, and it is time to make the most of it. The most important person is the one you are facing right now. The most important thing to do is what you are doing right now. The most important time is right now. Live your life before it is too late. Life is what you make it.

Thought of the Day 13 Your thoughts are the seeds of your mind

Land will grow whatever seeds you plant regardless of whether you plant flowers or poison. Land does not control what seeds are planted into it—farmers do. They plant the seeds they want to grow then tend to the land to continue removing unwanted, harmful plants. Your thoughts are the seeds of your mind, your character is the land, and you are the farmer that lets them grow. You become what you think about because that's what you allow to grow. Your choices will create who you become. Positive thinking produces positivity and negative thinking produces negativity. You reap what you sow.

Thought of the Day 14 Do not judge or condemn

Please, do not judge or condemn others because they are not like you, think like you, or do what you do. It does not mean they are wrong. All of us see the world as we are, not as t really is. There was a time that you, too, did something based off what you knew and believed at the time, that you would not agree with today. Now that you know better and differently, you can also do better and have better understanding. Forgive others for this process, too. We are all learning and it is a lifelong journey to become better than what we used to be.

Thought of the Day 15 Change yourself first

If you want to make a positive difference, inspire others to reach their potential, or to change the world, then you must first change yourself. You must make your life your masterpiece. Only by example can you become an inspiration to all life, just by showing how you lived yours. It all begins with changing your thoughts, then you can change your life.

Thought of the Day 16   Become the highest and truest versions of ourselves

We are born for a reason. We do not fully understand the meaning of life and how we should live. However, I do know this much to be true. We are given a lifetime to renew ourselves each day to become the highest and truest versions of ourselves as human beings. At the end of our lives, it would be the greatest accomplishment to fully exist as the best that we are capable of being.

Thought of the Day 17 The ultimate goal: being, doing, & using

Becoming who I truly am, doing what I am called to do and using all my potential to make a difference is the ultimate goal of mine. I have not found what is more meaningful than that. No amount of wealth, fame, nor power can replace or buy the happiness of being myself, having love of my vocation, and empathy toward others.

Thought of the Day 18 Your thoughts are your most powerful tools

Do you believe that your thoughts today connect to your future, and every feeling and action initiates from your thoughts? Once you truly understand that it is your mind, not just heredity or your environment that controls you or makes you sick and unhappy, then you understand that your thoughts can also make you well and happy. Your thoughts are your most powerful tools for a successful life. You can be a slave or a master depending on what you think. What you think, you become. What you feel, you attract. What you imagine, you create. Once you realize how powerful a thought is, why would you want to use the power of a negative one?

Thought of the Day 19 Think and act independently

Open your mind to every possibility, imagination, and uncertainty to obtain the knowledge which will set you free. But you must remain attached to nothing. I am I and you are you. I think and act independently, free from people's opinions which are based on their own preconceptions and judgment. Things are neither good nor bad. It is my interpretation of it that makes it so.

Thought of the Day 20 You become what you think about

You are the most important person in this world, and nothing exists without you. The most important thing in life is what kind of relationship you have with yourself. You become what you think about. If you believe your life is not worth living, you will see everything else as unworthy because your belief is the window through which you see the world.

Thought of the Day 21 Reap what you sow

How you see yourself is how you see the world. If you change the way you see the world, the world you see will change. How you speak to yourself is how you speak to others. How you treat yourself is how you treat the world. More than anything else, love yourself first. If you don't have love in you, how can you give away what you don't have? The truth is you get out what you put into it: you reap what you sow. GIGO! (Garbage In-Garbage Out)

Thought of the Day 22 The true measure of a man

Success in life is not measured by what you have, what you do, or what you accomplish in your life. No amount of wealth, positions, nor accomplishments for yourself can replace what you were born to be. Hence, the true measure of a man is to become who you truly are. The choices you have made determine the gap between who you were born to be and the man you pretend to be. The journey of your lifetime is to get close to your true self by knowing God and walking through the valley of life with Him because He is the creator of all things. Only then would I know the meaning of life and would see all things as what they are, not as what I see in my distorted eyes.

Thought of the Day 23 Change your thoughts, change your life

If you are happy with your life, keep doing what you have always done. But be careful what you wish for because your habits will lead you there whether it is good or bad. On the other hand, if you are not happy with your life, there are two ways you can change. One is to change the conditions you are in, which is not always possible. The second is the easiest: change the way you see the world. When you change the way you think, you change your emotions, and then you will act on these emotions. When you change the way you act, you can change your life. It all starts with changing your thoughts.

Thought of the Day 24 You are the conductor

You are the conductor of your own orchestra. You don't have to know how to play every instrument, but you must know how it's supposed to sound. Hence, let them serve their roles in accordance with the bigger picture. Every role must work together in harmony to create the heavenly sound. Life is your orchestra. You cannot do right in one area of your life while you are busy doing wrong in other areas.

Thought of the Day 25 I am kind & I am love

I am kind to those who are kind to me.

I am equally kind to the unkind because it's my nature.

I love and respect those who love me and respect me.

I still show love and respect to those who hate me and disrespect me.

Not as a reflection of who they are, but as the true nature of who I am.

I choose to see everything as my own self.

Thought of the Day 26 Self-confidence

A self-confident person undoubtedly believes in his own capability that he acts confidently and independently in the direction of his vision. He is open to all ideas and possibilities but not easily influenced by the opinion of others. Hence, self-confidence is the most attractive quality a man can have. How can anyone see how awesome a person you are if you cannot see it yourself?

Thought of the Day 27 Circumstances reveal your character

The bad circumstances can never break you, nor make or ruin your day. It only happens to reveal your character. There is no such thing as a good or bad circumstance. Your attitude on how to respond to what happens to you makes it so.

Thought of the Day 28 Do the right thing

Sometimes you will find yourself being the only one standing up for your own beliefs, refusing to obey immoral rules while everyone else is sitting down, doing nothing and looking the other way. Sometimes you will find yourself being the only one sitting down for your rights while everyone else acts as followers. There are only two ways to live: if it is right, do it no matter how difficult and unpopular it is. If it is wrong, don't do it no matter how small it is even when nobody cares. Small leaks sink ships. Small snowflakes become avalanches.

Thought of the Day 29 Five senses

We have beautiful eyes to see the good in all people and beauty in ugliness.

We have beautiful lips to speak only words of kindness, love, and encouragement.

We have beautiful ears to listen to the angelic voices of loved ones.

We have a beautiful nose to smell the richness in life and the beauty of nature.

We have beautiful skin to touch lovingly and give lovingly.

We have been given everything we need.

We don't need anything else other than to appreciate what are given and to love one another.

Thought of the Day 30 Who Am I?

I am not what I have.

I am not what I do.

I am not what I accomplish.

I am not who I think I am.

I am not who you think I am.

I am me.

I am made by the image of God.

God is in me and I in Him.

I don't need anyone else's permission to be happy or to be myself.

I know who I am.

I am unique.

I am worthy.

I am beautiful.

I am strong.

I am lovable.

And I love myself as I am.

Thought of the Day 31 Light and love

Martin Luther King, Jr. once said, "Darkness cannot drive out darkness: only light can do that. Hate cannot drive out hate: only love can do that." It is easy to respond, "An eye for an eye, and a tooth for a tooth." The truth of the matter is that it is unnatural for love to hate. A hater will always hate you who embodies love. It is better to light a loving candle in you in order to brighten up the world than to do nothing and curse the darkness. Be good to others even if they are not.

Thought of the Day 32 I learned something new today

If I have not learned anything today, my behavior would be the same today and tomorrow as it was yesterday because I am going to think the same thoughts, make the same choices, have the same experiences and feel the same feelings. Nothing would be different, and nothing would change. Then why do I need today or tomorrow if I repeat the same life over and over again as yesterday?

Thought of the Day 33 Freedom and happiness

The fundamental principle of all human beings is that we are all alike and want the same thing: freedom and happiness. It is ironic and pointless to search outside of our body when it is given to us for free the moment we were born —and cannot be taken away from us. We are born free, but we choose to live in an open cage as a captive bird. If we are not happy with what we have, no amount of wealth could satisfy our thirst for more even if we are the richest man on Earth because we always want more.

Thought of the Day 34 Do the little things with great love

You can only do a little, but the little things you do can make a big difference on someone who is going through a difficult time. Do not refuse to do something you can do for others when the opportunity comes to you. I believe it is the highest privilege to do something for someone without expecting anything in return. Never underestimate what you can do. A simple smile can save a person who thinks nobody cares.

Thought of the Day 35 Greatest assets or worst enemy

A drop of water either gives life to all beings or it becomes a flood that destroys everything that stands in its path with a single blow. Your thoughts are either your greatest assets or your worst enemy. You can either choose to live in the past as a prisoner or live today and tomorrow as a pioneer. Regardless of the path you choose, your thoughts will reconstruct such a world for you. I hope you realize how powerful your thoughts are. Then, you would never think a negative and toxic thought—not even for one second of your life.

Thought of the Day 36 Prepare to win

Many people hope to succeed in life but fail to prepare to win. When you face adversity, it might seem too difficult to overcome but you must have a heart of a champion. Believe in yourself and welcome all adversities as opportunities to grow and show what you are capable of. Your attitude must be, "Bring it on. It is not the first time I was knocked down, stepped on, and spat on. I always rose stronger than ever before. I am so happy that I get a chance to show what I was preparing for, training for, and living for."

Thought of the day 37 Two minds: conscious and subconscious

The hardest part of changing your life is not doing the same things you did yesterday. If you are repeating what you always have done over and over again without even thinking, you will always have the same life, and nothing would change. In order to truly change, your desire in the conscious mind must be greater than the subconscious body that is automatically driven by your habits. You must believe you are a limitless person who has all the potential and ability to become who you truly are. If you do that, you are not easily influenced by the opinions of others and their polluted eyes. You must do your work—learning new things with an open mind, relearning what you already learned in the past with new eyes, and letting go of all the belief systems that are holding you hostage.

Thought of the Day 38 Three types of regrets

There are three types of regrets. One is in the past which you cannot do anything about. Second is what you are dealing with right now which you can fix. Third is the one you can prevent now from happening in the future. You will not regret things that you have tried but failed. The only regret you would have in the end are chances you could have taken but did not when you could.

Thought of the Day 39 Fall in love with yourself

You have to fall in love with yourself. The world can be dark, cruel, and lonely when you feel no one understands what you go through and no one seems to care about you. That is why you have to fall in love with yourself so you could love others again. If you like the person you are alone with, you would never be lonely. If you cannot stand to be alone with yourself, you have to reexamine your inner self to find the barriers preventing you from seeing the truth, and then change the way you see things. Only then the things you see change. You would be content with your life and accept things as they are.

Thought of the Day 40 Anyway Part I

Anybody can be good to good people.

Be good anyway even if they are not, and you must overcome evil with good, not be defeated by it. You will be disappointed not by their bad behaviors but by your own unreasonable expectations.

Anybody can be kind to kind people.

Be kind to the unkind anyway and do not expect anything in return because you never know what a hard battle they are fighting. Only your kind heart can heal their broken and lonely hearts.

Anybody can be honest to honest people.

Be honest to the dishonest anyway, yet it is absurd to expect honesty from dishonest people.

Thought of the Day 41 Anyway Part II

Anybody can love those who love you back unconditionally.

Love the unlovable anyway even though they don't deserve your love. Love yourself first so you can give what you have. You are love and hate is not in you.

Anybody can respect those who respect you.

Show respect to people who don't respect you anyway, not as a reflection of their characters but as a reflection of who you are. If you respect yourself, others will respect you by nature.

Anybody can forgive those who deserve forgiveness.

Forgive the unforgivable anyway as you are already forgiven for all of your sins. To forgive is to see divine in every person the way God sees in them.

Thought of the Day 42 The highest form of being

At first, it was merely a whisper in your ears passing through. The more you got away from it, it became louder and louder that you could no longer silence the voice inside of you telling you to write. You would never become the person you were meant to be or be happy with yourself if you had been doing anything else but to write. Therefore, you must write.

If you are called to be a musician, be a musician to make music. That is what you do best. If you are called to be a baker, and that is what you love to do; then, you must bake. If you see yourself as a nurse then you could not be satisfied with anything else but as a nurse, you are the happiest when you take care of patients who need it the most.

The highest form of being is to become who you truly are and doing what you were born to do by using God given gifts to make a difference in this world.

Thought of the Day 43 Period vs. semicolon

Whether you have lived all of your life or had it cut short at a young age in quiet desperation, no human being wants their life to end with a period. We want it to be a semicolon; a continuous journey to the next life. We are spiritual beings having temporary and physical human experiences. Our physical body might be dead and buried but our spirit transcends and returns to the source—heaven.

The secret of life is you don't have to end this life to go to heaven. Heaven on earth is not the place you must find; it is the choice you must make. However, you choose to live your life becomes the reality, period!

Thought of the Day 44 Treasures buried inside of me Part I

When I was born, everybody knew what a lovable, unique, and worthy human being I was, except me. I was, then, too young, ignorant, and limited to know I was born for a reason.

When I was just a lad, I did what I knew how to do: I thought like a child and acted like a child. I perceived everything I heard and saw to be true because I didn't know better.

When I was a young man, I longed to leave my comfortable and safe home environment to venture towards a new life.

Thought of the Day 45 Treasures buried inside of me Part II

When I got older, I desperately sought the life I wanted, but the world was such a cruel and hostile place that would not put up with my childish behaviors and negative attitude.

When I finally came to face my own grave, I suddenly realized I still had all the talents and treasures buried inside of me that I had never utilized nor given away while I lived.

Thought of the Day 46 You are the sum total of all the choices

Settling for "good" is the enemy of greatness. You do not suddenly become excellent at what you do. It is the little things you do every moment in your life. You are the sum total of all the choices you have made up until this moment. If you don't like what you have become and what you are doing, you always have a choice and power to change by changing your automatic and unconscious habits. You are not a stone or a tree. You can change or move!

Thought of the Day 47 Your attitude and the choices

You are what you are, not because of your dysfunctional family environment, heredity, or bad circumstances, but rather your attitude and the choices you make after all those things happen in your life. Everyone has an undesirable background and faces unavoidable circumstances, but not everyone succeeds in life. It is about how you interpret the circumstances that happen. It would be the greatest lesson in life to choose your personal growth and fulfillment while others choose madness and adversity. Ask not why bad things happen to you repeatedly; instead, ask what you can do to make it a great opportunity and accomplishment.

Thought of the Day 48 C is between B and D

Bob Dylan sings, "A man is a success if he gets up in the morning and goes to bed at night and in between does what he wants." You and I have a very simple life because there would always be C between B and D: you make a choice in space between birth and death. There is no exception to this rule. You are free to make whatever choices, and your choices will always come with consequences, for every action, there is an equal and opposite reaction.

Thought of the Day 49 Know the difference between opinion and facts Part I

An opinion is formed by a belief or a preconception about someone or something. Your opinion is based on your feelings, your past experiences and what you are taught to be true. It is very personal and biased; hence, it is not necessarily based on fact or truth. That means you can be either right or wrong.

Thought of the Day 50 Know the difference between opinion and facts Part II

Each of us believe our own opinion to be true. When the opinions of others are different from us, we automatically think they are wrong. It only means we have not seen from their point of view.

When people say their opinions about you, you must understand it is their opinion and based on their personal experiences, feelings, beliefs, and perceptions. You don't have to accept or consent to their opinion.

Thought of the Day 51 Sphinx asked a riddle

Which creature walks with four legs in the morning, two at noon, and three in the evening?"

When I walked on four legs, I thought I was the center of the universe and was treated as such. I knew nothing about God and His existence.

When I walked on two legs, I believed in God for justice, rewards, and strength: punishing and rewarding people according to their deeds and as He gave me strength to accomplish worldly achievements.

When I walked on three legs, I wanted to know God to be like Him. And I wanted to be used for His purpose and spread His love to all of His creation.

Thought of the Day 52 I am the owner of my mind Part I

My mind is good and pure by nature. If I don't keep it good and pure by constant repair, anyone and anything can come into my mind and walk all over me with their dirty feet and their dirty minds. Then, that person or thing can occupy my mind and claim to be the new owner of me. I was kicked out of my own residency because I was unable to think for myself, and I allowed it to happen.

Thought of the Day 53 I am the owner of my mind Part II

I am reclaiming my own power and control back from everyone and everything I am attached to that has too much power over me. I must reclaim my mind and I have always been the owner of my mind and will kick them out of my mind and never invite them again. Nothing and no one can make me small and inferior without my consent, and I vow I will never consent to that.

Thought of the Day 54 Reflection of who you are Part I

It makes me upset when I treat somebody nice, and they are not nice to me. Is it not a golden rule to treat others the way we want to be treated and that we reap what we sow? Then, how come when I love some people, they don't love me back? I sow love in them, but I never reap what I sow. I am a good and kind person and treat others with goodness and kindness. They don't treat me the same way I have treated them. So, I don't reap what I sow!

Thought of the Day 55 Reflection of who you are Part II

If you love someone wholeheartedly but that person does not love you back, it does not mean you do not reap what you sow. It comes unexpected, unannounced, and at an unexpected time and place in a different form. You have planted a seed of love in them and you never know when and for whom it is going to bloom. We must love and respect them even if they are unlovable and disrespectful, not as a reflection of who they are, but a reflection of who you are.

Thought of the Day 56 Reflection of who you are Part III

"The Lord is good and His love endures forever." It is the act of God in you, and let it be done through you without expecting anything in return. It is foolish of us to want love from a person who does not know what love is, let alone does not know how to show it. Having someone to love is better than being loved by them.

Thought of the Day 57 Nothing is left undone

"I do nothing, but nothing is left undone" means seeing yourself as a vital part of an interconnected Universe. You are to live in alignment with the Universe and allow all things to live their own lives and to accept them as they are. You are not doing anything at all and yet everything gets done with no effort and by itself as long as you align your intention with your thoughts, feelings, actions, and goals.

Thought of the Day 58 I received everything I needed Part I

I asked to live in peace and serenity, free from chaos.

I was put in a sinful world to light my candle rather than to curse the darkness and do nothing.

I asked for wisdom that it might set me free.

I was born free and troubles in my life helped me to seek the truth. Now I have learned that wisdom in my head meant nothing if I did not live by it. All wisdom should lead to virtuous actions.

Thought of the Day 59 I received everything I needed Part II

I asked for unconditional and endless love.

Even though people have done many wrongs and hurtful things, Forgive them and love them anyway, for I am love and hate is not within me.

I asked for all the things that might allow me to enjoy life.

I was given life to fulfill His will through me, and that made all the difference.

After all, I received nothing I asked for.

But I received everything I needed.

Thought of the Day 60 I don't need your permission

I am love and worthy.

It's okay if you don't see me the way I see myself and accept me as I am.

My worth and happiness is not determined by you.

In fact, I don't need your permission to feel worthy and happy.

That is who I am regardless of how you feel about me or what you think of me.

I am lovable, worthy, and happy, not because you say I am, but because I choose to see it as such.

Acknowledgments

Tennessee Williams once wrote, "If the writing is honest, it cannot be separated from the person who wrote it." As the person who wrote this book, I must confess in all honesty that my writings don't reflect a book showcased in the front façade of every bookstore; rather it is my personal journal or diary to be kept in a cache, a secret place hidden from anyone. However, in the beginning of this writing journey, I was a man battling against the North winds. The harder that the wind blew and heaved, the more I refused to remove the layers and layers of clothing that shielded my true self. Today, at the end of this two year writing journey, I place down my pen as a person that has become a man, vulnerable and naked under the sun, but humble and kind.

It is paradoxical that these writings all began in my journal, where I could be brutally honest and truthful to myself because no one was going to read it. My journal isn't a leather-bound notebook or a fancy, blank journal you would receive as a gift on your birthday. I scribbled on napkins and scraps of paper when my thoughts flowed naturally and without force; then I stapled them together to save for the day I'd want to retrieve them again. Yet at the same time, I wanted to broadcast my story over the air, reaching as wide of a reach of readers as possible that would want to take this journey with me, the one in search for the meaning of life so each of us could live a life worth living.

The moment I decided to publish my life in the form of a book, releasing the words I stored in a cache, hoarded away, concealing the lifelong process in which my heart has transformed, my initial thought was whom would be the right editor. My daughter has proofread and edited the first drafts of my previous books. She did some chapters in this book as well, but she did not have time to finish this one due to being consumed with work. Because of my writing style and having learned English after coming to America at the age of seventeen, it was vital to find an editor who knows me as a person first, not as a writer. After my daughter has touched my writings here and there, she's relayed my messages in such a way that even a three-year-old child could understand!

In my writings, the content of the message is much more important than the words that are written. I placed my complete trust in God that he would send me the right person at the right time; meanwhile, all I needed to do was to keep writing patiently and without worry. Within a week after I transcribed my own illegible handwriting to text, the right person for the job showed up at the perfect moment. We have exchanged numerous emails and text messages, yet I have not physically met her yet. I hope to meet her in person by the time this is in print. Nonetheless, I feel like she knew the inside of my mind, like my own daughter. She knew exactly the contexts I wanted to convey and made my writing so much clearer and more precise.

For **Lakynn**,

Thank you so much for believing in me and that I have something worth telling. You volunteered to edit my entire book after you learned that my purpose for publishing this book was to give out to the adolescents at the hospital that I work, and I cannot express how much I cherish and value your willingness and altruistic nature. Thanks to my dear friend Dilya who recommended you to me. Dilya said she knew the perfect individual for my mission and what I was looking for, and you are truly the God sent editor for this book. I hope you work with me well into the future. I continue to write in my journal daily, and if fate brings these writings into print as well, then I know you are the bridge that connects my ordinary life to the world of literacy.

For **my wife Sue**,

I have two desks: one in the master bedroom because of the beautiful outdoor view in front of it, and the other in a study room full of books. I know that I have been annoying, roaming in and out of the rooms while everyone was sleeping, opening the windows wide during freezing cold temperatures, trying to find the inspiration for the words that flow through my heart. I know there have been times during this writing journey that I have been rude and unpleasant, a stranger fighting against the invisible battle that is writer's block. Not once have you complained, and you support and understand that this is something I love, regardless of whether I sell a single book or not. I love you very much.

For **my daughter Ahrahm and two sons Hannie and Doun**

Tagore once wrote, "Spring has passed. Summer has gone. Winter is here... and the song that I meant to sing remains unsung. For I have spent my days stringing and unstringing my instrument." When I spend time with you, I want to be completely, utterly present with you, knowing that I don't get to see you all as much as you live your own lives. Writing is one of my ways of spending time with you. One day all of us must depart from this Earth and when I leave before you, I want these books to remind you of how much I have loved you and that I am still right here in your heart. Thank you for encouraging me to be myself, as many of my stories in this book are your stories, too. Thank you for being my friends even more than my children. I love you so much.

For my three sisters: **Ok, Young Ae, Young** and brother **Chi**

My three sisters and younger brother may think that they have not done anything to contribute to this book, but they are dead wrong. I am only an interpreter, a storyteller of events. The protagonists of many of the events I've detailed in my stories have been my brother and three sisters, even in times I've altered names to protect their innocence. We have been through many ups and downs, with sometimes more downs, yet you have continued to show me the value of family. Thank you for your love and your encouragement.

For **Adolescents** I serve at my hospital,

This book would simply not be possible if it weren't for the eight-hundred adolescents per year that have come to the hospital I have been working at for the past seven years. Let me put it this way: I don't know how many people would still show up for work if they had twenty million dollars in the bank, yet I wholeheartedly believe that I would. Nothing in this physical world could take away how much I value these adolescents and how much I cherish showing up for them each day. I'm honored for the opportunity to make a difference and to do what I am called to do. So, thank you for allowing me to show up everyday to do what I do the best, and that is planting a seed of love and worth in your hearts to continue living a life worth living.

For my **coworkers**

We have an amazing team of dedicated staff in my Adolescent Unit from Dr. Billyar and our administrators to nurses, therapists, social workers, counselors, housekeepers, cooks, and adjunctive therapists, to only name a few. I don't have to look hard or far to rekindle in my heart why we do what we do and to be reminded or inspired to make a difference in the lives of the patients we have the privilege to serve. No mountain is high enough and no ocean is deep enough to prevent us from conquering any of the issues that face us. We can do this!

For my best friend **Dr. James Perdue**, Professor of Perseverance
I have known James ever since high school (yes, that was several decades ago). He taught my children when he was a coach and teacher at a local middle school: his team won a state championship, and he became an award-winning educator. Then, he went back to college and earned a doctoral degree to become an accomplished writer and motivational speaker to spread his message; his quadriplegic body would neither define nor confine his chosen life. A total freak accident playing football in his backyard left him quadriplegic, and he was to be placed in a nursing home due to his inability to function independently at the age of nineteen. All those aforementioned accomplishments happened after he became quadriplegic. His unimaginable and personal obstacles helped him to become an expert in mental toughness, perseverance, and resiliency. You are reading my 9th book, and James has been the one who helped me publish all of them. I would not trade our friendship for anything, and it is my great pleasure having you as my life-long friend. I love you, Man!

For **my customers at Franklin Cleaners**
Not many of my customers know that I have been working in healthcare for over twenty years and am now working as an adolescent counselor, yet when I go to our family business to help my wife, in Franklin, many customers have mentioned that I seem genuinely happy every time they see me. I can't help but think that this happiness comes from how much I love what I do. I am so grateful that God sees me fit to be the best counselor that I can be for the adolescents that I meet and gives me the resources I need to help them, and I hope that this gratitude radiates to all other areas of my life too. Hence, working at my family business with my wife and my sister is so therapeutic and for whatever reason, we have the best customers who treat us as their family members. Thank you for being our customers!

For **my Rotary Family**
I have saved the best for the end of this acknowledgment. Finally, I owe thanks to my Rotary family for helping me find my place in this world. What I do at the hospital is merely an extension of my volunteerism in the name of Rotary. When I became a ShelterBox first disaster responder, deploying to save lives from disaster, I was called

insane or mad because no right-minded man would sacrifice his life for somebody else and expect nothing in return. Nobody can pay me enough for what I am doing right now for adolescents; however, no amount of money can buy my personal fulfillment as a human being and the happiness it has brought me to see the difference in patients' lives. As one of 1.2 million Rotarians in the world, I hope I live by our motto "Service Above Self" each and every day of my life.

Accomplishments and Awards for Community Service

- Past President of the Rotary Club of Hendersonville 2008-2009
- Rotary International District Governor 2014-2015
- SRT (ShelterBox Response Team)—International First Disaster Responder.
- Alumnus of L'Evate Leadership
- Alumnus of Leadership Sumner
- Past Board of Directors & Executive Director for Korean-American Social Service in Nashville.
- The Frist Humanitarian Award in 2011
- Lifetime Distinguished Service Award 2011
- Rotarian of the Year, Hendersonville Rotary Club in 2004
- Rotarian of the Year, Rotary International District 6760
- Distinguished Service Award, Rotary International District 6760 in 2010
- President's Service Award from President Barack Obama in 2011 & 2012
- Tennessee Hospital Association Meritorious Service Award in 2011
- The highest honor Service Above Self Award from Rotary International in 2011.
- Sumner County Order of the Horse in 2012
- President's Service Award from President Donald Trump in 2018
- Numerous proclamations and resolutions from Sumner County, U.S. Congress, and Philippines

PART V: BOOKS THAT I READ

#	Y/M/D-Score	제목 TITLE	지은이 AUTHOR
1	19750000-5	조선불교유신론 * 님의 침묵	한용운
2	19760500-5	석가여래 일대기	김대웅
3	19760600-1	환경오염과 식물	차종환
4	19780200-4	하늘을 우러러	김동길
5	19780300-5	자기 앞의 생	에밀 아자르
6	19780700-4	사랑을 위하여	고은
7	19780700-3	말콤엑스 (상)	Alex Haley
8	19780700-3	말콤엑스 (하)	Alex Haley
9	19780800-5	룸비니에서 구시나가라까지	불교교육회편저
10	19790100-4	겨울날	김광섭
11	19790300-5	불가능은 없다 (속)	카네기
12	19790424-3	내일은 비	김병총
13	19790700-2	셍고르시전작집	레오뽈 세다르 셍고르
14	19791000-5	효경 (외)	이민수 엮음
15	19791017-3	한국 청년에게 고함	김동길
16	19791031-2	가시를 삼킨 장미	김문화
17	19791101-3	The Origin of Species	Darwin
18	19791101-3	솔가지 위에 쌓인 눈	김 철 외 13인
19	19791102-3	사랑하며 용서하며	이향봉 스님
20	19791103-4	하버드대학의 공부벌레들	존 제이 오스본
21	19791104-4	서 있는 사람들	법정
22	19791104-4	하느님 나의 하느님	김동길
23	19791123-4	돛대도 아니달고	김인호
24	19791205-3	케네디가의 도전	오오마에 마사히게
25	19800000-5	The Old Man And the Sea	Ernest Hemingway
26	19800000-5	Imagineering	Michael LeBoeuf
27	19800000-3	Little House on the Prairie	Laura Ingalls Wilder
28	19800100-1	KAL 타고 왔읍니다	유재수
29	19800100-4	만다라	김성동
30	19800200-3	내일을 위한 대화	김형석
31	19800300-3	갈 수 없는 나라	조해일
32	19800300-1	청	현지은 외 다수
33	19800300-3	명상의 늪가에서	김동리
34	19800500-3	나의 누이여 나의 신부여	H.F.페터스
35	10800523-4	무소유	법정
36	19800523-4	명사십리	한용운
37	19800600-4	진실을 찾아서	간디
38	19800700-5	소크라테스, 불타. 공자, 예수	칼 야스퍼스
39	19800800-3	옷을 벗지 못하는 사람들	정다운
40	19800927-3	참회록	룻소
41	19801000-4	무설전	이향봉 스님
42	19801000-2	Death Be Not Proud	John Gunther
43	19801001-2	Lev Tolstoy 톨스토이	Janko Lavrin
44	19801003-3	죽음에 이르는 병	키에르케고르
45	19801009-4	영혼의 모음	법정
46	19801009-5	금강반야바라밀경	김해안
47	19801009-5	지와 사랑, 데미안-, 싯달타	헤르만 헤세
48	19801009-4	유리알 유희	헤르만 헤세
49	19801009-3	사랑학 개론	정다운
50	19801017-5	간디자서전/시민의 불복종	함석헌 번역

51	19801021-3	경정상담	주자청
52	19801027-5	논어	차주환엮음
53	19801027-4	날자, 한번만 더 날자꾸나	오규원 엮음
54	19801100-2	흰돌의 초상	원영동
55	19810000-3	그래도 이 손으로	방귀희
56	19810100-3	선, 그 세계	스즈끼 박사
57	19810300-3	무엇이 죽어 새가 되는가	박범신
58	19810300-2	아들의 겨울	김주영
59	19810400-4	처세론	Arthur Schopenhauer
60	19810402-4	The Outsiders	S.E. Hinton
61	19810600-4	속.영원과 사랑의 대화	김형석
62	19810700-3	사랑이 무엇이더뇨	김일엽
63	19810700-3	돌아 눕는 혼	박범신
64	19811100-3	어둠의 자식들	황석영
65	19820200-1	속세에 던진 잿빛청춘	이경원
66	19820316-4	나의 누이와 나	프리드리히 니체
67	19820322-3	하늘의 별처럼 들의 꽃처럼	김형석
68	19820400-3	청춘을 불사르고	김일엽
69	19820400-2	백색인간 1	김성종
70	19820400-2	백색인간 2	김성종
71	19820408-3	나는 죽음을 선택했다	Ann & Samuel Charters
72	19820700-2	걸레스님 중광	김정휴
73	19820800-1	임금님께 고함	김원각
74	19820800-3	일곱개의 장미송이	김성종
75	19820900-3	죽으면 살리라	안이숙
76	19821000-3	꽃이 지면 눈이 시려라	김일엽
77	19821000-5	형장의 신	박범신
78	19821000-3	사바세계를 무대로 멋지게 살아라	경봉스님
79	19821000-4	조선불교유신론 * 님의 침묵	한용운
80	19821100-1	거짓예언자 함석헌	조순명
81	19821200-4	극락에 길이 없는데 어떻게 왔는가	경봉스님
82	19821200-5	왜 사느냐고 묻거든	Luise Rinser
83	19821200-3	죽으면 죽으리라	안이숙
84	19821200-3	오막살이 집한채	김성동
85	19821205-2	새해의 선물	박유평
86	19830000-5	Love Story	Erich Segal
87	19830000-4	백범일지	백범 김구
88	19830100-4	칼	이외수
89	19830100-3	미지의 흰새	박범신
90	19830110-3	위대한 침묵	정다운
91	19830111-3	Uncle Tom's Cabin	스토우
92	19830112-4	니르바나의 종	정다운
93	19830115-3	야반삼경에 문빗장을 만져보거라	경봉스님
94	19830116-3	낮은 데로 임하소서	이청준
95	19830117-4	사람의 아들 (단편)	이문열
96	19830118-3	젊은 날의 초상	이문열
97	19830129-3	현대불교수필전	
98	19830129-5	풀잎처럼 눕다 1	박범신
99	19830130-5	풀잎처럼 눕다 2	박범신
100	19830130-2	인간시장 1	김홍신
101	19830131-2	인간시장 2	김홍신

102	19830131-2	인간시장 3	김홍신
103	19830200-1	쓰레기들의 행진	종황
104	19830200-3	살아있는 날의 소망	박완서
105	19830201-2	인간시장 4	김홍신
106	19830202-2	인간시장 5	김홍신
107	19830203-2	인간시장 6	김홍신
108	19830204-2	인간시장 7	김홍신
109	19830205-2	인간시장 8	김홍신
110	19830202-4	바보새	함석헌
111	19830213-3	머리없는 세상	Elias Canetti
112	19830222-5	백년 동안의 고독	Gabriel G. Marquez
113	19830300-3	누가 지우랴 이 한 점의 먹물을	김일엽
114	19830300-3	미로의 저쪽 1	김성종
115	19830300-3	미로의 저쪽 2	김성종
116	19830400-3	태양제 1	박범신
117	19830400-3	태양제 2	박범신
118	19831100-2	링컨의 일생	김동길
119	19831100-2	젊은이여 인생을 달하자	김동길 외
120	19840100-3	전설따라 삼천리	
121	19840100-3	나를 키워 준 이 말 한 마디	서정주외 99인
122	19840224-3	내영혼 황혼을 바라보며	이용우
123	19840300-4	미로일지	이문열
124	19840300-3	생각하며 산다	김동길 외
125	19840400-4	대학별곡	김신
126	19840400-4	영원과 사랑의 대화	김형석
127	19840400-4	소설 손자병법 1	정비석
128	19840400-4	소설 손자병법 2	정비석
129	19840400-4	소설 손자병법 3	정비석
130	19840400-3	애정의 조건	래리 맥머트리
131	19840600-3	안개 속에 지다 1	김성종
132	19840600-3	안개 속에 지다 2	김성종
133	19840600-3	부랑의 강	김성종
134	19840700-5	컬러 탈무드	n/a
135	19840700-4	내가 부르다 죽을 노래여	김동길
136	19840800-5	산방한담	법정 스님
137	19840900-5	오싱 1	하시다 스가꼬
138	19840900-5	오싱 2	하시다 스가꼬
139	19840900-5	오싱 3	하시다 스가꼬
140	19840900-5	오싱 4	하시다 스가꼬
141	19840900-5	오싱 5	하시다 스가꼬
142	19840900-5	오싱 6	하시다 스가꼬
143	10841100-3	늘 깨어 있는 사람	법정 스님외 다수
144	19841100-4	이 모든 괴로움을 또 다시	전혜린
145	19841200-5	레테의 연가	이문열
146	19841200-4	그리고 아무 말도 하지 않았다	전혜린
147	19850000-4	If Tomorrow Comes	Sidney Sheldon
148	19850000-4	The Color Purple	Alice Walker
149	19850100-1	금병매	소소생
150	19850100-2	금병매	소소생
151	19850300-2	아름다운 밀회 1	김성종
152	19850300-2	아름다운 밀회 2	김성종

153	19850401-4	사랑의 말	김남조
154	19850700-1	인간 시라소니	정용택
155	19850700-2	청맹과니들의 노래	김수용
156	19850800-3	그대 영혼을 적시는 차 한잔	안병욱 외 다수
157	19851000-3	아제아제 바라아제	한승원
158	19851100-2	The Class 하버드 동창생	Eric Segal
159	19851100-3	허튼소리 1	중광
160	19851100-3	허튼소리 2	중광
161	19860300-4	마음	이청담
162	19860600-3	나는 너에게 너는 나에게	김동길
163	19860600-3	사랑은 희생이었읍니다	김동길
164	19861100-1	한국종교 가롯유다의 후예인가 데바닷타의 후예인가	유보산
165	19870000-3	It	Stephen King
166	19870000-2	Wallis and Edward	Mighael Blogh edited
167	19870202-4	우리가 이 땅에 사는 이유	김동길
168	19870204-3	반야심경	송운거사
169	19870207-4	사랑의 길 자유의 길	김동길
170	19870210-4	동창을 열고	김동길
171	19870211-2	그릴 수 없는 사랑의 빛깔까지도	이중섭
172	19870218-3	황제를 위하여	이문열
173	19870224-4	콩밭에 소를 매고도	김삼웅 엮음
174	19870302-5	삶이 그대를 속일지라도	구상 외 10인
175	19870304-3	사랑이여 빛일레라	구상 외 다수
176	19870309-5	사랑과 지혜 그리고 창조	안병욱
177	19870310-3	하루에도 팔만 사천 번씩 절망하며	김성동외
178	19870314-3	생각이 흐르는 강물	김동리
179	19870317-5	하늘 땅에 바른 숨 있어	함석헌
180	19870324-2	사다트 자서전	안와르 사다트
181	19870400-4	젊음이여 어디로 가는가	이어령
182	19870400-4	저물레에서 운명의 실이	이어령
183	19870410-4	떠도는 자의 우편번호	이어령
184	19870414-5	축소지향의 일본인	이어령
185	19870422-5	불꽃놀이	박범신
186	19870422-4	한국현대인물사론	송건호
187	19870426-4	푸는 문화 신바람의 문화	이어령
188	19870426-3	밀월	박범신
189	19870429-3	아함경 이야기	
190	19870500-5	독일국민에게 고함	Johann Gottlieb Fichte
191	19870505-3	둥지 속의 날개	이어령
192	19870600-3	Ethics 윤리학	Aristoteles
193	19870600-4	Apologia Socrates	Platon
194	19870605-3	토끼와 잠수함	박범신
195	19870608-3	식구	박범신
196	19870610-3	The Importance of Living	Lin Yu Tang 임어당
197	19870618-5	명심보감	미상!
198	19870619-3	달팽이의 외출	이문열
199	19870627-5	도산 안창호 논설집	안창호
200	19870710-5	안도산전	주요한
201	19870720-4	한그루 진실의 나무를 심을때	안병욱
202	19870801-5	뜻으로 본 한국역사	함석헌

203	19870817-3	객지	황석영
204	19871000-3	미행	박범신
205	19871200-3	생의 불앞에 두 손을 쪼이며	안병욱 외 다수
206	19871221-3	우리들 뜨거운 느래	박범신
207	19880000-2	국군은 죽어서 달한다	모윤숙
208	19880000-3	홀로 서기	서정윤
209	19880000-3	홀로 서기 2	서정윤
210	19880300-3	위대한 침묵 후편	정다운
211	19880300-5	Zen Comics 스님들기 보는 단화책	요안나 살라잔
212	19880300-3	옷을 벗지 못하는 사람들 2	정다운
213	19880328-4	단재 신 채호/ 그 생애와 정신	임중빈
214	19880403-3	항상 마음은 넉넉하게	손경산 스님
215	19880405-5	도산 안창호/ 그 생애와 정신	임중빈
216	19880407-3	님의 발길따라	서경보 스님
217	19880407-3	큰스님 손안에 뜬달	서경보 스님
218	19880410-3	무심유심	서경보 스님
219	19880411-3	바람되어 구름되어	정다운, 이향봉
220	19880419-3	풍경소리 마음소리	서경보 스님
221	19880421-3	큰스님 피리와 기침소리	서경보 스님
222	19880423-3	서산대사	서경보 스님
223	19880425-3	사명대사 임난기	
224	19880427-4	산은 산 물은 물	이성철 스님
225	19880428-3	마음에서 마음으로	이청담 스님
226	19880504-4	머물며 흘러가며	구산 스님
227	19880505-3	벼랑끝에 서서 길을 묻는 그대에게	김선유-편집인
228	19880507-4	마음이 곧 부처	해안 스님
229	19880511-2	태어나서 죽을 때까지	정다운
230	19880514-3	무엇이 이 외로움을 이기거 하는가	이향봉
231	19880514-3	사람귀하	이향봉
232	19880515-2	인생십이진법	정다운
233	19880517-3	소설 정감록 1	정다운
234	19880519-3	소설 정감록 2	정다운
235	19880522-3	소설 정감록 3	정다운
236	19880524-4	원효	황영진외
237	19880606-3	할말은 애야지요	중광 스님 외 11 스님
238	19880606-4	말과 침묵	법정스님
239	19880607-4	물소리 바람소리	법정스님
240	19880611-3	아직도 못다한 사랑이여	이육사
241	19880613-3	불의 나라 1	박범신
242	19880614-3	불의 나라 2	박범신
243	19880614-3	불의 나라 3	박범신
244	19880617-3	사랑학 개론 (후편)	정다운
245	19890100-4	Bulfinch's Mythology	Thomas Bulfinch
246	19890131-3	사랑하는 이여 나의 빛이여	김동길외
247	19890428-4	The Glass Menagerie	Tennessee Williams
248	19900606-3	A Farewell to Arms	Ernest Hemingway
249	19900610-2	우리글 바로쓰기	이오덕
250	19900701-4	사람의 아들	이문열
251	19900711-4	그대 다시는 고향에 가지못하리	이문열
252	19900830-3	Q씨에게	박경리
253	19900906-4	텅 빈 충만	법정스님

254	199C0908-3	숲은 잠들지 않는다 1	박범신
255	199C0909-3	숲은 잠들지 않는다 2	박범신
256	199C0918-3	떠도는 넋은 언제 잠드는가	김성동
257	19910114-4	미국사	앙드레 모로아
258	19910205-3	Buddhist Scriptures	Edward Conze
259	19910223-5	The Oedipus Plays of Sophocles	Sophocles
260	19910309-3	꿈과 쇠못	박범신
261	19910606-3	물위를 걷는 여자	신달자
262	19910625-2	인간업보	삼중 스님
263	19910702-3	진실한 삶의 길	성열
264	19910921-1	불교와 기독교의 비교연구	마스다니 후미오
265	19911120-5	소설 동의보감 1	이은상
266	19911122-5	소설 동의보감 2	이은상
267	19911123-5	소설 동의보감 3	이은상
268	19920127-4	Kokoro	Natsume Soseki
269	19920206-3	The Wild Geese	Ogai Mori
270	19920304-3	Seven Japanese Tales	Junichiro Tanizaki
271	19920304-3	Thirst for Love	Yukio Mishima
272	19920403-4	The Box Man	Kobo Abe
273	19920417-4	Masks	Fumiko Enchi
274	19920526-3	깊고 푸른 밤 (이상문학상)	최인호 외
275	19921010-3	수요일의 도적	박범신
276	19921013-3	시인	이문열
277	19921014-2	삭발하고 본 세상	박일엽
278	19921025-3	덫	박범신
279	19921026-4	변경 1	이문열
280	19921029-4	변경 2	이문열
281	19921030-4	변경 3	이문열
282	19921201-1	단식 건강법	김동극
283	19921203-1	4시간 수면비법	슈우세이요오
284	19921205-3	까치밥	이향봉
285	19921226-3	황금가면	이승우
286	19921227-2	제 5 열 1	김성종
287	19921228-3	서울 에펠탑 (상)	강형원
288	19921228-3	서울 에펠탑 (하)	강형원
289	19921228-2	제 5 열 2	김성종
290	19921228-2	제 5 열 3	김성종
291	19930105-4	변경 4	이문열
292	19930107-3	그 많던 싱아는 누가 다 먹었을까	박완서
293	19930313-3	비명	장세연
294	19930316-4	최후의 증인 1	김성종
295	19930316-4	최후의 증인 2	김성종
296	19930410-5	풍요로운 삶의 길	이규호 엮음
297	19930506-3	변경 5	이문열
298	19930807-5	소설 목민심서 1	황인경
299	19930811-5	소설 목민심서 2	황인경
300	19930811-5	소설 목민심서 3	황인경
301	19930812-5	소설 목민심서 4	황인경
302	19930813-5	소설 목민심서 5	황인경
303	19930819-5	벽오금학도	이외수
304	19830820-3	소설 사명대사 1	이종익

305	19830821-3	소설 사명대사 2	이종익
306	19830825-3	소설 사명대사 3	이종익
307	19930827-4	The Uses of Enchartment	Bruno Bettelheim
308	19930827-4	The Heart of Social Psychology	Arthur & Elaine N. Aron
309	19930827-4	꿈꾸는 식물	이외수
310	19931222-1	한국불교전설	최정희
311	19940000-5	Financial Peace	Dave Ramsey
312	19940412-4	고운이름 한글이름	배우리
313	19940417-2	숲속의 방	강석경
314	19940419-4	여명의 눈동자 1	김성종
315	19940420-4	여명의 눈동자 2	김성종
316	19940421-4	여명의 눈동자 3	김성종
317	19940421-4	여명의 눈동자 4	김성종
318	19940422-4	여명의 눈동자 5	김성종
319	19940423-4	여명의 눈동자 6	김성종
320	19940423-4	여명의 눈동자 7	김성종
321	19940424-4	여명의 눈동자 8	김성종
322	19940425-4	여명의 눈동자 9	김성종
323	19940426-4	여명의 눈동자 10	김성종
324	19940627-5	The Life Time Reading Plan	Clifton Fadiman
325	19940830-4	The Client	John Grisham
326	19950312-3	The First-Time manager	Loren B. Belker
327	19951229-4	Making the Most of Your Money	Jane Bryant Quinn
328	19960120-5	The 7 Habits of Highly Effective People	Stephen Covey
329	19960717-5	The 10 Natural Laws of Successful Time & Life Management	Hyrum W. Smith
330	19960900-5	Financial Peace Revised	Dave Ramsey
331	19970301-4	나는 똥이올시다	중광
332	19970306-3	공부가 가장 쉬웠어요	장승수
333	19970318-5	Chicken Soup for the Soul	Jack Canfield
334	19970410-X	구역조직을 가정교회로 바꾸라	최영기목사
335	19970421-3	Personal Finance for Dummies	Eric Tyson
336	19970421-3	위대한 약속	양정신
337	19970813-4	여보게 저승갈때 뭘 가지고가지	석용산스님
338	19970911-5	지와 사랑, 데미안, 싯달타	헤세
339	19970918-5	First Things First	Stephen Covey
340	19971006-4	먼데서 오는 새벽	김남조
341	19971007-2	The Art of Real Estate Appraisal	William L. Ventolo,jr
342	19971126-	새벽을 깨우리로다	김진홍
343	19971203-1	여자는 죽어야 한다 (상)	김성종
344	19971205-1	여자는 죽어야 한다 (하)	김성종
345	19980109-4	젊은 베르테르의 슬픔	Goethe
346	19980127-5	The 7 Habits of Highly Effective Families	Stephen Covey
347	19980209-3	영혼의 새벽	김남조
348	19980213-4	사랑방 손님과 어머니	주요섭
349	19980219-3	구름을 잡으려고	주요섭
350	19980219-	미행	박범신
351	19980301-3	생명 1	하시다 스가꼬
352	19980303-3	생명 2	하시다 스가꼬
353	19980307-3	생명 3	하시다 스가꼬
354	19980309-3	생명 4	하시다 스가꼬

355	19980312-2	젊은 시인의 사랑	신동엽
356	19980319-5	그리고 삶은 떠나가는 것	김성종
357	19980321-5	Over the Top	Zig Ziglar
358	19980322-3	영원한 나를 찾아서	대행스님, 혜원편
359	19980411-4	끝나는 고통 끝이없는 사랑	김남조
360	19980427-5	The Giving Tree	Shel Silverstein
361	19980427-5	A 2nd Helping of Chicken Soup for the Soul	Jack Canfield
362	19980522-4	The Millionaire Next Door	Thomas Stanley
363	19980615-5	큰 그릇은 더디게 만들어진다	남동진, 이향규 엮음
364	19980617-3	부모님을 편안하게 모시는 58가지 방법	백창화
365	19980617-5	Awaken the Giant Within	Anthony Robbins
366	19980704-5	Unlimited Power	Anthony Robbins
367	19980709-2	내가 연봉 18억원을 받는 이유	윤윤수
368	19980713-5	Demian	Hermann Hesse
369	19980716-3	어두울 때는 등불을 켜라	윤재근
370	19980717-2	30대에 하지 않으면 안될 50가지	나카타니 아키히로
371	19980721-3	무궁화 꽃이 피었습니다 1	김진명
372	19980721-3	무궁화 꽃이 피었습니다 2	김진명
373	19980722-3	무궁화 꽃이 피었습니다 3	김진명
374	19980727-3	Tapping Potential	Kenneth J. Lodi
375	19980729-2	성공하는 사람은 생각이 다르다	김양호
376	19980801-3	The English Patient	Michael Ondaatje
377	19980803-2	때를 알아라	안병욱
378	19980806-3	The One Minute Manager	Kenneth Blanchard
379	19980812-3	목걸이	모파상
380	19980819-5	The Think and Grow Rich Action Pack	Napoleon Hill
381	19980820-2	Father Knew Best	Dave & Elsa Hornfisher
382	19980829-3	The Memory Book	Harry Lorayne
383	19980902-4	지혜로운 어부는 그물을 촘촘히 짜지 않는다	최홍일 엮음
384	19980911-4	장자에서 얻는 지혜	이기동
385	19980913-4	못생긴 나무가 산을 지킨다	고도원
386	19980916-3	마더 테레사	신홍범
387	19980925-4	The 9 Steps to Financial Freedom	Suze Orman
388	19981001-4	Do What You Love, the Money Will Follow	Marsha Sinetar
389	19981005-5	인생 백년을 읽는 한권의 책	안길환
390	19981006-3	밤이면 내리는 비	박범신
391	19981008-3	황야 1	박범신
392	19981010-3	황야 2	박범신
393	19981012-3	황야 3	박범신
394	19981017-3	성공은 성공의 어머니	김영호
395	19981019-3	바보가 되거라	김현준
396	19981022-4	The Power of Positive Thinking	Norman Vincent Peale
397	19981026-X	미국의 소득세 가이드	김창수
398	19981104-4	Don't Sweat the Small Stuff...& it's all small stuff	Richard Carlson
399	19981116-T	Food Service Management	Anne Powell Knoll
400	19981119-3	Don't Worry, Make Money	Richard Carlson
401	19981130-4	마음을 비우는 지혜	정빈
402	19981204-2	모든 생활은 철학이다	황필호
403	19981205-	저마다 깨친 인연이 있었네	김원환
404	19981205-3	Wisdom Made in America	
405	19981209-4	두려워하면 갇혀버린다	이거룡

406	19981209-2	붉은 대지 1	김성종
407	19981209-2	붉은 대지 2	김성종
408	19981211-2	붉은 대지 3	김성종
409	19981213-2	붉은 대지 4	김성종
410	19981213-2	붉은 대지 5	김성종
411	19981209-2	More Than Enough	Dave Ramsey
412	19981228-5	Grow Rich! With Peace of Mind	Napoleon Hill
413	19990102-5	글쓰기를 두려워 말라	박동규
414	19990107-5	Mere Christianity	C. S. Lewis
415	19990114-4	신은 모든 곳에 있을 수 없기에 어머니를 만들었다	정채봉, 류시화엮음
416	19990115-5	Proverbs for Daily Living	Johenner Troyer edited
417	19990120-T	Serving Safe Food	National Rest. Associa'
418	19990121-4	말을 잘하고 글을 잘 쓰려면 꼭 알아야 할 것들	리의도
419	19990131-T	Man to Man	장재진
420	19990201-4	The Road Less Traveled	M. Scott Peck
421	19990210-3	글 쓰기에 성공하는 책	장진한. 후타쓰기 고조
422	19990221-5	불교성전	불교성전간행회
423	19990304-5	The Seat of the Soul	Gary Zukav
424	19990304-T	Excel 97 Introduction	Comp USA
425	19990305-3	아우야! 세상엔 바브란 없단다	안의정
426	19990307-3	욕심일랑 벗어두고 걸림없이 살게나	윤청광
427	19990309-T	Excel 97 Intermediate	Comp USA
428	19990310-3	죽비 깎는 아침	지묵스님
429	19990312-T	Word 97 Introduction	Comp USA
430	19990314-4	배짱으로 삽시다	이시형
431	19990315-T	Power Point 97 Introduction	Comp USA
432	19990316-T	Window 98 Introduction	Comp USA
433	19990325-T	Access 97 Introduction	Comp USA
434	19990326-5	몸으로 가르치니 따르고 입으로 가르치니 반항하네	청학동 훈장
435	19990400-2	불교와 세계종교	최정인
436	19990405-3	The Edison Trait	Lucy Jo Palladino
437	19990408-3	생명을 풀무질하는 농부	유재현
438	19990420-3	세계는 넓고 할 일은 많다	김우중
439	19990423-4	이 땅에 태어나서	정주영
440	19990427-4	조율사	이청준
441	19990427-1	경세지략	홍매지음, 임국웅 옮김
442	19990427-T	Internet Fundamentals	Comp USA
443	19990429-3	자기 완성을 위하여	Seicho Taniguchi
444	19990430-4	너의 꿈을 펼쳐라	이원숙
445	19990502-T	Sample Business Pans	Courtney Price
446	19990503-5	Till We Have Faces	C. S. Lewis
447	19990503-T	The Entrepreneur's Planning Handbook	
448	19990513-4	마쓰시다 고소스케의 생애	다이 히사미쓰
449	19990517-2	They Never Said It	Paul F. Boller,Jr
450	19990517-2	Mother Knew Best	Dave & Elsa Hornfischer
451	19990517-5	You Can If You Think You Can	Norman Vincent Peale
452	19990519-5	하늘이여 땅이여 1	김진명
453	19990520-2	그대는 별로 뜨고	김소엽
454	19990520-2	님바라기	남궁연희 엮음

455	19990520-5	하늘이여 땅이여 2	김진명
456	19990521-2	빈 산에 사람없어도 꽃은 피고 물 흐르더라	법광스님
457	19990521-4	Man's Search For Meaning	Viktor E. Frankl
458	19990525-2*	The Booklover's Almanac	Robert Brittain Edited
459	19990526-1	숫타니파타	법정옮김
460	19990610-T	Employee Handbooks in TN	Cindy C. Ettingoff, etc.
461	19990612-5	The Road Less Traveled & Beyond	M. Scott Peck
462	19990621-5	As I Lay Dying	William Faulkner
463	19990626-5	The Giver	Lois Lowry
464	19990630-3	오늘 다 못다한 말은	이외수엮음
465	19990701-4	들개	이외수
466	19990702-3	Grand Ole Opry	Jerry Strobel edited
467	19990705-4	황금비늘 1	이외수
468	19990705-4	황금비늘 2	이외수
469	19990721-4	Unlimited Power: A Black Choice	Anthony Robbins
470	19990723-3	Illuminations: Visions for Change, Growth & Self-Acc	Stephen C. Paul
471	19990729-4	The Restaurant from Concept to Operation	Donald E. Lundberg
472	19990801-2	집 상편	김성동
473	19990805-1	집 하편	김성동
474	19990808-3	The Pursuit of Happiness	David G. Myers
475	19990810-2	쓸쓸한 이야기	김성동
476	19990816-4	에세이 명심보감	이규호 편저
477	19990816-4	논어에서 얻는 지혜	이기동
478	19990823-4	The Power Principle	Blaine Lee
479	19990824-3	출가	백금남
480	19990826-3	인연이야기	법정
481	19990828-3	진짜 나와 가짜 나	석용삼 스님
482	19990907-4	Tuesdays with Morrie	Mitch Albom
483	19990921-3	에밀	Rousseau
484	19991002-3	The Courage to be Rich	Suze Orman
485	19991004-4	버리고 떠나기	법정
486	19991012-3	What They Don't Teach You at Harvard Business School	Mark Mc Cormack
487	19991016-4	새들이 떠나간 숲은 적막하다	법정
488	19991017-3	관음예문	송담스님
489	19991017-5	여래장	황산덕
490	19991021-3	고뇌하는 이들을 위하여	오록원스님외 17인
491	19991026-5	홍어	김주영
492	19991029-3	The Richest Man in Babylon	George S. Clason
493	19991101-5	Rich Dad Poor Dad	Robert T. Kiyosaki
494	19991103-T	What Every Mgr Should Know About Financial Analysis	Alan S. Donnahoe
495	19991105-3	Getting Into Money	Cheri Fein
496	19991108-2	쫄병시대	김신
497	19991110-2	인간루쉰	왕샤오밍
498	19991113-2	통도사 가는 길	조성기
499	19991118-4	Dubliners	James Joyce
500	19991120-3	생의 의문에서 그 해결까지	광덕스님
501	19991121-3	퇴마록 (혼세편) 1권	이우혁
502	19991121-3	퇴마록 (혼세편) 2권	이우혁
503	19991123-3	퇴마록 (혼세편) 3권	이우혁

504	19991124-3	The Power of Self-Esteem	Nathaniel Branden
505	19991130-3	인생을 위하여 지성을 위하여	김동길외
506	19991207-4	Living the 7 Habits	Stephen R. Covey
507	20000115-4	The Right to Write	Julia Cameron
508	20000122-4	꼭 읽어야 할 현대시 222선	오선영 엮음
509	20000123-3	"Surely You're Joking, Mr. Feynman!"	Richard P. Feynman
510	20000125-3	Chicken Soup for the Christian Soul	Jack Canfield
511	20000131-3	잠 못 이루는 밤을 위하여	Carl Hilty, 박충하 번역
512	20000207-4	How to Open & Run a Successful Restaurant	Christopher Egerton-Thomas
513	20000215-5	How to Open Franchise Business	Mike Powers
514	20000225-5	The E-Myth Revisited	Michael E. Gerber
515	20000316-5	New Life in Christ 그리스도 안에 있는 새생명 제 1권	n/a
516	20000319-5	The Franchise Fraud	Robert L. Purvin, Jr.
517	20000320-3	Pay It Forward	Catherine Ryan Hyde
518	20000324-3	석양에 홀로 서서	김동길
519	20000324-2	Hamburger Magic	Jenny Stacey
520	20000328-5	Fellowship with Christ 그리스도와의 교제 제 2권	n/a
521	20000328-4	산다는 것과 믿는다는 것	마헨드라나드 굽타
522	20000407-4	Harry Potter & the Sorcerer's Stone	J.K. Rowling
523	20000503-4	Angela's Ashes	Frank McCourt
524	20000505-2	Surprised by Joy	C. S. Lewis
525	20000517-4	How to Give Away Your Faith	Paul E. Little
526	20000528-5	How to Manage a Restaurant	John W. Stokes
527	20000529-4	How to Become a Millionaire	Mark L. Alch, Ph.D.
528	20000727-5	성경전서	
529	20010108-3	무릎으로 사는 그리스도인, 무명의 그리스도인	이진희옮김
530	20010317-4	지금 알고 있는 걸 그때도 알았더라면	류시화엮음
531	20010325-3	시험이 없는 신앙생활은 없다	옥한흠
532	20010426-3	수필 어떻게 쓸 것인가	윤모촌
533	20010620-5	이것을 믿는다 I Know What You Believe	Paul E. Little
534	20010620-3	Personal Bankruptcy & Debt Adjustment	Kenneth J. Doran
535	20010626-4	정의가 나를 부를 때	박영창
536	20010703-5	그리스도의 재림을 대비하라Prepare now for the second	Homer Duncan
537	20010706-3	성경 바로 읽기	민영진
538	20010706-3	The Screwtape Letters	C.S. Lewis 김선형옮김
539	20010708-4	The Secret of Intercession	Andrew Murray
540	20010708-4	Take Each Day One Step at a Time	Various Poets
541	20010804-5	The World Is My Home(A Memoir)	James A. Michener
542	20010809-3	사랑아, 네가 어찌 그리 아름다운지	김하원
543	20010813-4	믿는 만큼 자라는 아이들	박혜란
544	20010820-2	한눈으로 보는 성경 이야기 1	폴임
545	20011219-3	한눈으로 보는 성경 이야기 2	폴임
546	20011219-3	The Forest People	Colin M. Turnbull
547	20020102-5	Power for Living	Jamie Buckingham
548	20020108-3	성자가 된 청소부	바바 하리다스
549	20020201-3	When God Whispers Your name	Max Lucado
550	20020311-2	부모의 마음에 따라 자녀는 자란다	차원재
551	20020512-3	함께읽는 신약성서	한국신학연구소 지음

552	20020620-4	A Complaint is a Gift	Janelle Barlow
553	20020621-4	Gung Ho!	Ken Blanchard
554	20020626-3	함께읽는 구약성서	한국신학연구소 지음
555	20020710-4	The Right to Write	Julia Cameron
556	20020727-3	외지 2	재미시인작품
557	20030216-3	Outgrowing the Pain	Eliana Gil, Ph.D.
558	20030316-4	Religion: The Social Context	Meredith B. McGuire
559	20030520-5	A Single Shard	Linda Sue Park
560	20030522-4	When My Name Was Keoko	Linda Sue Park
561	20030603-2	After the Rain	Norma Fox Mazer
562	20030605-3	빙점 The Freezing Point	미우라 아야꼬
563	20030608-3	빛이 있는 동안에	미우라 아야꼬
564	20030608-3	이 질그릇에도	미우라 아야꼬
565	20030614-4	Chicken Soup for the College Soul	Jack Canfield
566	20030619-5	Chicken Soup for the Unsinkable Soul	Jack Canfield
567	20030625-4	Financial Peace Revisited	Dave Ramsey
568	20030700-4	Criminology	Adler & Mueller
569	20030711-3	(속) 빙점	미우라 아야꼬
570	20030721-3	말속의 말	이어령
571	20030808-3	The One Minute Father	Spencer Johnson, M.D.
572	20030811-5	A Light in My Heart	Young Woo Kang
573	20030904-4	Chicken Soup for the Volunteer's Soul	Jack Canfield
574	20030913-3	아버지와 아들의 꿈	강영우
575	20030918-1	내 안의 성공을 찾아라	강영우
576	20030921-1	교육을 통한 성공의 비결	강영우
577	20030923-5	Sand and Foam	Kahlil Gibran
578	20031022-3	The Prophet	Kahlil Gibran
579	20031027-3	우리가 오르지 못할 산은 없다	강영우
580	20031028-3	Just Like Jesus	Max Lucado
581	20031114-3	Dickens	Peter Ackroyd
582	20031217-5	Delinquency in Society	Robert M. Regoli
583	20031229-3	우리 옆에 왔던 부처	이청
584	20040101-4	Chicken Soup for the Parent's Soul	Jack Canfield
585	20040103-2	A Step from Heaven	An Na
586	20040105-5	The English Patient(A Screenplay)	Anthony Minghella
587	20040108-3	어둠을 비추는 한 쌍의 촛불	강영우/석은옥
588	20040112-2	이런 사람이 무자격 부모다	Dr. Susan Forward
589	20040113-1	I'm Having a Baby	Ellen Sue Stern
590	20040114-4	모든 것은 기도에서 시작됩니다	Mother Teresa
591	20040118-3	행복한 죽음	까뮈지음 이애경 옮김
592	20040214-4	Cider House Rules	John Irving
593	20040217-2	신의 꽃 1	우덕현
594	20040218-2	신의 꽃 2	우덕현
595	20040219-2	릴케의 명시	Rainer Maria Rilke
596	20040225-1	예수평전	모리악
597	20040305-5	The True Joy of Positive Living	Norman Vincent Peale
598	20040316-5	The Purpose Driven Life	Rick Warren
599	20040323-5	What Matters Most	Hyrum W. Smith
600	20040327-4	훈장, 중편소설집	이외수
601	20040407-4	시와 삶의 노트	구상
602	20040416-5	편지	명정스님, 성성욱엮음

603	20040418-4	백악관을 기도실로 만든 대통령 링컨	전광
604	20040425-5	Aesop's Fables	
605	20040501-3	Olive's Ocean	Kevin Henkes
606	20040510-2	Soul Stories	Gary Zukav
607	20040512-3	Thoughts From the Seat of the Soul	Gary Zukav
608	20040604-4	생각하는 즐거움 성각하는 괴로움	조지훈, 박목월, 박두진
609	20040719-3	Mystic River	Dennis Lehane
610	20040720-0	바그다드 천사의 시	제인 워렌, 김영선 옮김
611	20040721-2	불교설화산책	송지홍엮음
612	20040724-2	익명의 섬	이문열
613	20040725-2	새하곡	이문열
614	20040727-3	Beyond the Words	Bonni Goldberg
615	20040729-3	구로아리랑	이문열
616	20040731-4	사색	이문열
617	20040731-2	우리가 행복해지기까지	이문열
618	20040810-4	Korea Unmasked	Won-bok Rhie
619	20040818-3	How to Live Within Your Means	Robert A. Ortalda, Jr.
620	20040818-2	광란자	바스콘셀로스
621	20040824-3	The Success of 7 eleven Japan	Akira Ishikawa
622	20040829-4	How to Start & Manage a Convenience Food Store Bus.	Jerre G. Lewis
623	20040907-5	Service, Service, Service	Steve Albrecht
624	20040912-4	로미오와 줄리엣	셰익스피어
625	20040915-4	The 4 Ways To Grow Your Business	Kraft Bros.
626	20040917-4	Making the Most of Your Money	Jane Bryant Quinn
627	20040918-3	Customers for Keeps	Lois K. Geller
628	20040920-2	Green Eggs and Ham	Dr. Seuss
629	20040920-5	Antigone	Sophocles
630	20040921-5	Who Moved My Cheese?	Spencer Johnson, M.D.
631	20040925-5	Charlotte's Web	E.B. White
632	20040927-4	Moby Dick	Herman Melville
633	20040928-4	Anne of Green Gables	Lucy Maud Montgomery
634	20041005-5	The Da Vinci Code	Dan Brown
635	20041006-3	Because of Winn-Dixie	Kate DiCamillo
636	20041008-0	Love in the Time of Cholera	Gabriel Garcia Marquez
637	20041017-4	The Total Money Makeover	Dave Ramsey
638	20041023-4	Angels & Demons	Dan Brown
639	20041024-3	Smart Guide to Buying a Home	Alfred Glossbrenner
640	20041026-4	Building Real Estate Riches	Chris Condon
641	20041128-3	Smart Couples Finish Rich	David Bach
642	20041130-3	The Automatic Millionaire	David Bach
643	20041204-4	The One Minute Manager Meets the Monkey	Kenneth Blanchard
644	20041206-3	The One Minute Sales Person	Spencer Johnson, M.D.
645	20041225-4	The Effective Executive	Peter F. Drucker
646	20050111-5	The 8th Habit	Stephen R. Covey
647	20050111-3	A Hero In Every Heart	H.Jackson Brown Jr.
648	20050118-5	Living the 7 Habits, The Courage to Change	Stephen R. Covey
649	20050205-5	The Psychology of Blacks	Thomas A. Parham
650	20050213-4	Afrocentricity	Molefi Kete Asante
651	20050223-3	The Falsification of Afrikan Consciousness	Amos N. Wilson
652	20050303-4	봄 여름 가을 겨울	법정스님

653	20050313-4	The Positive Principle Today	Norman Vincent Peale
654	20050413-5	Stay Alive All Your Life	Norman Vincent Peale
655	20050418-4	The Little Guide to Your Well-Read Life	Steve Leveen
656	20050422-5	What Matters Most	Hyrum W. Smith
657	20050423-4	Cultural Misorientation	K. Kambon
658	20050424-3	The Sky is Falling	Sidney Sheldon
659	20050425-2	"L" is for Lawless	Sue Grafton
660	20050428-5	Getting to Yes	Roger Fisher
661	20050429-3	The Prayer of Jabez	Bruce Wilkinson
662	20050429-5	The Present	Spencer Johnson, M.D.
663	20050502-5	Building Your Field of Dreams	Mary Manin Morrissey
664	20050503-5	Getting to Yes	Roger Fisher
665	20050503-1	The Motley Fool Investment Guide	David & Tom Gardner
666	20050505-3	Kane & Abel	Jeffrey Archer
667	20050508-3	The Birth of Venus	Sarah Dunant
668	20050510-3	What To Do With Your Money Now	David & Tom Gardner
669	20050512-3	Their Eyes Were Watching God	Zora Neale Hurston
670	20050514-4	Song of Solomon	Toni Morrison
671	20050521-4	How to Develop & Use a Personal Mission Statement	Steven R. Covey
672	20050522-3	The Money Book for the Young Fabulous & Broke	Suze Orman
673	20050524-4	Focus	Stephen R. Covey
674	20050525-4	The 7 Habits of Highly Effective People	Stephen R. Covey
675	20050526-3	The Money Answer Book	Dave Ramsey
676	20050527-3	The 4 Disciplines of Execution	Stephen R. Covey
677	20050528-4	Gone For Good	Harlan Coben
678	20050601-2	The Scarlet Letter	Nathaniel Hawthorne
679	20050603-4	The Last Promise	Richard Paul Evans
680	20050604-4	Writing About Your Life	William Zinsser
681	20050608-4	Good Harbor	Anita Diamant
682	20050609-4	Essentials of Alternative Dispute Resolution	Susan Patterson
683	20050609-2	The Modern Gladiator	Hyrum W. Smith
684	20050611-4	Heaven & Earth	James Van Praagh
685	20050612-2	This Present Darkness	Frank E. Peretti
686	20050613-4	A Farewell to Arms	Earnest Hemingway
687	20050614-2	The Stars Shine Down	Sidney Sheldon
688	20050616-5	Death's Acre	Dr. Bill Bass
689	20050619-4	African-American Audio Experience	Richard Wright
690	20050621-4	A Man's Journey to Simple Abundance	Sarah Ban Breathnach
691	20050624-5	Bud, Not Buddy	Christopher Paul Curtis
692	20050626-3	The Shipping News	Annie Proulx
693	20050628-5	Even the Rat Was White	Robert V. Guthrie
694	20050628-3	The Black Image in the White Mind	Robert M. Entman
695	20050629-4	A Beautiful Mind	Sylvia Nasar
696	20050701-4	Pet Sematary	Stephen King
697	20050703-1	The Television Writer's Handbook	Constance Nash
698	20050701-3	Wisdom	Leonard Roy Frank
699	20050703-4	The Body Farm	Patricia Cornwell
700	20050705-3	Cause of Death	Patricia Cornwell
701	20050706-3	Cruel & Unusual	Patricia Cornwell
702	20050712-3	The Guardian	Nicholas Sparks
703	20050713-4	Body of Evidence	Patricia Cornwell

704	20050714-3	A Farewell to Arms	Ernest Hemingway
705	20050715-4	All That Remains	Patricia Cornwell
706	20050719-4	Short Cuts	Raymond Carver
707	20050724-3	The Face	Dean Koontz
708	20050725-4	The Body Artist	Don Delillo
709	20050727-3	Death Du Jour	Kathy Reichs
710	20050728-4	Ethics for the New Millennium	Dalai Lama
711	20050728-3	The Joy of Books	Eric Burns
712	20050730-1	Slaughterhouse-Five	Kurt Vonnegut
713	20050731-3	The Genesis of Justice	Alan M. Dershowitz
714	20050803-3	Coaching Youth Soccer	Am. Sport Education
715	20050804-4	Deception Point	Dan Brown
716	20050805-3	The Psychology of Winning	Dr. Denis Waitley
717	20050806-3	Our Journey Home	Gary Bauer
718	20050808-3	People of the Century	narrated by Dan Rather
719	20050810-3	Survival Is Not Enough	Seth Godin
720	20050811-4	Enthusiasm Makes the Difference	Norman Vincent Peale
721	20050812-3	Speak Up with Confidence	Jack Valenti
722	20050813-0	The Book of Secrets	Osho
723	20050814-3	Don't Know Much About the Bible	Kenneth C. Davis
724	20050815-1	Poland	James A. Michener
725	20050817-3	Nothing Is Impossible	Christopher Reeve
726	20050817-5	A Century of Service	David C. Forward
727	20050831-5	The African Unconscious	Edward Bruce Bynum
728	20050907-3	Hidden Prey	John Sandford
729	20050909-2	The King of Torts	John Grisham
730	20050911-3	The Brethren	John Grisham
731	20050913-3	Barbaric Mercies	Gaylord Brewer
732	20050914-4	Just One Look	Harlan Coben
733	20050916-3	Digital Fortress	Dan Brown
734	20050916-3	Men Are From Mars, Women Are From Venus	John Gray, ph.D
735	20050919-1	Portrait of a Killer, Jack the Ripper Case Closed	Patricia Cornwell
736	20050921-3	What's So Amazing About Grace?	Philip Yancey
737	20050924-3	Heaven on Earth	Danny Seo
738	20050926-4	Just As I Am	Billy Graham
739	20050928-4	The Total Money Make Over	Dave Ramsey
740	20050930-3	Certain Prey	John Sandford
741	20051003-3	A Passion to Win	Sumner Redstone
742	20051005-4	1st To Die	James Patterson
743	20051008-4	Honeymoon	James Patterson
744	20051009-0	Changing Directions Without Losing Your Way	Paul & Sarah Edwards
745	20051010-5	The Prince of Tides	Pat Conroy
746	20051011-5	My Losing Season	Pat Conroy
747	20051012-3	The Lake House	James Patterson
748	20051017-2	Lifeguard	James Patterson
749	20051020-3	Violets Are Blue	James Patterson
750	20051025-3	The Loop	Nicholas Evans
751	20051026-0	The Queen of the Damned	Anne Rice
752	20051026-3	Fish! Sticks	Stephen C. Lundin
753	20051027-3	Lessons from a Father to His Son	John Ashcroft
754	20051028-3	How to Run a Successful Meeting-in 1/2 the Time	Milo O. Frank

755	20051029-1	The Homing	John Saul
756	20051031-3	Speak from the Heart	Steve Adubato
757	20051102-3	Great Expetations	Charles Dickens
758	20051104-3	Who Took My Money?	Robert T. Kiyosaki
759	20051105-4	Built to Last	James C. Collins
760	20051107-0	Hard Times	Charles Dickens
761	20051110-3	Chicken Soup for the Soul	Jack Canfield
762	20051111-0	The Clan of the Cave Bear	Jean M Auel
763	20051113-3	8 Weeks to Optimum Health	Andrew Weil, M.D.
764	20051114-3	The Five People You Meet in Heaven	Mitch Albom
765	20051116-4	On Writing	Stephen King
766	20051121-4	The Last Juror	John Grisham
767	20051122-3	Writing and Being	G. Lynn Nelson
768	20051127-4	Good To Great	Jim Collins
769	20051128-3	The Good Earth	Pearl S. Buck
770	20051129-3	Harvard Business Review on What Makes a Leader	Harvard Business School
771	20051204-4	Little Red Book of Selling	Jeffrey Gitomer
772	20051208-4	The Rule of Four	Ian Caldwell
773	20051220-4	The World According to Garp	John Irving
774	20051220-3	Executive Intelligence	Justin Menkes
775	20051225-3	True Believer	Nicholas Sparks
776	20060127-3	Jesus Freaks	dc Talk
777	20060208-4	The 80/20 Principle	Richard Koch
778	20060322-5	Hardwiring Excellence	Quint Studer
779	20060326-2	EZ-101 Finance	Joel G. Siegel
780	20060409-3	The Five Dysfunctions of a Team	Patrick Lencioni
781	20060515-4	Napoleon Hill's Keys to Success	Matthew Sartwell
782	20060521-3	The Art of Thank You	Connie Leas
783	20060528-1	거울없는 방	권경희
784	20060610-5	First, Break All the Rules	Marcus Buckingham
785	20060708-2	My Pocket Mentor	Sandra Gaviola
786	20060708-3	Journey to the Center	Matthew Flickstein
787	20060716-4	The Oz Principle	Roger Connors
788	20060731-4	Winning with People	John C. Maxwell
789	20060921-3	You've Got to Read This Book!	Jack Canfield
790	20060926-3	QBQ!	John Miller
791	20061017-3	Managing Up	Rosanne Badowski
792	20061119-5	If Disney Ran Your Hospital	Fred Lee
793	20070111-4	Prayer	Philip Yancey
794	20070113-3	The Winning Attitude	John C. Maxwell
795	20070126-3	Developing the Leaders Around You	John C. Maxwell
796	20070204-4	Becoming a Person of Influence	John C. Maxwell
797	20070218-4	The Tipping Point	Malcolm Gladwell
798	20070221-5	The 21 Irrefutable Laws of Leadership	John C. Maxwell
799	20070304-3	Blink	Malcolm Gladwell
800	20070312-T	신앙의 출발 1	
801	20070312-T	Living Budedha, Living Christ	Thich Nhat Hanh
802	20070318-3	Going Home Jesus & Buddha as Brothers	Thich Nhat Hanh
803	20070317-T	새로운 생활 2	
804	20070328-T	성장의 생활 3	
805	20070415-3	Fred Factor	Mark Sanborn

806	20070414-T	교회의 생활 4	
807	20070422-T	경건의 생활 5	
808	20070423-T	헌신의 생활 6	
809	20070606-3	흐린세상 건너기	이외
810	20070610-3	Disney Way	Bill Capodagli
811	20070909-5	The Water Is Wide	Pat Conroy
812	20071005-3	The District Governor in Action	Mrs. Bonnie Fakes
813	20071014-0	유머손자병법	유머화술연구회
814	20071118-4	The Goal	Eliyahu Goldratt
815	20080101-5	7 Habits of Highly Effective People	Steven R.Covey
816	20080118-3	For Whom the Bell Tolls	Ernest Hemingway
817	20080125-3	The Power of Intention	Wayne W. Dyer
818	20080129-4	The Art of Happiness at Work	Dalai Lama
819	20080201-3	101 Secrets of Highly Effective Speakers	Caryl Rae Krannich
820	20080208-3	Wobegon Boy	Garrison Keiller
821	20080216-3	Benjamin Franklin: Am American Life	Walter Isaacson
822	20080223-3	Speaking of Rotary	Randal Adams
823	20080308-4	Life of Pi	Yann Martel
824	20080320-4	Primal Leadership	Daniel Goleman
825	20080424-4	The World Is Flat	Thomas L. Friedman
826	20080525-3	Life Is a Gift	Bob & Judy Fisher
827	20080527-3	내 마음 그리스도의 집	Robert Boyd Munger
828	20080602-3	Eat That Frog!	Brian Tracy
829	20080618-3	How to Wow	Frances Cole Jones
830	20080624-4	The Essential Wooden	John Wooden
831	20080803-4	Failing Forward	John C. Maxwell
832	20080809-4	Execution	Bossidy & Charan
833	20081020-3	The Innocent Man	John Grisham
834	20081104-5	The Shack	William P. Young
835	20081106-3	사랑할 땐 별이 되고	이해인
836	20081112-2	Human Moments	Edward Hallowell
837	20081121-4	Robert's Rules of Writing 101	Robert Masello
838	20081122-1	Speak	Laurie Halse Anderson
839	20081126-5	The Elements of Style	Strunk & White
840	20081207-3	The Last Lecture	Randy Pausch
841	20090105-4	The Zen Book	Daniel Levin
842	20090125-3	The Sphere Project	The Sphere Project
843	20090208-4	Safety First	Save the Children
844	20090213-3	Landmine & Explosive Remnants of War	Safety Handbook
845	20090419-4	Present Like a Pro	Cyndi Maxey
846	20090907-4	The Heavenly Man	Brother Yun
847	20091103-5	The Lords of Discipline	Pat Conroy
848	20091108-3	The Dream Giver	Bruce Wilkinson
849	20091201-3	이상문학상 1977 1회	박완서, 한수산등
850	20100108-5	Your Best Life Now	Joel Osteen
851	20100114-5	Knowing God	J.I.Packer
852	20100122-2	Come Thirsty	Max Lucado
853	20100401-4	Half Time	Bob Buford
854	20100527-5	High Five!	Ken Blanchard
855	20100609-4	The Quick and Easy Way to Effective Speaking	Dale Carnegie
856	20100616-3	The Barbarian Way	Erwin R. McManus

857	20100709-4	The Amazing Results of Positive Thinking	Norman Vincent Peale
858	20100712-3	Upside Down Leadership	Michael C. Blackwell
859	20100725-3	Leadership Jazz	Max DePree
860	20100803-4	Ships of Mercy	Don Stephens
861	20100817-3	Chicken Soup for the Romantic Soul	Jack Canfield
862	20100902-5	the Case for Servant Leadership	Kent M. Keith
863	20101001-4	The Daily Writer	Fred White
864	20101116-5	Reaching for the Invisible God	Philip Yancey
865	20101118-3	Room to Write	Bonni Goldberg
866	20101129-5	On Writing Well	William Zinsser
867	20110101-4	Human All Too Human	Friedrich Nietzsche
868	20110122-5	Worse Than War	Daniel J. Godlhagen
869	20110213-4	To Have Or To Be	Erich Fromm
870	20110219-4	Things Fall Apart	Chinua Achebe
871	20110309-4	사랑	이광수
872	20110313-3	Fathers and Sons	Ivan S. Turgenev
873	20110331-4	The Adventures of Huckleberry Finn	Mark Twain
874	20110409-4	On Life	Leo Tolstoi
875	20110411-3	The Tempest	William Shaksespeare
876	20110510-4	Don Quixote	Miguel de Cervantes
877	20110629-4	Die Verwandlung 변신	Franz Kafka
878	20110820-3	나는 당신을 만나기 전부터 사랑했습니다	우광호
879	20110824-3	사랑합니다 감사합니다	고도원
880	20110829-4	Pensees	Blaise Pascal
881	20110915-5	성경전서	
882	20111002-4	아버지	김정현
883	20111005-4	우리들의 행복한 시간	공지영
884	20111005-4	하늘과 바람과 별과 시	윤동주
885	20111009-4	엄마를 부탁해	신경숙
886	20111011-4	자전거 도둑	박완서
887	20111014-5	접시꽃 당신	도종환
888	20111023-4	우리들의 일그러진 영웅	이문열
889	20111023-3	Hans Christian Andersen Fairy Tales	Hans Christian
890	20111107-3	7년의 밤	정유정
891	20111107-4	황태자비 납치사건	김진명
892	20111121-5	Beach Music	Pat Conroy
893	20120101-5	The Fountainhead	Ayn Rand
894	20120103-5	Black Boy	Richard Wright
895	20120202-5	Atlas Shrugged	Ayn Rand
896	20120213-5	To Kill A Mockingbird	Harper Lee
897	20120220-4	My Reading Life	Pat Conroy
898	20120326-4	Madame Bovary	Gustave Flaubert
899	20120409-4	Honoring Our Past: The Words & Wisdom of Paul Harris	Paul Harris
900	20120615-3	The American Dream	Dan Rather
901	20120623-4	My Road to Rotary	Paul Harris
902	20120624-4	쓰나미의 과학	이호준
903	20120716-5	A Portrait of the Artist as a Young Man	James Joyce
904	20121129-5	Catch-22	Joseph Heller
905	20121211-4	One Day in the Life of Ivan Denisovich	Aleksandr Solzhenitsyn
906	20121222-5	The Catcher in the Rye	J.J. Salinger

907	20121228-4	The Grapes of Wrath	John Steinbeck
908	20130101-5	The Pearl	John Steinbeck
909	20130101-4	Of Mice and Men	John Steinbeck
910	20130107-4	Poor Folk	Fyodor Dostoevsky
911	20130404-2	Ulysses	James Joyce
912	20130406-4	Start with Why	Simon Sinek
913	20130413-4	Resurrection	Leo Tolstoi
914	20130417-4	Anthem	Ayn Rand
915	20130507-4	Of Human Bondage	William S. Maugham
916	20130609-4	We The Living	Ayn Rand
917	20130612-3	One More Play	James M. Perdue
918	20130616-5	Meditations	Marcus Aurelius
919	20130617-4	The Time of Our Lives	Tom Brokaw
920	20130619-5	Dear Chandler, Dear Scarlett	Mike Huckabee
921	20130624-4	Theodore Boone: The Activist	John Grisham
922	20130628-4	Proof of Heaven	Eben Alexander, M.D.
923	20130630-3	The Divine Comedy of Dante Alighieri	Dante Alighieri
924	20130701-4	David Copperfield	Charles Dickens
925	20130703-3	A Christmas Carol	Charles Dickens
926	20130709-4	Manon Lescaut	Abbe Prevost
927	20130725-3	Making Good Habits, Breaking Bad Habits	Joyce Meyer
928	20130801-3	The Rescue	Nicholas Sparks
929	20130805-3	The Bridge	Karen Kingsbury
930	20130813-5	Slaughterhouse-Five	Kurt Vonnegut
931	20130821-5	South of Broad	Pat Conroy
932	20130905-5	The Great Santini	Pat Conroy
933	20130908-5	Night	Elie Wiesel
934	20130913-4	To Have and Have Not	Earnest Hemingway
935	20130920-4	Leaves of Grass	Walt Whitman
936	20131006-4	Life Is What You Make It	Peter Buffett
937	20131010-5	Unbroken	Laura Hillenbrand
938	20131115-4	Benjamin Franklin: An American Life	Walter Isaacson
939	20131118-4	25 Ways to Win with People	John C. Maxwell
940	20131118-4	7 Steps to Fearless Speaking	Lilyan Wilder
941	20131130-5	Sum It Up	Pat Summitt
942	20131207-3	Creating True Peace	Thich Nhat Hanh
943	20131210-4	Wobegon Boy	Garrison Keiller
944	20131212-4	Leonardo da Vinci	John Phillips
945	20131216-4	Grammar Snobs Are Great Big Meanies	June Casagrande
946	20131219-3	100 Ways to Motivate Yourself	Steve Chandler
947	20131222-5	Wheat Belly	William Davis, MD
948	20131231-5	Kite Runner	Khaled Hosseini
949	20140104-5	A Thousand Splendid Suns	Khaled Hosseini
950	20140121-4	Tis	Frank McCourt
951	20140126-5	The Secret life of Bees	Sue Monk Kidd
952	20140215-5	The World Until Yesterday	Jared Diamond
953	20140221-3	The Heart of a Woman	Maya Angelou
954	20140302-5	The Immortal Life of Henrietta Lacks	Rebecca Skloot
955	20140307-3	How Full Is Your Bucket?	Tom Rath
956	20140313-4	The Lexus and the Olive Tree	Thomas L. Friedman
957	20140420-4	Low Pressure	Sandra Brown

958	20140424-3	Ford County	John Grisham
959	20140430-4	I Am Malala	Malala Yousatzai
960	20140507-4	Drive	Daniel H. Pink
961	20140509-3	Think Big Act Small	Jason Jennings
962	20140515-3	The Innocent Man	John Grisham
963	20140528-4	Killing Jesus	Brian O'Reilly
964	20140622-5	The Hunger Games	Suzanne Collins
965	20140701-5	I Am a Rotarian	Kim Kim
966	20140703-5	My Life in Letters	Kim Kim
967	20140704-4	Are You There, Vodka? It's me, Chelsea	Chelsea Handler
968	20140708-3	The Other Typist	Suzanne Rindell
969	20140713-4	Life's Greatest Lessons	Hal Urban
970	20140718-4	The Shining	Stephen King
971	20140722-4	Carrie	Stephen King
972	20140729-4	The Graduate	Charles Webb
973	20140803-4	The Confession	John Grisham
974	20140807-4	The Appeal	John Grisham
975	20140815-3	The King of Torts	John Grisham
976	20140820-5	The Litigators	John Grisham
977	20140827-3	Standing for Something	Gordon B. Hinckley
978	20140830-3	The Racketeer	John Grisham
979	20140902-4	Angels at the Table	Debbie Macomber
980	20140906-3	Dolores Claiborne	Stephen King
981	20140910-3	Nothing's Sacred	Lewis Black
982	20140921-3	Under the Banner of Heaven	Jon Krakauer
983	20140925-3	Redemption	Karen Kingsbury
984	20140927-3	Remember	Karen Kingsbury
985	20141002-3	Emotional Intelligence	Daniel Goleman
986	20141013-5	Who Asked You?	Terry McMillan
987	20141015-4	In Cold Blood	Truman Capote
988	20141021-4	The Perks of Being a Wallflower	Stephen Chbosky
989	20141022-3	Salem's Lot	Stephen King
990	20141024-3	The Butler: A Witness to History	Will Haygood
991	20141101-4	Parting the Waters: American in the King Years 1954-63	Taylor Branch
992	20141108-3	Sundays at Tiffany's	James Patterson
993	20141114-3	Playing for Pizza	John Grisham
994	20141121-4	Sycamore Row	John Grisham
995	20141205-4	How to Stop Worrying & Start Living	Dale Carnegie
996	20141208-4	How to Talk to Anyone, Anytime, Anywhere	Larry King
997	20141213-4	The Longest Ride	Nicholas Sparks
998	20141214-4	The Course of Human Events	David McCullough
999	20141219-5	Rome 1960	David maraniss
1000	20141223-3	Team of Rivals	Doris Kearns Goodwin
1001	20150101-3	The Choice	Nicholas Sparks
1002	20150108-4	The Fault in Our Stars	John Green
1003	20150119-4	The Five Love Languages	Gary Chapman
1004	20150124-3	Folk Tales from Korea	Zong In-Sob
1005	20150126-4	Holes	Louis Sachar
1006	20150127-2	Suspicion Nation	Lisa Bloom
1007	20150208-4	The Last Child	John Hart

1008	20150212-4	Thrive	Arianna Huffington
1009	20150222-4	I Declare	Joel Osteen
1010	20150310-4	The Death of Santini	Pat Conroy
1011	20150324-5	Gone Girl	Gillian Flynn
1012	20150327-3	Lost Light	Michael Connelly
1013	20150330-2	A Clockwork Orange	Anthony Burgess
1014	20150403-3	Our Endangered Values	Jimmy Carter
1015	20150410-5	Book Thief	Markus Zusak
1016	20150414-3	Brave New World	Aldous Huxley
1017	20150419-3	Second Honeymoon	James Patterson
1018	20150423-3	City of Bones	Michael Connelly
1019	20150430-4	Gray Mountain	John Grisham
1020	20150501-3	Grace	Max Lucado
1021	20150505-4	Fahrenheit 451	Ray Bradbury
1022	20150506-2	D is for Dead Beat	Sue Grafton
1023	20150515-4	Lovely Bones	Alice Sebold
1024	20150523-5	The 7 Habits of Highly Effective People	Steven R.Covey
1025	20150529-4	Teacher Man	Frank McCourt
1026	20150601-3	How to Talk So Kids Can Learn	
1027	20150607-3	Lucky	Alice Sebold
1028	20150616-4	Blood Memory	Greg Iles
1029	20150626-5	The Gods of Guilt	Michael Connelly
1030	20150628-4	The 7 Habits of Highly Effective Teens	Sean Covey
1031	20150701-3	Coping with Difficult People	Arlene Matthews Uhl
1032	20150705-5	Accused	Lisa Scottoline
1033	20150709-3	Terrorist	John Updike
1034	20150713-5	Whale Done!	Ken Blanchard
1035	20150717-3	Fierce Conversations	Susan Scott
1036	20150720-3	Chasing the Dime	Michael Connelly
1037	20150729-4	The Break Out Principle	Herbert Benson, M.D.
1038	20150808-3	Absalom, Absalom!	William Faulkner
1039	20150810-4	True Evil	Greg Iles
1040	20150811-5	We Are Rotarians	Kim Kim
1041	20150813-4	Turning Angel	Greg Iles
1042	20150818-5	No Country For Old Men	Cormac McCarthy
1043	20150825-3	Life is a series of presentations	Tony Jeary
1044	20150908-3	A mind at a time	Mel Levine
1045	20150921-5	Jane Eyre	Charlotte Bronte
1046	20151006-3	Chicken Soup for the Preteen Soul	Jack Canfield
1047	20151007-3	The 7 Best Things Smart Teens Do	John C. Friel
1048	20151008-5	The Bone Tree	Greg Iles
1049	20151009-4	The Black Pearl	Scott O'Dell
1050	20151010-1	Chicken Soup for the Teenage Soul	Jack Canfield
1051	20151022-5	Beloved	Toni Morrison
1052	20151025-4	Mr. Mercedes	Stephen King
1053	20151027-4	My Antonia	Willa Cather
1054	20151104-5	Change of Heart	Jodi Picoult
1055	20151110-4	The Secret	Rhonda Byrne
1056	20151128-4	Goldfinch	Donna Tartt
1057	20151208-4	How to Be Alone	Jonathan Franzen
1058	20151213-3	Throw Out Fifty Things	Gail Blanke

1059	20151214-5	The Schopenhauer Cure	Irvin D. Yalom
1060	20151217-3	Love Wins	Rob Bell
1061	20151218-4	Into the Wild	Jon Krakauer
1062	20151225-4	What Are They Thinking?	Aaron M. White, PhD
1063	20151226-5	Ahrahm Kim	Kim Kim
1064	20151227-5	Hannie Kim	Kim Kim
1065	20151228-5	Doun Kim	Kim Kim
1066	20151228-5	Words That I Live By	Kim Kim
1067	20151229-5	Words That You Live By	Kim Kim
1068	20160102-4	Persuasion	Jane Austen
1069	20160104-3	The Leadership Pill	Ken Blanchard
1070	20160109-4	Blackbird	Jennifer Lauck
1071	20160118-5	1984	George Orwell
1072	20160123-3	The Color of Earth, Water, Heaven	Kim Dae Hwa
1073	20160131-3	Become a Better You	Joel Osteen
1074	20160201-3	Mrs. Dalloway	Virginia Woolf
1075	20160208-3	Why Do I Love These People?	Po Bronson
1076	20160209-5	Animal Farm	George Orwell
1077	20160211-3	The Strange Library	Haruki Murakami
1078	20160214-1	The Secret of Everything	Barbara O'Neal
1079	20160309-4	Gnostic Gospels	Elaine Pagels
1080	20160311-4	Dark Places	Gillian Flynn
1081	20160315-3	This Land Is Their Land	Barbara Ehrenreich
1082	20160318-4	If I Stay	Gayle Forman
1083	20160328-4	Travels with Charley in Search of America	John Steinbeck
1084	20160412-4	Betrayed	Lisa Scottoline
1085	20160416-5	The Brothers Karamazov	Fyodor Dostoevsky
1086	20160423-4	Son	Lois Lowry
1087	20160425-5	The Education of Little Tree	Forrest Carter
1088	20160503-3	Eve	WM. Paul Young
1089	20160511-4	Looking for Alaska	John Green
1090	20160601-5	Doing Good in the World	David C. Forward
1091	20160610-3	One Year in Coal Harbor	Polly Horvath
1092	20160613-1	The Last Sin Eater	Francine Rivers
1093	20160627-3	Divergent	Veronica Roth
1094	20160701-4	Rotary Presidents: Themes & Visions	Rotary International
1095	20160705-5	Animal Farm	George Orwell
1096	20160710-4	The Beautiful Stories of Life	Cynthia Rylant
1097	20160712-5	The Wright Brothers	David McCullough
1098	20160722-4	Catching Fire	Suzanne Collins
1099	20160728-4	Mockingjay	Suzanne Collins
1100	20160810-3	The Spontaneous Fulfillment of Desire	Deepak Chopra
1101	20160822-3	Insurgent	Veronica Roth
1102	20160826-3	Here She Went	Gayle Forman
1103	20160830-5	War and Peace	Leo Tolstoy
1104	20160901-4	Ward No. 6	Anton Chekhov
1105	20160907-5	Good Earth	Pearl S. Buck
1106	20160910-3	Teaching Hope	Erin Gruwell
1107	20160914-3	The Curious Case of Benjamin Button	F. Scott Fitzgerald
1108	20160917-3	An Abundance of Katherines	John Green
1109	20160922-4	Freedom Writers Diary	Erin Gruwell

1110	20160925-4	The Metamorphosis	Franz Kafka
1111	20160928-5	Sharp Objects	Gillian Flynn
1112	20161008-4	The 7 Habits of Highly Effective Families	Steven R.Covey
1113	20161011-3	Rosalie Lightning	Tom Hart
1114	20161012-3	Smart Thinking:3 Essential Keys to...	Art Markman, ph D
1115	20161014-3	Time Management from the Inside Out	Julie Morgenstern
1116	20161020-4	The Great Gatsby	F. Scott Fitzgerald
1117	20161023-4	Breakfast at Tiffany's	Truman Capote
1118	20161029-4	The Road	Cormac McCarthy
1119	20161101-1	Golden Age	Jane Smiley
1120	20161107-5	Leadership Challenge	James Kouzes
1121	20161112-3	Crucial Conversations	Kerry Patterson
1122	20161113-3	A Separate Peace	John Knowles
1123	20161118-4	The Cosmic Ocean	Paul K. Chappell
1124	20161130-4	Go Set a Watchman	Harper Lee
1125	20161208-5	The Social Animal	David Brooks
1126	20161210-3	Three Willows	Ann Brashares
1127	20161213-5	Greek Myths	James Baldwin
1128	20161220-3	The Road to Character	David Brooks
1129	20161224-4	Boundaries	Henry Cloud
1130	20161230-4	Emotional Awareness	Paul Ekman
1131	20170110-4	Speak Spanish to Learn Spanish	Pimsleur
1132	20170115-5	A Little Life	Hanya Yanagihara
1133	20170121-3	Darkness at Noon	Arthur Koestler
1134	20170210-3	Confessions of Zeno	Italo Svevo
1135	20170311-4	Salt, Sugar, Fat	Michael Moss
1136	20170424-5	Crime and Punishment	Fyodor Dostoevsky
1137	20170428-3	Redirecting Children's Behavior	Kathryn J. Kvols
1138	20170505-4	Stumbling on Happiness	Daniel Gilbert
1139	20170512-4	Helping Teens Who Cut	Michael Hollander
1140	20170529-5	The Tipping Point	Malcolm Gladwell
1141	20170609-4	Codependent No More	Melody Beattie
1142	20170628-5	How: Why How We Do Anything Means Everything	Dov Seidman
1143	20170629-3	Public Lives Private Prayers	Mary Reath
1144	20170709-5	The Master and Margarita	Mikhail Bulgakov
1145	20170714-3	East of Eden	John Steinbeck
1146	20170820-5	Gone with the Wind	Margaret Mitchell
1147	20170823-4	My grandmother asked me to tell you she's sorry	Fredrik Backman
1148	20170827-3	Alice's Adventures in Wonderland	Lewis Carroll
1149	20170829-3	Through the Looking Glass	Lewis Carroll
1150	20170902-4	David and Goliath	Malcolm Gladwell
1151	20170908-4	Understanding Children	Jerome Kagan
1152	20170915-4	Rebecca	Daphne DuMaurier
1153	20170919-4	Counseling and Psychotherapy	Dugald Arbuckle
1154	20170920-2	Summer Crossing	Truman Capote
1155	20170927-4	Me, Myself, and Why	Jennifer Ouellette
1156	20171001-4	The Girl on the Train	Paula Hawkins
1157	20171013-4	The Book of Virtues	William J. Bennett
1158	20171020-4	The Moral Compass	William J. Bennett
1159	20171021-4	Glenn Beck's Common Sense	Glenn Beck
1160	20171024-3	Let's All Be Brave	Annie F. Downs

1161	20171026-4	Triggers	Marshall Goldsmith
1162	20171104-5	Feeling Good	David D. Burns, M.D.
1163	20171110-3	Understanding Teenage Depression	Nicholas Bakalar
1164	20171113-4	Conscious Business	Fred Kofman
1165	20171114-3	Quotations for Successful Living	H.A. Levin
1166	20171120-4	The Zookeeper's Wife	Diane Ackerman
1167	20171125-5	Psycho-cybernetics	Maxwell Maltz, M.D.
1168	20171201-2	The Zen Path through Depression	Philip Martin
1169	20171210-4	The Magic Power of Self-Image Psychology	Maxwell Maltz, M.D.
1170	20171216-5	Age of Opportunity	Laurence Steinberg, Ph. D.
1171	20171219-5	The Compound Effect	Darren Hardy
1172	20171220-4	Watership Down	Richard Adams
1173	20171225-4	Untangled	Lisa Damour, Ph.D.
1174	20171226-3	NPR Classic Driveway Moments	
1175	20171227-3	Driven to Distraction	Edward Hallowell, M.D.
1176	20171228-4	The Entrepreneur Roller Coaster	Darren Hardy
1177	20180121-4	The Feeling Good Handbook	David D. Burns, M.D.
1178	20180124-4	The Future of the Mind	Michio Kaku
1179	20180216-3	Brainstorm	Daniel J. Siegel, M.D.
1180	20180221-3	The Six Pillars of Self-Esteem	Nathaniel Branden
1181	20180225-3	Self Esteem the New Reformation	Robert H. Schuller
1182	20180309-4	The Good Teen	Richard M. Lerner, Ph.D
1183	20180314-4	The Power of Your Subconscious Mind	Joseph Murphy, Ph. D
1184	20180318-3	The Art of Clear Thinking	Rudolf Flesch
1185	20180325-3	The Psychology of Self-Esteem	Nathaniel Branden
1186	20180325-1	What Do They See When They See You Coming?	Stephen M. Gower
1187	20180329-5	A Better Way to Think	H. Norman Wright
1188	20180405-4	The Truth About Addiction & Recovery	Stanton Peele, Ph. D
1189	20180407-4	Preparing for Adolescence	James Dobson, Ph. D
1190	20180417-4	Toxic Parents	Dr. Susan Forward
1191	20180420-5	What to Say When You Talk to Your Self	Shad Helmstetter, Ph. D
1192	20180513-4	불교정신치료 강의	전현수박사
1193	20180514-3	세상을 바꿀 수 없다면 자신을 바꿔라	Gao Yuan
1194	20180514-4	채식주의자	한강
1195	20180520-3	법정 마음의 온도	김옥림
1196	20180520-4	멈추면, 비로소 보이는 것들	혜민 스님
1197	20180520-3	1일1독	박지현
1198	20180521-3	조금 더 편해지고 싶어서 거리를 두는 중입니다	Stefanie Stahl
1199	20180521-5	Adolescence	John W. Santrock
1200	20180522-4	청소년의 자살 그리고 더 많은 이야기	수원시자살예방센터
1201	20180523-5	심리학, 열일곱 살을 부탁해	이정현 정신과 전문의
1202	20180525-5	10대와 통하는 심리학 이야기	노을이
1203	20180525-3	망상과 환상 속에서 사는 아이들	Raquel E. Gur
1204	20180527-5	정신의학의 탄생	하지현
1205	20180529-3	의식은 언제 탄생하는가?	마르첼로 마시미니
1206	20180531-4	몸, 뇌, 마음	Judith Rustin
1207	20180611-5	Motivational Interviewing	Miller & Rollnick
1208	20180624-5	DBT Principles in Action	Charles R. Swenson
1209	20180630-1	알다, 보다, 잡다	김문성
1210	20180705-5	The Happiness Trap	Russ Harris M.D.

1211	20180706-5	Nonsuicidal Self-Injury	David Klonsky
1212	20180706-5	백범일지	백범 김구
1213	20180709-3	Lecture on Psychopathology	양병환
1214	20180716-5	감정은 어떻게 만들어지는가?	리사 펠드먼 배럿
1215	20180717-4	The Ant and the Elephant	Vince OpsCenter
1216	20180804-5	How Emotions Are Made	Lisa Feldman Barrett
1217	20180808-4	Think Less Learn More	Srini Pillay, MD
1218	20180815-4	You Are What You Think	David Stoop, Ph. D
1219	20180816-5	Unstoppable	David L. Black, Ph D
1220	20180818-4	When Breath Becomes Air	Paul Kalanithi
1221	20180821-5	Reclaiming Youth at Risk	Larry K. Brendtro
1222	20180826-3	나를 사랑해야 치유된다	선안남
1223	20180903-3	Breaking Through to Teens	Ron Taffel
1224	20180917-4	Life Unlocked	Srinivasan S. Pillay, MD
1225	20180918-5	성문 종합영어	송성문
1226	20180922-3	Life Strategies for Teens	Jay McGraw
1227	20181004-5	The Healing Brain	Robert Ornstein
1228	20181013-3	Brain Wars	Mario Beauregard
1229	20181016-3	Parenting Today's Adolescent	Dennis & Barbara Rainey
1230	20181021-4	The Search for Meaning	Thomas H. Naylor
1231	20181026-3	10 Dumbest Mistakes Smart People Make	Arthur Freeman
1232	20181110-4	Descartes' Error	Antonio R. Damasio
1233	20181203-5	The Boy Who Was Raised As a Dog	Bruce D. Perry, MD, Ph.D
1234	20181208-3	In the Footsteps of Gandhi	Catherine Ingram
1235	20181217-3	Heads Up Psychology	Marcus Weeks
1236	20181222-2	Stuff That Sucks	Ben Sedley
1237	20190102-5	From Darkness to Sight	Dr. Ming Wang
1238	20190108-4	Who Says You Can't? You Do	Daniel Chidiac
1239	20190208-5	Evolve Your Brain	Dr. Joe Dispenza
1240	20190221-5	Breaking the Habit of Being Yourself	Dr. Joe Dispenza
1241	20190227-5	You Are the Placebo	Dr. Joe Dispenza
1242	20190314-3	무소유	김세중
1243	20190315-3	Buddha	Karen Armstrong
1244	20190316-3	Bowling Alone	Robert D. Putnam
1245	20190321-3	Live Your Dreams	Les Brown
1246	20190405-4	Put Your Dream to the Test	John C. Maxwell
1247	20190411-3	Loving Each Other	Leo Buscaglia
1248	20190428-3	A World Waiting to be Born	M. Scott Peck, M.D.
1249	20190502-4	I and Thou	Martin Buber
1250	20190604-4	Why Zebras Don't Get Ulcers	Robert M. Sapolsky
1251	20190605-3	Are Your Kids Naked Online?	Chris Good
1252	20190610-3	The 10X Rule	Grant Cardone
1253	20190612-3	The Mindset of Successful Thinking	Troy M. Smith
1254	20190723-5	Behave	Robert M. Sapolsky
1255	20190724-4	Unlimited Memory	Kevin Horsley
1256	20190725-5	The Strangest Secret	Earl Nightingale
1257	20190725-2	The Hardest Part About...	Sawyer Small
1258	20190726-4	Biology of Belief	Bruce H. Lipton, ph. D
1259	20190805-3	가짜 자존감 권하는 사회	김태형
1260	20190814-4	The Honeymoon Effect	Bruce H. Lipton, ph. D
1261	20190819-1	소소한 풍경	박범신

1262	20190819-4	Discover Your Possibilities	Robert H. Schuller
1263	20190823-5	There Are No Children Here	Alex Kotlowitz
1264	20190905-4	The Anatomy of Violence	Adrian Raine
1265	20190909-5	Psycho-Cybernetics	Maxwell Maltz, M.D.
1266	20190911-4	Emotional Intelligence 2.0	Travis Bradberry
1267	20190913-5	Psycho-Cybernetics	Maxwell Maltz, M.D.
1268	20190924-3	Reviving Ophelia	Mary Pipher, ph. D
1269	20191003-3	How to Be an Adult in Faith & Spirituality	David Richo
1270	20191003-2	No Boundaries	Jim Hadley
1271	20191017-3	On 1984	James Daley
1272	20191018-5	Psycho-Cybernetics	Maxwell Maltz, M.D.
1273	20191108-5	The New Psycho-Cybernetics	Maxwell Maltz, M.D.
1274	20191119-4	Psycho-Cybernetic Principle for Creative Living	Maxwell Maltz, M.D.
1275	20191124-4	Thoughts to Live By	Maxwell Maltz, M.D.
1276	20191201-4	Psycho-Cybernetics-Creative Living for Today	Maxwell Maltz, M.D.
1277	20191205-3	You Never Can Tell	Janice Holland
1278	20191207-4	Conquest of Frustration	Maxwell Maltz, M.D.
1279	20191219-5	Psycho-Cybernetics	Maxwell Maltz, M.D.
1280	20191222-4	Life Is What You Make It	Ronald L. Willingham
1281	20191223-3	Self Mastery Through Conscious Autosuggestion	Emile Coue
1282	20191225-5	Creative Mind	Ernest Holmes
1283	20191230-4	Treat Yourself to Life	Raymond Charles Barker
1284	20191230-3	Leadership Through the Ages	Rudolph W. Giuliani
1285	20200103-4	The Power of Decision	Raymond Charles Barker
1286	20200115-4	Choice Theory	William Glasser. M.D.
1287	20200120-4	Reality Therapy	William Glasser. M.D.
1288	20200123-3	비행운	김애란
1289	20200129-4	A Guide to Rational Living	Albert Ellis, Ph. D
1290	20200215-4	The Road Back to You	Ian Morgan Cron
1291	20200220-4	Excuses Begone	Wayne W. Dyer
1292	20200302-4	The Laws of Human Nature	Robert Greene
1293	20200308-4	Your Erroneous Zones	Wayne W. Dyer
1294	20200310-3	Conquering the Generational Challenge	David Butler
1295	20200318-5	Stoner	John Williams
1296	20200325-4	For the New Intellectual	Ayn Rand
1297	20200328-4	5 Ideas That Change the World	Barbara Ward
1298	20200329-2	Psychopathology	Von Karl Jaspers
1299	20200407-4	The Story of Philosophy	Will Durant
1300	20200407-1	People Tools	Alan C. Fox
1301	20200420-4	Six Questions of Socrates	Christopher Phillips
1302	20200413-3	P.R.O.S	Chris Hope
1303	20200415-3	Life's Best Chapter Retirement	Johnnie C. Godwin
1304	20200417-5	When Bad Things Happen to Good People	Harold S. Kushner
1305	20200419-5	The True Measure of a Man	Richard E. Simmons III
1306	20200420-4	The Richest Man Who Ever Lived	Steven K. Scott
1307	20200422-3	I Was Just Wondering	Philip Yancey
1308	20200501-4	A Father's Book of Wisdom	Jackson Brown, Jr.
1309	20200505-5	Anna Karenina	Leo Tolstoy
1310	20200510-5	Meditations	Marcus Aurelius
1311	20200510-5	Living the Wisdom of the Tao	Wayne W. Dyer
1312	20200513-3	He-Understanding Masculine Psychology	Robert A. Johnson

1313	20200513-4	She-Understanding Feminine Psychology	Robert A. Johnson
1314	20200514-5	The Words of Martin Luther King, Jr.	Coretta Scott King
1315	20200515-4	Bus 9 to Paradise	Leo Buscaglia
1316	20200521-4	Treating Addiction	William Miller
1317	20200523-4	Love	Leo Buscaglia
1318	20200524-3	All I Really Need to Know I Learned in Kindergarten	Robert Fulghum
1319	20200528-4	David	Charles R. Swindoll
1320	20200607-3	Pilgrim's Progress	John Bunyan
1321	20200609-5	This Man from Lebanon	Barbara Young
1322	20200618-4	Living on the Ragged Edge	Charles R. Swindoll
1323	20200620-3	The Story of My Life	Helen Keller
1324	20200621-3	The Path to Love	Deepak Chopra
1325	20200630-5	Wishes Fulfilled	Wayne W. Dyer
1326	20200704-5	The Power of Awareness	Neville Goddard
1327	20200705-3	Strengthening Your Grip	Charles R. Swindoll
1328	20200707-5	Dying to Be Me	Anita Moorjani
1329	20200714-4	The Happiness Project	Gretchen Rubin
1330	20200719-3	Better Than Before	Gretchen Rubin
1331	20200721-4	Awakened Imagination & the Search	Neville Goddard
1332	20200731-4	The Neville Reader	Neville Goddard
1333	20200804-5	Why We Get Fat	Gary Taubes
1334	20200806-5	Unstoppable	David L. Black, Ph D
1335	20200807-3	Even the Stars Look Lonesome	Maya Angelou
1336	20200807-5	The Love Poems of Rumi	Deepak Chopra (edited)
1337	20200812-5	The Power of Awareness	Neville Goddard
1338	20200817-3	Wild at Heart	John Eldredge
1339	20200830-4	Think & Grow Rich	Napoleon Hill
1340	20200831-4	Quotations of Franklin Delano Roosevelt	Applewood Books
1341	20200902-4	Life Wisdom: Quotes from Zig Ziglar	Zig Ziglar
1342	20200923-4	A whole New Mind	Daniel H. Pink
1343	20200928-3	You Can Heal Your Life	Louise L. Hay
1344	20201010-4	Nowhere Near the Bottom	Fred Bailey
1345	20201013-4	The Snow Goose	Paul Gallico

Made in USA - Kendallville, IN
1198285_9798551118213
11.21.2020 0838